World on a String

Bucky and me.

World on a String

A MUSICAL MEMOIR

John Pizzarelli
and
Joseph Cosgriff

Foreword by Jonathan Schwartz

Lincoln Center

WILEY

John Wiley & Sons, Inc.

Cover image: © Christopher Jacobs
Cover design: Wendy Mount

"I Like Jersey Best," words and music by Joseph Cosgriff, Green Monster Music (ASCAP) from (*John Pizzarelli Trio: Live at Birdland* (Telarc—2003) and *Pizzarelli's P.S. Mr. Cole* (RCA—1999).

Lyrics from Michael Franks "Eggplant" from *The Art of Tea* (Reprise—1976) courtesy of Mississippi Mud Music (BMI).

"The Waters of March," words and music by Antonio Carlos Jobim, Corcovado Music.

Photo credits: page ii: photograph by Jimmy Katz, from the personal collection of John Pizzarelli; pages 3, 6, 18, 21, 57, 104, 113, 138, 147, 169, 178, 187, 191, 192, 195, 227, and 228: personal collection of John Pizzarelli; pages 24, 35, and 40: personal collection of Bucky Pizzarelli; page 47: photograph by Russ Titelman, from the personal collection of John Pizzarelli; page 60: photograph by Joe Cosgriff, from the personal collection of John Pizzarelli; page 77: personal collection of Bucky Pizzarelli, courtesy of the Huddlestons; page 117: © 2009, used by permission of the Boston Red Sox; page 119: © Steve J. Sherman; pages 201 and 238: JohnPizzarelli.com, copyright John Pizzarelli, 2011; page 202: photograph by Russ Titelman; page 204: courtesy of the Jacob Burns Film Center; pages 218 and 219: photographs by Russ Titelman. Courtesy of the Carlyle Hotel and John Pizzarelli personal collection; page 240: photograph by Joe Cosgriff; page 241: Andrew Southam.

Lincoln Center and Lincoln Center for the Performing Arts names and logos are registered trademarks of Lincoln Center for the Performing Arts, Inc., in the United States and other countries. Used here by license.

Published by John Wiley & Sons, Inc., Hoboken, New Jersey
Published simultaneously in Canada

For general information about our other products and services, please contact our Customer Care Department within the United States at (800) 762-2974, outside the United States at (317) 572-3993 or fax (317) 572-4002.

Wiley also publishes its books in a variety of electronic formats. Some content that appears in print may not be available in electronic books. For more information about Wiley products, visit our web site at www.wiley.com.

Library of Congress Cataloging-in-Publication Data:

Pizzarelli, John.
  World on a string: a musical memoir/John Pizzarelli and Joseph Cosgriff; foreword by Jonathan Schwartz.
    pages; cm.
  Includes discography and index.
ISBN 978-1-118-06297-5 (cloth); ISBN 978-1-118-22228-7 (ebk);
ISBN 978-1-118-26096-8 (ebk); ISBN 978-1-118-22228-7 (ebk)

  1. Pizzarelli, John. 2. Guitarists—United States—Biography. I. Cosgriff, Joseph. II. Title.
  ML419.P593A3 2013
  787.87'164092—dc23

                                                                                    2013020852

Printed in the United States of America

10 9 8 7 6 5 4 3 2 1

We dedicate this book to Ruth and Bucky Pizzarelli, for creating a home where everyone is welcome and where love, music, and stories have always flowed generously.

I will say, too, that lovemaking, if sincere, is one of the best ideas Satan put in the apple she gave to the serpent to give to Eve. The best idea in that apple, though, is making jazz.

—Kurt Vonnegut, *Timequake*

Contents

Foreword

The plane made a sharp turn to the left, not far from the San Jacinto Mountains, already snowcapped early in October. Then the plane began to descend while keeping its beeline toward the mountains.

John Pizzarelli was sitting next to me, his Red Sox hat (the same as mine) settled at a cockeyed position on his head, probably encouraged by the wild tension within the musician who wore it. But there was no music now, as the mountains grew closer. Pizzarelli's face had turned into a wild white, as if it had been painted on. His eyes were cast downward in defeat. The end, I guessed he imagined, was merely seconds away.

This was a flight I had taken fifty or more times—L.A. to Palm Springs, on the American Airlines puddle jumper that seated about twenty passengers. On one of the flights years earlier, I'd been able to see the Pacific Ocean from a rear window and the desert floor from the front of the plane.

I was scared now, and thought of my daughter Casey asleep in bed in New York.

Then, suddenly, the plane veered right, ascended a bit, and landed comfortably. Pizzarelli remained frozen in time until I straightened his hat. "What was that about?" he asked, finally.

"They wanted to come in from the north. Simple matter," I told him.

In those days, I stayed at an inexpensive lodge with comfortable suites and a large pool. Some of the rooms, like mine, had kitchens. I'd been using the lodge for close to twenty years and was permitted to store things in an infrequently used closet, no deeper than an indentation, in the back of the lodge. I set up shop—typewriter, manuscripts, dictionaries, and books and CDs that I often used.

Pizzarelli, having fetched his guitar from the plane, settled into Room 108, right across the breezeway from my Room 320. I made a run for Scotch and beer, and then went back in my room. John began to play and sing, and I would sing, and he would play for me to sing. It must be noted that Pizzarelli is one of the finest accompanists for any singer, anywhere. He listens to what you're doing so that he becomes a part of the lyric.

And on this very first night, mellow and finally pleased with things, John began to sing Irving Berlin's "Better Luck Next Time." At the tail end of the bridge, approaching the line about an event that happens once in a lifetime, not twice, the room began shaking—the walls squealed, bottles and cans on the kitchen table plunged to the floor. As I recall, two bottles of Corona beer were smashed all over the place, but the bottle of Johnnie Walker Black Label Scotch remained intact.

An ashen-faced Pizzarelli was holding his guitar closely to his chest for, I think, an umbilical protection. One must understand that the guitar has indeed played a protective role in John's life. His father, Bucky Pizzarelli, and God knows how many Pizzarellis stretching back into an earlier century, made some sort of living by playing this instrument. John looked at me as though he were viewing *The Exorcist*.

I said simply: "Earthquake."

The Silence of the Lambs joined *The Exorcist* in the mutilated soul of what was once a guitarist and singer, and a man I deeply cared for.

An earthquake in the California desert usually lasts no longer than thirty seconds. I'd been through at least six or seven over the years, most of them arriving when I was writing at the very typewriter I'm using now (a Hermes 3000, if you really want to know).

Imagine: the plane, the mountains, the walls, the shaking room—all in about six hours.

We drank whiskey seriously and gradually forced the evening to an end.

John Pizzarelli's story is contained in the book you hold. In this little foreword, I'd like to fill in a few holes in the narrative that would otherwise remain quietly unknown.

The pages are filled with funny stuff, laugh-out-loud stuff, and Sinatra commenting on Pizzarelli's physical appearance. And musician talk (you'll find it for yourself). Most of all, this book documents, like no other, the nomadic life of any fellow or gal who picks up an instrument professionally: the discipline, the airplanes, the endless lack of sleep, and, to be sweet about it, the beer.

John, with whom I talk so very often, is a fifty-two-year-old man, and, in fact, a celebrity, who hides behind his craft. He is a dead-on mimic, a perceptive observer of the mediocre, and a benign and almost loving social critic. Occasionally, when the word *no* is called for, he's a hard man to find.

John's wife, Jessica Molaskey, a singer, dancer, actress, painter, gardener, and mother, is truly wonderful at all of the above. On a morning a while ago, Jessica, John, and their Red Sox expert of a daughter, Madeleine, set off for their cozy and desirable little house in, as I see it, a threatening forest that opens up finally at a perfect swimmable lake. Even around his own family on this serene drive he has become, without an essential *no* for miles around, Bob Dylan, Billie Holiday, Ted Kennedy, Tony Bennett, Wolf Blitzer, and Bucky Pizzarelli.

"Where's Daddy?" Madeleine asked Jessica.

"I'm not sure," she answered, as the voice of Chris Matthews joined us on the drive.

If my wife and children were out of town, I'd rather spend time with this guy Pizzarelli than with almost anyone else. Of course, there is something to be said for spending hours and hours with Jessica talking about myself.

—Jonathan Schwartz
New York City

Acknowledgments

We wish to thank our editors, Hana Lane and Tom Miller, assistant editor Jorge Amaral, and the entire team at Wiley, for their expert advice and assistance throughout the project.

Thanks to our agent, Doug Grad, for helping to make the book possible and for helping to shape what it became; to Jonathan Schwartz, for letting us know early we were onto something; to Johnny and Maddie, to Bucky and Ruth, Anne and Mary; to Martin Pizzarelli, for being there every night; and to Jessica Molaskey, for more reasons than I can possibly name.

To all the folks who informed my "wonder years": the teachers and students from Wandell, Bosco, the University of Tampa, and William Paterson; the counselors and my friends from KDC, Maurice and Charlotte. To Ron Byerly, whose work ethic remains an inspiration and whose words of wisdom continue to resound in me. To Dick Ables, who looked out for all the Pizzarellis. To Joe Cosgriff, for being a trusted friend for so long and for making this book into something special. To all the guys in all the bands who helped make some great music all over. To George and Fran at Nobody's, Danny and Larry at Giulio's, and Judy Barnett at J's. To Buddy Morra for righting the ship, to Joel Hoffner for being the rock, and to everyone else for supporting the cause for great music and memories.

—John Pizzarelli

I thank Steve Cosgriff, Paul Orlin, Steven Schnitzler, Jim Czak, Bucky and Ruth Pizzarelli, Aaron Weinstein, Russ Titelman, Martha Chang, Ren and Marilyn Harris, Frank Rogers, Richard Kind, Pam Starr, Peter

ACKNOWLEDGMENTS

Collery, Ray Duffy, Jerry Trupiano, Sherm Feller, Ike Delock, David Margolick, Denny Galehouse, Bob Sullivan, Nestor Chylak, Barberi Paull Feit, Budd Mishkin, Amy Jedlicka and our hockey family, Sobhy, Barbara, Emily, and Hannah Ahmed, Anthony Russo, Martin Pizzarelli, Dawne Dickenson, Joan Rider, Grace, Matthew, Eric, and Ryan Cosgriff, Duncan McCurrach, Mary and Joe Lauricella, Robin Smith, Pam and George Bloom, Paulo Jobim, Carolyn Sherman Gutierrez, Susan Goodenow, Frank and Kathy Dotzler, Steve Apkon, Kathy Bonomi, Mary Anne and Kara Armellino, Tony Tedesco, Larry Fuller, Tony Skrelja at the Café Carlyle, Tim Hennessey, Martin Vogelbaum, Dick Bresciani, Rich Carrara, Maddie Dames, Carl Butrum, Tony Monte, Maria Traversa, Ira and Susan Schulman, Gott's Roadside (formerly Taylor's Automatic Refresher), Stan and Heather Roth, Kevin Taylor, Harry Bauld, Craig and Brett Teper, Dave Shotland, Peter Puck, Matt Selton, Greg Amoral, Tom Juhase, Dr. Cathy Carron, Jill and Dale DeGroff, Ed Laub, Gianni Valenti, Christine Pedi, Peter Crowley, the Powers family, Suzie Frank, the Birnbaums, Scott and Melissa Oscher, Chris Wertz, Jeff Levy, David Niu, Mark Barry Cohen, Liza Page Nelson, Lorraine Gracey, Arturo Cortes, Brandon Steiner, Ed Randall, Doug Quinn, Joe Trustey, Marina and Paul Donahue, Paul Tvetenstrand, Sean Vokhshoor, Gene Orza, Arnie Peinado, Rob Rieger, Dan Russo, Chuck and Shelly Shotland, Jim Monaghan, Erwin Freire, Lance Cutler, Normann Larsen, Bill and Jim Jennings, Mary Bowers, John Bonanno, Henry Leung, Alison Prager, Jim Ribellino III, Bill Hatzichristos, Peter Gogolak, Tom Bailey, Susan Mason, Ron Carman, Boris Bereza, our Rangers' rep, and Mac Taylor. And Thesaurus.com.

John and I wish we could share this book with those no longer with us, especially Uncle Bobby and Uncle Peter, Uncle Frank Rieger, my parents and grandmothers, Pete Fornatale, Don Gardner, Howard Dickenson, James B. Powers, and my spirited and wonderful sister, Joan Russo.

—Joseph Cosgriff

We would also like to thank Lincoln Center for their support of John and this book. And both of us thank Paul Frank for the pats on the back and the occasional kicks slightly lower.

Preface

We have reached the introductory pages of the book—so, in the words of Bullwinkle's archnemesis, Boris Badenov, "Allow me to introduce myself." My name is John Pizzarelli, and 175 times a year—give or take—I lead the John Pizzarelli Quartet into action somewhere in the world.

Along with Larry Fuller on piano, Tony Tedesco on drums, and my brother, Martin Pizzarelli, on bass, I play an electric guitar (usually a sixteen-inch John Pizzarelli Model 7-String from Moll Custom Instruments when on the road) and sing tunes that are primarily drawn from a category of music called the Great American Songbook. I'll leave defining the Songbook to others (and discuss it later), but chances are that if Sinatra, Ella, Tony Bennett, Mel Tormé, or Peggy Lee recorded them before 1960, or if they were composed by Irving Berlin, Harold Arlen, Richard Rodgers, George Gershwin, Arthur Schwartz, Jerome Kern, Cole Porter, or Jimmy Van Heusen, those are the types of songs on my concert setlists.

As I often mention at my concerts, I am keenly aware that our audiences are made up of two distinct groups: (a) fans of the John Pizzarelli Quartet and our music and (b) those forced to attend by friends and loved ones in the first group. To our loyal supporters and social media friends, whom we estimated to be in the tens of millions when pitching this book, thank you for following me into a world that seems both familiar (relating stories) and uncharted (typing words onto a screen for people to read six months later). As Albert Brooks greeted listeners on one of his brilliant seventies comedy albums, "Congratulations on your purchase." It is my hope that this book will stimulate discussions, fill in some gaps, and continue the dialogue we've been having with those who like us and our music, adding to what we already do at concerts, on Facebook, on my website, and in conversations after my shows.

To those in the second group who had been hoping for a more sentimental gift (or even a different book), thanks for your enthusiasm—or for at least masking your disappointment. Unlike a lot of memoirs and autobiographies that force you to slug it out for two hundred pages before the subject's *parents* are even born, I'll be sixteen years old by the end of chapter 1, which reminds me of an old Louis Armstrong joke, perhaps apocryphal. When asked how his book was coming along, he replied that he'd completed six hundred pages and had only reached 1929. (He died in 1971.)

For friends of fans and for those of you who own the book because it was recommended by a beloved bookseller, here is a quick highlight reel of my career: I recorded a duo instrumental album with my father in 1980, put out my first vocal album in 1983, and over the past thirty years as a singer and bandleader released more than twenty LPs and CDs (and digital equivalents) on labels such as Stash, Chesky, RCA, and Telarc International. I opened for Frank Sinatra's World Tour in 1993, performed duets with Rosemary Clooney onstage and on recordings, starred (that's what it said in the ad) in a Broadway show, have been appearing on the late shows (Letterman, Conan, Leno—looking forward to Craig Ferguson) since 1991, headlined at Carnegie Hall, and in December 2011 led twenty-two hundred people in a singalong of "The Twelve Days of Christmas" at the Disney Concert Hall in Los Angeles. I have accompanied James Taylor, both in the studio and in concert, and in February 2012 I did a TV special with Sir Paul McCartney and played live with him at the Grammy Awards, a followup to backing him on rhythm guitar on his album of vintage covers, *Kisses on the Bottom*. In addition, I have sung the national anthem at Fenway Park, "Take Me Out to the Ballgame" at Busch Stadium, and "I Like Jersey Best" in São Paulo, Brazil.

When I began playing professionally in a guitar duo with my father over thirty years ago, I never dreamed it would lead to the opportunities and experiences I have listed in the previous paragraph. (I just read the paragraph again *twice*.) But I have been playing the guitar, singing, and writing songs since I was a teenager. There's something to be said for putting in your time or, as Hemingway described his greatest responsibilities—"to last and to get my work done."

In November 2011, Joe Nocera of the *New York Times* characterized my career (along with my wife's) as "the opposite of 'overnight sensations.'" I love the description. And while it is mind-blowing to step back and realize that I actually make my living walking out onto a stage every night, there are many nights when what I do and what our quartet does begins and ends with less glamorous work. The plane arrived late, the luggage got lost, the sound system was made in shop class by a ninth-grader, and my voice deserted me four nights ago (no jokes, please). But when five hundred people go out of their way to purchase tickets and expect to be transformed to the joyful place where we always try to take them, it is my job to ignore the distractions and make sure we (as my father says) "deliver the ball."

What I have learned from the best—Zoot Sims, Ray Brown, Rosie Clooney, Tony Bennett, and my dad—is to keep at it. Zoot always reminded us to work as hard when there are two people in the house as when there are a thousand and two. In a similar vein, Bruce Springsteen speaks of focusing on the imaginary couple in the upper reaches of the arena who might be seeing him perform for the first time. And what I carry forward from my time with Rosie was how she put her head down and went about her work, even when her health, her voice, and other factors she couldn't control weren't close to being perfect.

Why am I writing a book? Besides having it "suggested" by more than one outspoken audience member over the years, I reached my fiftieth birthday—Il Vagabondo, great meal, stupendous wines from friends' vineyards, solid guest list—and embraced it as a good opportunity to examine where I've been, what I've learned, and where I might be going. Someone that night gave me a quote from Muhammad Ali that said (paraphrasing) that if you look at things the same way at fifty as you did at twenty, then you just wasted thirty years of your life. When I first entertained the idea of writing things down, it wasn't necessarily for a book project, it was more to look back at my first thirty years as a working musician and jot down whatever I could remember. In the spirit of Jimmy Buffett's "A Pirate Looks at Forty," this project began more like "Pizzi Looks at Fifty."

Those of you who attend my concerts are well aware that I am prone to talking extensively between songs. In a 140-character world at least three of my favorite stories have more than 140 actual characters—all with names and speaking lines. I have long made it clear that stories and storytelling have always been a central part of my life. Jean Shepherd, Bob & Ray, Garrison Keillor, Phil Schaap, Ralph Kiner, Larry Josephson, and Jonathan Schwartz were my radio heroes. Josephson, who worked for Pacifica stations nationally and WBAI locally in New York, became so inspired after hearing the Beatles' "Lady Madonna" for the first time in March 1968 that he played the song on a loop for two consecutive hours. It's a stunt that sounds even more impressive in our current era of all-programmed stations, when commercial radio doesn't even back announce song titles and artists. Just traffic and weather—and mattress commercials.

I have also been fortunate to have grown up in a home that was always a popular and warm landing spot where musicians felt as though they were welcome to visit anytime (thanks, Mom). And since my dad's generation was one of musicians who spent at least the early part of their careers traveling with big bands, their skills in the field of spoken-word improvisation developed along with a command of their instruments over the course of hundreds (and sometimes thousands) of all-night bus rides. And they didn't talk like "six-year-olds on helium," either. (Thank you, David Ives, for nailing that one.) There was no "It was like, awesome, and she was like, 'Whatever.'" When my father's friends came to our home, they always brought articulate and entertaining accounts of what was happening on the road, often with accompanying fallout to their personal lives at home. My brother and I had the good sense during those days to grab front-row seats and become active and appreciative listeners.

So with all proper respect for the elders, I wish to become part of the tradition of passing along what I have seen and heard—and what I believe—while I am still around to play music, sing lyrics, and maybe try writing prose again at some point. The film mogul Samuel Goldwyn said, "I don't think anyone should write his autobiography until after he's dead," but that's easier said than done. Goldwyn also said, "If I could drop dead right now, I'd be the happiest man alive!"—which sounds more like Ralph Kiner. It's an added bonus to be able to knock out a version of things while a significant number of the participants in the narrative are still with us.

There are two authors' names on the front cover, and with all the ghost-writing controversies out there (subject of an instructive install-ment of Kurt Andersen's *Studio 360,* produced by PRI), it's probably worthwhile to fill you in on the process that resulted in the words making it onto these pages (or digital representations). First of all, Joe Cosgriff is a person who has always urged me to write things down, if only for my own self-keeping, memory preservation, and eventual reading pleasure. Odds are that we most likely would have written this book together, whether it was part of a formal project or simply for posterity. We've been collaborating successfully for over thirty years on songwriting, jokes, special lyrics, Red Sox luncheons, after-dinner speeches, monologues, Carnac bits, friends' liner notes, online baseball articles—you name it. So while there was never a question about whether I had enough to say, I was confident that Joe had solid instincts about what worked and how to organize those ideas into chapters and categories. It also helped that he'd been on the road with us during the Sinatra tour, had met Rosemary Clooney many times, and knows well the cast of characters who float through my life.

At the beginning we worked in a structure we envisioned Woodward and Bernstein using—we sat across from each other at a table, shared ideas, named names, and wrote them down. It had been successful in the past when we brainstormed for material—but we'd never before needed to produce the sheer number of pages required for a book. It was great fun, but the glacial pace at which we were getting words onto the page projected to a completion date of Bucky Pizzarelli's 111th birthday. Told by the powers-that-be to get things moving, we stumbled upon a seemingly dysfunctional system that inexplicably worked—I began talking through the microphone and into the software we use to record our radio show, and then e-mailed the files or snail-mailed CDs to Joe for transcribing. This method was surprisingly effective for any number of reasons, and it produced a series of unforeseen benefits, particularly in getting the details of stories into the book. One such unexpected bonus was that recalling and dictating a story would invariably help to elicit others, some of which hadn't appeared on my radar screen in ten or twenty years. And seeing the transcripts of my spoken words motivated me to write more, enough so that over the second half of the project, I submitted all new material in written form and spent considerable time revisiting the text of the spoken stories to make sure they would work on the printed (and digital) page.

I recognize that when it comes to purchasing books, readers have no shortage of authors from whom they can choose. An early 2012 visit to the local Barnes and Noble stores on Fifty-Fourth Street and Third Avenue led me to books by authors as diverse as Keith Richards, Tina Fey, Martin Amis, Samantha Power, Don DeLillo, Seamus Heaney, and Dr. Seuss, all within a twenty-foot radius. Then there are those writers referred to by my publisher's marketing department as "secondary competitors"—Dante Alighieri, Søren Kierkegaard, Aristophanes, and Anton Chekhov. It is one thing to be judged within the Grammy Awards' Traditional Pop Vocal category against Rod Stewart—it's a far more imposing challenge slugging it out for position on book-shelves and on e-book websites with an author who lived in the fourth century BC.

Thank you for joining me as I share my story and my stories. It's meant to be a celebration of the music, the people who play it, and those who love and support it. In the face of the daunting list of talented authors whose works are deserving of the time you set aside to read, I am grateful beyond words that you have chosen to buy (or accept) my book.

John Pizzarelli
New York City

1

When I Was a Little Boy

All my life I've always wanted to be somebody. Now I see I should have been more specific.

—Jane Wagner

The date written on the back of one of our family's most cherished photographs indicates that it was taken in mid-October 1966. Those were the days when Captain Kangaroo and Mister Green Jeans were sending me off to the first grade every day, Batman (on the new color TV) had replaced black-and-white Superman as my new caped hero ("Quick, Robin—hand me the shark-repellent Bat-spray!"), and *Meet the Beatles* was no. 1 on the Pizzarelli family hi-fi. The photo itself, an interior scene of people seated together at a dinner table, brought back fond (and fuzzy . . . I wasn't yet seven years old) memories of our weekly family gatherings at the home of my uncle Pete and aunt Honey in Clifton, New Jersey.

What I clearly recall about those Sundays is the roar of everybody trying to talk at the same time, kids running around in all directions, and gallons of red sauce simmering in immense vats on the stove. And as much as we all loved to be with one another, it was Aunt Honey's cooking that brought in the sellout crowds. As true masters do, she played to her strengths, which in her case happened to be homemade pasta, veal and chicken cutlets, and eggplant parmigiana—with and without meat—served in and around an endless vat of tomato sauce. That was the menu every Sunday—profound in its simplicity. We joke now that Uncle Pete and Aunt Honey's dining room must have been constructed by the same people who made Sansabelt trousers, given how the modest square footage of the dining room appeared to expand to accommodate the number and girth of the family members and their guests in attendance. Twelve or fifteen (or sometimes more) of us could gather at the table without anyone feeling crowded—at least until certain members of the family (no names, please) went for their third helpings of ziti and veal parm.

At some point in the proceedings my father and his uncle Bobby (Uncle Pete's younger brother) would grab my attention—or just grab *me*—lead us to a relatively quiet area of the house, and hand me a Paramount tenor banjo. That summer I had begun taking lessons with Uncle Bobby in a tiny downstairs cubicle at Victor's House of Music in Ridgewood, New Jersey, about ten minutes from our home in Saddle River, and he always wanted to break away from the group to play a few songs with me whenever the families got together.

The quiet banjo sessions with Uncle Bobby and my dad struck a stark contrast with the rollicking family sing-alongs that always followed Aunt Honey's incredible meals. Two things about Uncle Pete, Uncle Bobby, and those incredibly happy Sundays remain clear in my memory after all these years—the brothers' lightning-fast hands and their ear-to-ear smiles of joy while they were strumming. The setlist was made up of everybody's all-time banjo hits: "Bye, Bye Blues," "Yes, Sir, That's My Baby," "Bye Bye Blackbird," and "Alabamy Bound." Now that I think about it—it must have been more than a little out of the ordinary for a six-and-a-half-year-old to be picking up on the obscure musical references ("Well, I'm Alabamy bound") in Bugs Bunny cartoons. And I was even able to play the basic chords to the song on the banjo!

My dad—who has the same name as I do, although everyone called him Bucky, short for "Buckskin," a nickname bestowed by his onetime Texas cowhand father who eventually settled on the plains of Paterson—would often sit in with his uncles, usually playing Uncle Pete's guitar. I recall sitting at their feet, staring at their hands, and thinking, *How do they do it? How do they even know what strings to play?* The force of the music coming from the three instruments (all unplugged!) literally shook the lamps in the living room, as well as the pots and pans that hung in the kitchen. The sound of the banjos and the guitar during those sing-alongs was as glorious as anything I'd ever heard. It also marked one of the first (of many) moments when I said to myself, *This is what I want to do—all the time.*

Pete and Bobby Domenick were my dad's mother's brothers and were the men who taught my father how to play the banjo and guitar. Bobby (born in 1915) lived his life as a professional musician, switching from banjo to guitar and spending the better part of two decades on the road with several big bands—including those of Bob Chester (where Sinatra sang before he signed with Tommy Dorsey), Buddy Rogers

My uncle Bobby (front with banjo) and Uncle Pete (second row) taught me how to play banjo and guitar, just as they taught my father before me.

(Mary Pickford's husband), and Clyde McCoy, whose relatives liked to drop the gloves with the Hatfields.

Bobby also spent time with pianist and bandleader Raymond Scott, whose music was arranged and adapted by the incredible Carl Stalling for use in hundreds of Warner Brothers cartoons. Few people remember these bands of the thirties and forties, but they were all fairly popular name bands in their day. Throughout those years, Bobby would return home from his tours "looking like a million bucks," according to Bucky, always dressed in a spiffy suit and two-toned shoes, driving a new Buick, and sporting a glamorous actress or singer on his arm. He'd also bring home "a suitcase full of stories" and a slew of cutting-edge chords and harmonics he'd learned from other musicians, which he couldn't wait to share with his brother Peter and my father.

When Bobby came off the road permanently, he was able to support himself and Aunt Anita with steady studio work in the fifties and sixties (which included sessions with Louis Armstrong), as well as in duo acts with one of "the Joes"—either the blind accordion player, pianist, organist, songwriter ("Nowhere," "Have Another One, Not Me," "Meet Me at No Special Place"), and underappreciated vocalist Joe Mooney, or the jazz violinist and All-World practical joker Joe Venuti. Because Mooney was blind, and his small groups did not use sheet music, he'd call out the licks and the chords to his sidemen—or just allow them to feel where things were going. Bucky was steeped in this tradition—he first recorded with Mooney in 1951—and always emphasized to my brother Martin and me the importance of listening closely to hear the changes. As for Joe Venuti—more on him later. His recordings with Eddie Lang are the gold standard among records made by early guitarists.

Bobby never missed an opportunity to credit Uncle Pete's support of the family back home for making his own professional career possible. Having remained at home to work in the silk mills of Passaic, New Jersey, Peter (b. 1908) came to be my dad's primary teacher and mentor throughout the thirties and forties. Many years later I would learn of Uncle Pete's impeccable reputation among professional musicians, even though his full-time job limited him to weekend club dates and weddings. He won particularly favorable recognition from none other than my dad's good pal and our frequent houseguest, electric guitar pioneer Les Paul, who lived nearby in Mahwah, New Jersey, in those days. Somehow Uncle Bobby and Uncle Pete found themselves hired as the opening act for Les at an outdoor gig in northern New Jersey— outside a firehouse—and their playing that day threatened to over-shadow the headliner. But Les encouraged the brothers and wanted to hear more, the result being *Banjorama*, a record on Mercury released in the late fifties featuring my father, pianist Dick Hyman (credited as "The Renowned Ricardo"), Uncle Bobby, and Uncle Pete, led by guitar/banjo ace Carmen Mastren (original price: $2.98). Sporting one of the coolest LP album covers out there, it's worth the ten dollars you'll pay for it on eBay, a bargain for the album art alone. *Fun fact*: Mastren spent some time in the 1930s working for an R. Crumb Hero of Jazz, Joe "Wingy" Mannone, the one-armed trumpet player, bandleader—and author (*Trumpet on the Wing*).

From the *Banjorama* sessions came the story Les would often tell about Uncle Pete, who, while a music veteran, had not spent a lot of time in recording studios. Mortified at hitting an off-note close to the conclusion of one of the *Banjorama* cuts, Peter became upset and began apologizing personally and profusely to everyone in the studio, which meant the spectators, the maintenance staff, and sixty-seven banjo players—only a slight exaggeration. He probably would have begun a second complete lap around the apology circuit had Les not explained to him that he'd fix things—they'd simply splice from an earlier cut or have Peter redo a few seconds of his part. Les said that he'd never seen someone go from deep embarrassment to utter joy as quickly as Uncle Pete did when he understood that he'd been saved by the magic of the recording process. And if you were going to fix an error in a recording session during the late fifties, there was no one more qualified to do so than Les Paul.

It wasn't lost on me that I was learning the fundamentals of the banjo and guitar from the same two men who had taught my dad to play. And not only was I learning from Dad's teachers—I was playing the stringed instruments in the same order that my dad had learned them—first banjo, then guitar. Dad has always been a believer that the banjo trains guitarists to correctly develop and strengthen wrist action. Also, he never misses a chance to tell interviewers, students, and college master classes that learning the banjo provides the proper foundation for learning rhythm, which he believes to be an essential-yet-overlooked skill for anyone serious about playing the guitar.

It's probably a good idea at this point to dispel the notion that it was all banjos, guitars, and music lessons at the Pizzarelli house 24/7/365. I had been a decent pitcher and shortstop in Little League until, in just one daunting off-season, I lost my mojo (story to follow), the other kids had growth spurts, and their pitches seemed to gain in velocity. I survived for another season as a good-field/no-hit, concave-chested outfielder, making highlight-reel running catches in the outfield before there was ESPN and Web Gems. Reflecting on those days, I wonder whether I might have spent too little time on batting practice and too

A Pizzarelli team photo before Martin appeared on the scene. From left, Anne, an early-career me, Mom, Mary, and Dad.

much time on batting *stances*. Or mumbled my evening prayers, so that instead of winding up as the best banjo-playing baseball player, I asked to be the best banjo-hitting player.

Like most Little Leaguers in the late sixties and early seventies, I imitated the players with the most distinctive batting stances. As I did successfully by imitating the icons of the guitar—Uncle Bobby and Uncle Pete, George Barnes, Freddie Green, and Dad—I should have modeled myself after some of the greats in the game—Willie Mays, Ted Williams, Hank Aaron, Jimmy Piersall. But instead, my favorite baseball stances to replicate in front of the mirror each day in those years belonged to Horace Clarke, Steve Whitaker, Joe Pepitone, and Ron Woods of the shockingly bad Yankee teams that followed the Bombers' consecutive World Series appearances of 1960–64. All four of these players looked great *getting ready* in the batter's box—until they were forced to deal with the harsh reality of professionally pitched baseballs, which turned all four into virtually automatic outs. The same way certain numbers are memorable to me—1492, 1776, 1812, and 1915 (Sinatra born)—I recall .117—Steve Whitaker's batting average in 1968. Even in an era dominated by extraordinary pitching, .117 was just *too* low. Whitaker, the man I imitated in front of the mirror each day, was let go in the expansion draft. Learning that one of my mirror guys had been sent packing was a traumatic moment for an eight-year-old, who spent sleepless nights in fear of the "expansion draft," wondering if he, too, could be "left unprotected."

Additional information for the back of my *Jazz Heroes of Jersey* trading card would include the fact that I was captain of the Wandell School's eighth-grade basketball team. Our squad found itself pitted against nearby towns such as Upper Saddle River, Ho-Ho-Kus, and Hackensack, all of which seemed to be producing eighth-graders who were six foot two with Joe Torre–like five o'clock shadows. If their ages were to be believed, they must have reached puberty in the third grade. Or the kids must have red-shirted kindergarten. I remember my mother's support—showing up for the games, encouraging me at all times, and urging me to calm down after being called for questionable fouls, one for having my jaw inconveniently in the path of an opponent's flying elbow. But our team's problems began squarely with the team captain—I could not make a layup to save my life, a sentence you will not read in basketball legend Jerry West's critically acclaimed memoir. Whatever the outcome (and it was always the same), Mom's cooking, especially her fabulous pot roast, ensured that the agony of defeat did not extend one minute past the start of dinner hour.

When I was about to turn twelve, my mom and dad faced a significant family decision. For the previous six years, my father had a dream job, holding *The Tonight Show*'s guitar chair after sharing it with Gene Bertoncini and Tony Mottola at various times during the mid-sixties. But when Johnny Carson announced that *The Tonight Show* was leaving New York and heading to Burbank, California, where the show would be based full-time beginning in May 1972, my parents were forced to decide whether our family would be following the Carson entourage out to the West Coast.

Bucky had started on the show full-time in 1966, working for one of his true pals in all of music, Skitch Henderson. Things happened fast, so here goes—Skitch, in his second stint as *The Tonight Show*'s bandleader (he had skipped the Jack Paar years after working for Steve Allen) was replaced for about ten minutes by Milton DeLugg. (Carson's first choice was said to have been Ray "The Very Thought of You" Noble, of whom George Van Eps had always spoken so highly.) DeLugg was quickly succeeded by Carl "Doc" Severinsen in 1967. So in a little over a year it was Skitch, DeLugg (instead of Ray Noble), then Severinsen.

Doc brought the musical chairs to an end, taking over Carson's band until Johnny's final show in 1992, after a twenty-five-year run as *The Tonight Show*'s bandleader and a forty-year stint with the program in its various incarnations. Known best for his collection of flashy shirts and leisure suits—and later, linoleum sport jackets—that complemented his hipster persona (and gave fits to camera operators and color TV manufacturers), Doc helped raise the profile of Carson's orchestra to rock-band status in the seventies. And for all his style and sizzle, Severinsen was known among musicians as someone who had earned his stripes. A fixture in Skitch's first trumpet chair since 1952, he was known among the guys as a musician's musician—a man who knew the music and the arrangements, and who, even at the top of his career, still practiced for several hours each day. Stories still circulate among his colleagues in the band who can recall instances of Doc losing himself in practice sessions at his home studio for up to a full day, blowing through scheduled appointments and mealtimes. For his part, Bucky loved working with and for Doc Severinsen, although he is quick to point out that Doc "dressed like a Princeton kid right up until he got the leader's job."

As much as my dad likes to get on Doc for the way he dressed in those days, not many musicians escaped the early and mid-seventies unscathed—the 1972–78 period features a little more Doc in my dad's wardrobe than he'd like to admit, as we remind him when we dig out his old album covers.

Skitch and Doc had assembled an all-star lineup of jazz musicians in New York—Clark Terry, Ed Shaughnessy, Snooky Young, Tommy Newsom, Grady Tate, Walt Levinsky, and Bob Haggart. To this day, my father's face lights up when he speaks of *The Tonight Show* years, and not simply for the obvious blessing it was for a musician and the father of four kids to have a steady, well-paying gig. It was exciting, he still says, to go to work every day with guys who were both the best musicians in town and his closest friends.

Yet as much as my dad loved Doc, the guys on the bandstand, and job security, our family's roots and our hearts were in the New York/New Jersey area. It was where our relatives lived (and ate), it was home to Dad's studio work, and it was where he was in demand at the best jazz clubs in the world. Also, my parents were outspoken about not wanting Anne, Mary, Martin, and me to grow up in Los Angeles, at least not the city they viewed from afar in 1972. So the decision was made that we would be staying in New Jersey.

Let the record show that the *Tonight Show* did not allow my father to leave the band without some behind-the-scenes pleading for a change of heart. I remember picking up more than a few phone calls from Doc during that time, and his message would always be the same: "Tell your Dad we need him!" But Mom and Dad's decision stood firm, and we stayed in New York. I did get to see the final concert given by the New York *Tonight Show* Orchestra at Lincoln Center's Avery Fisher Hall before the band left for the West Coast. My grade-school buddy Bill Burke still recalls the concert vividly, especially going backstage and meeting drummer Grady Tate, a singular character and a wonderful, distinctive drummer. Check out Grady on Stan Getz's *Sweet Rain* album. Or his work with Wes Montgomery. Or singing "Naughty Number Nine" and "I Got Six" on *Schoolhouse Rock*.

A few short months after we made the decision to remain in New Jersey and near our close-knit relatives, our family's world was turned upside down. A week after breezing through his annual physical exam, Uncle Bobby died suddenly of a heart attack at the age of fifty-seven. His death shook our family to its core. With Uncle Bobby's passing, Dad and I began a new routine—the Sunday drive from Saddle River to Clifton to take lessons with and to comfort Uncle Pete. An important part of learning the basics from Uncle Pete was the tablature he made with numbers, where he listed the number of strums and put a circle around the melody note. This allowed me to play songs ("Bye, Bye Blues") while I was learning the full range of chords, an approach that allowed me to strum away like a big leaguer even as a banjo novice. I am convinced that being taught by my father's mentors ramped up my learning curve on the early duo gigs with Bucky, when my father would essentially throw me into the water, and his eyes would shout, "Swim!"

While I sat for lessons with Pete, my dad would go pick up a tub of Country Club Ice Cream. At the conclusion of my lesson we'd each knock back a bowl or two, then grab our instruments—Dad would play Uncle Pete's guitar, with Pete and me on banjo—and begin a joyful jam. And as Bobby had done when he and I played songs together, Pete and my father had a way of accompanying me that made the music sound far better than the notes and chords I was actually playing. After a few songs, one of us would ask, "Hey, how about some more ice cream?" so we'd take a short break, then pick up the instruments again. This was a great time in my life—learning from my dad's teacher, playing notes and chords that seemed impossible only a few years before, trading licks with my dad and our beloved uncle, unlimited ice cream. Twelve years old. It didn't get better than this.

The Sunday lessons and ice cream–fueled jam sessions ended abruptly and sadly about five months later, when Uncle Pete died on Christmas Eve, also of a heart attack and far too early in his life. While Uncle Pete had always perked up for our Sunday sessions, Aunt Honey believed that her husband never got over his younger brother's sudden and unexpected passing. Even as we played and tried to have fun, Peter would often grow melancholy during the breaks in our Sunday banjo lessons, reminding us, "It's just not the same without Bobby." The deaths of both uncles within a five-month period left a gaping hole in the center of our large extended family. Even though it was not in my father's DNA to deal with sadness by talking things out, I could tell in his eyes and by the way he carried himself that this was a particularly rough period for him. All these years later, when my dad, Martin, and I reminisce about Pete and Bobby, usually when we're strumming guitars on my parents' porch, I have begun to fully understand how much Dad was affected when he lost the two men who had sat next to him for over forty years and filled his head and heart with music. Our conversations about Pete and Bobby led to the cathartic experience of making the 2007 album *Sunday at Pete's*, which paid tribute to my uncles' lives, their music, and the impromptu guitar and banjo gatherings that brought joy to our family for so many years. Whenever I find myself taking part in a family sing-along, and it doesn't need to be *my* family, I invariably think of Bobby and Pete and make sure I strum hard enough to rattle the pots and pans.

Without a teacher who knew the method I had learned from my uncles, I stopped taking banjo lessons. Part of it was sadness; I had lost my two beloved uncles and teachers almost overnight, and I needed to mourn them and all they meant to me. I also didn't want to start from scratch with a new teacher who'd be using new methods. Make no mistake: Dad was still encouraging me to play, but this was the beginning of his post-Carson days, which meant his working all day in studio sessions, often coming home for dinner with Mom and the kids, then heading back to Manhattan to play with George Barnes and various duos at night. But one day I picked up one of Dad's Gibson guitars from the couch, studied the tablatures in an Elton John songbook one of my sisters was using, and figured out the rest from playing along with the records. A lightbulb appeared, along with an uncomplicated epiphany that ranks up there with "They're undefeated in games in which they scored more runs than their opponent"—*The guitar plays just like the banjo—it just has more strings.*

A pal who had stuck with me through grammar school and then Don Bosco Preparatory High School, guitarist and bassist Steve Lafiosca would visit our home often in those days, always eyeing the music equipment that occupied every room of our house. "Hey," Steve told me one day, "we can start a rock band—you have a bass, an amp, *and* a guitar." Had Steve paid more attention, he'd have noticed that we had at least one bass, amp, and guitar *in every room*. But while I might have had the hardware to start a band, I didn't know much about actually playing the instruments. What I did know was that I liked plugging in and experimenting with all the electronic features, especially the wah-wah pedal. It all sounded so cool to us. Soon, mostly through trial-and-error, we produced sounds close enough to the ones we were *trying* to create—sounding like Peter Frampton in the Humble Pie days or early Robin Trower. Or Johnny Winter on "Bony Moronie." Almost immediately, my rehearsing and playing with that first band quickly moved beyond fooling around with knobs, dials, bells, and whistles, and became more about wanting to become a more serious guitar player.

Let's backtrack here—I always loved music and participated in a handful of "rock" bands in the sixties and seventies; the good news is that none of them required me to wear mascara. Okay, I am not sure if the official scorer will be counting the Tomahawks, with yours truly on the Susan Dey–model tambourine, Bill Hunt on the Melodica, and anchored on the drums by Bill Burke. Our band's performances at school included the Monkees' covers and a few originals about war and peace (lower case, not the Tolstoy version), all within the confines of a hard seven o'clock bedtime. As I spent my early high school days learning solos from rock records and playing in more bands, my dad casually listened from a distance, showing me a few things but always taking a hands-off approach, allowing me to play the music I liked and never forcing his tastes or his style on me. Then when I was about sixteen, Dad came into the room after hearing me play and threw down the gauntlet. "Okay, you've learned all these Frampton licks. How about learning 'Rose Room' from this Django Reinhardt record?" He even tossed in a five-dollar kicker if I could play it all the way through in one take. *Five dollars.* Adjusted for inflation (1976) and for the exchange rate in "Bucky Bucks," this would equate to roughly twenty-five thousand dollars today.

Two things immediately became apparent: (a) learning "Rose Room" would be more difficult than playing "Country Comfort" and "Show Me the Way" and (b) I was blown away by Django's guitar playing, which I later learned he'd achieved with two- or three-fingered chords—his third and fourth fingers were fused together and not usable after being burned in a home fire. But in the process of falling a couple of choruses (okay, more than a couple of choruses) short of the five-dollar reward, I succeeded in wearing out the grooves on the Django record, first finding my way to the other cuts of that album (like "Nuages"), and then moving on to albums by other artists in that same world, such as Clifford Brown and Billie Holiday. It wasn't far from there to the impressive George Barnes parts from a duo album that he and my dad made in 1971 (*Guitars Pure and Honest*). Barnes's playing always made sense to me at an age when I was casting about for a sound of my own. Even today, when I listen closely to playbacks at recording sessions, I can still pick up hints of George's sound lurking within my playing.

At that time I frequently accompanied my father to his solo club gigs and solo concerts in the New York/New Jersey area, one of my dad's acoustic guitars in hand—sometimes to warm up with him off-stage, mostly for more credibility when I'd put my head down and mumble to gain access to the clubs and concert halls without a ticket.

Then one night I couldn't believe my ears—it was Dad's voice coming from the stage. "Bring up your guitar, John," he announced. "My son is going to play 'Honeysuckle Rose.'" I remember that introduction from my dad the same way ballplayers talk about their first introduction by the peerless Bob Sheppard over the old Yankee Stadium public address system ("Numbah 7, Mickey Mantle, centa-field, numbah 7"). In the spirit of Uncle Pete and Uncle Bobby when they accompanied me, my dad made me sound better than I deserved to that night (as he still does today) by a factor of several hundred.

In 1976 my dad and I began working together occasionally, starting with a song or two whenever I accompanied him to gigs. When I played with Dad in those days, I accompanied him on an Aria copy of a Gibson ES175, a six-string guitar similar to the one George Barnes and all the jazz guys were playing in those days. Around the house my dad would often hand me the George Van Eps model seven-string, which Van Eps had designed for Gretsch—the seventh string being the low A below the E—and demonstrate all the different keys and walking baselines that this guitar and the additional string made possible.

Though my dad was nothing but supportive and reassuring about my progress, these sporadic, trial-by-fire experiences represented an obvious wake-up call. As much as audiences like rooting for an underdog, I would need to show considerable improvement and expand my repertoire beyond two songs if I wanted to amount to something more than an earnest kid who'd been brought out to show how the guitar lessons were coming along.

2

Rock and Roll High School

I don't think I'd have been in such a hurry to reach adulthood if I'd known the whole thing was going to be ad-libbed.

—Bill Watterson

"Higher, higher."

"Lower, lower."

I had arrived at the hotel in the wee small hours, hadn't gotten much sleep, and was startled to be awakened in the morning by a series of odd commands coming from the other side of the room. I recognized the voice to be my father's—good thing, since he was the occupant of the room's other bed when I fell asleep. Fortuitously, I had awakened in a position that faced away from whatever was transpiring.

"Higher, higher," he soon repeated.

"Now lower . . . *lower!*"

Uh-oh. I had heard all about the unspoken jazz musicians' code—that whatever happens on the road stays on the road. And we were in New Orleans, a town that had been marching to its own drummers—and trumpet, clarinet, and tuba players—even before Napoleon sold it to Jefferson in the Louisiana Purchase (known in France as the Louisiana Sale) for a player to be named later. Maybe decadence was in the water down here. All I could think at that moment was "Say it isn't so"—both the Billie Holiday version and the little boy's plea to Shoeless Joe Jackson outside a courthouse in 1920. The kid (if there was a kid) might have said, "Say it ain't so." I used both, adding the words "Please" and "God."

As I held the pillow over my ears, the demands persisted:

"Higher, higher."

"Lower, lower."

As I have mentioned, Dad replaced what had been *The Tonight Show* part of his schedule with bookings in clubs and recording studios, though he never missed an opportunity to meet up with his old NBC pals on those rare occasions when they performed back east. A year or so after the guys had moved west, I drove with Bucky to Long Island to see and hear Doc perform with a touring band at the Westbury Music Fair. Renamed the NYCB Theatre at Westbury a few years ago, the Westbury Music Fair began as a tent in 1956 and still has quirks, such as its circular stage in the middle of the theater that is rigged with hydraulics that allow it to revolve during the performances. (No revolving stage for Doc at this show, however.) The big moment for us came when Doc spotted Dad in the audience. "Hey, isn't that Bucky in the second row?" he announced to the audience, at which point he stopped the music, directed a spotlight at Dad (and me), and came to the edge of the stage. He reached across the first row and hugged my dad, then treated my father to the introduction of his life: "He's a winner of the Nobel Prize and the Purple Heart, he's the world's greatest living human, a close, personal friend of Trummy Young's . . ." After the concert, we went backstage to visit with Doc and ran into Johnny Frosk, Doc's replacement as the lead trumpet player of the *Tonight Show* band, who also didn't make the move to Burbank. (Johnny would later play beautifully on my *Naturally* and *All of Me* releases on RCA.)

In a voice filled with frustration, Doc said to Johnny and my dad, "But you two were the only guys I *wanted* to go with me to L.A."

A side note: it was Doc Severinsen whose great sound and powerful presence in front of the band inspired me to choose the trumpet as my school band instrument back in the fourth grade. And having discovered that Doc was a composer after catching one of his extended pieces on *The Tonight Show*, I decided to compose a piece for two trumpets to be played at our sixth-grade concert. To this day my mother talks about that concert, recalling the moment when she picked up the program, opened to the credits page, and read my name over and over again next to the word "Composer." She claims she spent the rest of the week wondering where, when, and how I had managed to *write* music. What I remember is that the performance itself had its bumps, given the three takes it took for Bill Hunt and me to play the piece all the way through without having to start again from the top. Good thing we were seated while playing, because Bill was so mortified by the do-overs that his legs almost didn't lift him up to acknowledge the wild applause that greeted our one successful pass at the piece.

When Dad no longer had the steady *Tonight Show* job, he was busier than ever with nightclub engagements at places like Upstairs at the Downstairs, the King Cole Room of the St. Regis Hotel, the Soerabaja on Seventy-Third Street and Lexington Avenue (now Vivolo), and the Guitar. He wouldn't have a long-term gig again until he and his trio were booked at the Café Pierre at the Pierre Hotel in the early eighties. For the Soerabaja engagement in the early seventies, the tenor sax player Zoot Sims, whose apartment was nearby, would often drop by and sit in when he wasn't on the road. To the bewilderment of my dad, Zoot *kept* sitting in, going so far as to send Al Cohn to sub for him when he couldn't make it. Yes, this wasn't even an official (or paying) gig for Zoot, and yet he believed it was necessary to send a sub when he couldn't make it. (And Al Cohn—arranger, tenor ace, Woody Herman alum—was no ordinary sub, kids.) Zoot did negotiate to have my dad drive him home, agreeing on a rate that would pay Bucky a dollar per block or a dollar per pothole, whichever came out to more money for my father.

Zoot had played with everybody—Count Basie, Artie Shaw, Benny Goodman, Woody Herman, Stan Getz, Gerry Mulligan, and, for almost thirty years, Al Cohn. His unscheduled, unbilled visits had turned Dad's solo gig at the Soerabaja into one of the hottest shows in town. Soon afterward, Dad and Zoot found themselves together on an international tour with Benny Goodman, followed by a live album with Benny in Copenhagen. They forged a lifetime friendship on that Goodman tour and began booking duo gigs when they got home.

For about a four- or five-year stretch, Zoot and his wife Louise visited on the day after Christmas, the feast of Saint Stephen for Catholics, but "Zoot Sims Day" in the Pizzarelli household. Zoot's holiday routine was a simple one—it involved finishing whatever holiday food was left over, taking on all comers in Ping-Pong, and, of course, leading a rousing jam session with whoever wanted to join in. The only person we knew who owned a carrying case for his table tennis paddle, Zoot took his Ping-Pong almost as seriously as he took his saxophone. After he beat about six of us in a row without breaking a

In a photo taken in the early eighties at Waterloo Village in New Jersey, I share the stage with Bucky and one of the all-time great guys, Zoot Sims.

sweat, Bucky took us aside and came clean to us that Zoot's Manhattan apartment had a full-size Ping-Pong table built to fit over the dining room table, which allowed Zoot to challenge musicians to after-hours matches that would sometimes last until five o'clock in the morning or later. I bet his neighbors loved that.

Having moved to nearby Nyack, New York, by the mid-seventies Zoot had become a year-round fixture in our home, and we loved having him around. Whenever he and I were in a room together, he'd invariably begin the conversation with the same all-purpose nugget of lifestyle advice: "You gotta get laid." *You gotta get laid?* I was fifteen years old. Aside from that, I was spending eight hours a day at an all-boys high school, my patter with girls was beyond pathetic, and my nose took up three-quarters of my acne-ravaged face. Get laid? The Wandell School had a better chance of beating Jerry West's Lakers.

When my brother Martin and I look back on those days, one midwinter music session in our living room comes to mind often. Zoot had decided after dinner one night that instead of heading home, he wanted to play for a little while. But he hadn't brought his sax. First, we had to find him an instrument. The closest thing we had to a tenor sax was my sister Mary's school band clarinet. That was okay with Zoot; he assured us that he'd played any number of instruments when he toured with his parents "back in the vaudeville days," before switching to tenor as a teenager. His parents, Pete, a dancer, and Kate, had been vaudeville performers for over forty years, and Zoot had played clarinet and drums in the early acts. Man, it must be cool to have "Vaudeville Days" on one's résumé, instant street cred to drop into any conversation or interview situation.

Now that Zoot had a horn to blow, we needed to find a song we could all play, including Martin, who was then a beginner on the stringed bass. We finally settled on "Out of Nowhere," a Johnny Green tune from the thirties that had been Bing Crosby's first no. 1 hit and became a jazz classic following the Coleman Hawkins–Django Reinhardt–Benny Carter recording. With the song selection in place, Zoot appointed Martin as the Keeper of the Flame, instructing him not to allow the fireplace to fizzle out under any circumstances.

Dad, Martin, Zoot, and I were soon playing the tune, and we were having a ball! Zoot was flying, both musically and figuratively (with a primary assist from a certain Mr. Johnnie Walker), sometimes calling out, "That was a Goodman lick!" after he'd play a riff or two on the clarinet. Even on a plastic Bundy that had spent too many summers locked in the musty band room at my sister's high school, Zoot could swing hard and make it look effortless. With everyone taking multiple solos, the song stretched beyond a half hour in duration, with no one feeling any pain. That is, no one except Martin, who, being new to the bass, had yet to develop protective calluses, at least not ones that would sustain him through a forty-five-minute "Out of Nowhere." The high action of the strings on my father's half-sized high school bass, the one on which Martin was learning, did not help his cause either. Before my brother knew it, he was dealing with three or four serious blisters, all threatening to blow at any moment. At a point when he could barely keep his hands in contact with the strings, the appointed Keeper of the Flame then did some fast thinking.

"Hey Zoot," he called out, abandoning his bass. "I think the fire's dying. I'd better get to it." Zoot knew Martin had been in distress and reminded everyone of my brother's fast-thinking exit line ("I think the fire's dying") whenever he saw us.

Another superior musician, Joe Pass, was also a visitor to the Pizzarelli home during my high school years. Joe Pass, like many of my dad's colleagues, was another musician whose reputation and celebrity status had eluded me. A bona fide star among guitar players, he had been on the cover of *Guitar Player* magazine when I just started high school and shortly before one of his visits—around 1976. (I perused *Guitar Player* during my high school years with the same intensity my friends brought to their affinity for *Playboy* during the Barbi Benton era.) Joe happened to be sitting in the living room with Bucky talking music and guitars when Dad handed him an old Gibson L-5 that he had recently purchased. My father then called in my sister Mary, who knew the chords to "When Sunny Gets Blue." In no time, she and Joe were off and running, with Mary playing rhythm and Joe taking the melody. And when I say that he "took the melody," it doesn't do justice to what we witnessed that day. Within maybe fifteen seconds I knew that I had never heard single-string playing like that in my life. And I'd heard *everyone*, both at our house and on records. I was floored. He was also an engaging and funny guy, so I made sure I sat next to him at lunch and tried not to miss a word of his stories.

Perhaps ten years later, at the Umbria Jazz Festival in Perugia in central Italy, we heard that Joe would be giving a master class as part of the event's lecture schedule. Martin and I *had* to go! We arrived to see him lecturing to a room almost completely made up of Italian-speaking guitar students, none of whom appeared to be fluent (or even remotely conversant) in English. Joe started things off by calling a kid to the stage.

"Play something . . . anything," Joe suggested.

"How 'bout 'Summertime'?" the kid said in broken English.

Probably sensing he wouldn't be heard, Joe then muttered to no one in particular, "Why is it that everyone always wants to play 'Summertime'?"

The song selection, Perugia's summertime heat, the language barrier in the hall, and probably a good case of jet lag, all seemed to

Joe Pass (far left) with Herb Ellis, Bucky, and me in Denver in 1984.

converge and whack Joe at the same time. So when the kid decided to play only a couple of bars of the melody before he began blowing his solo, Joe exploded.

"Hey, you gotta play the melody, for cryin' out loud! You guys all want to get to the jazz, and you forget the melody!"

This was one of his favorite pet peeves, and Joe hit his stride with three or four minutes of serious venting, which was curiously met by the nodding heads and smiling faces of the guitar students. But Joe hadn't intended his rant to be taken as humor. Soon Martin and I figured out that we were the only people in the room who understood English or had the slightest idea of what Joe was saying. It was as though the Italian guitar students were head-bobbing as they would to a parent; they were aware of the cadence, but not a single word was getting through.

My friendship with Joe continued for many years as I kept running into him at jazz festivals. Backstage one night, Joe asked me to play for him, and I chose Ray Noble's ballad "I Hadn't Anyone Till You." After I played the first line, Joe stopped me and suggested a hip little chord—a D-flat 7 (sharp-11)—on the word "till," which he said he would allow me to "borrow." We then switched guitars, prompting Joe to shake his head at the seven-string, which I was playing full-time at this point. "Whaddya do with this goddamned extra string anyway?" he would always ask. I wanted to refer him to George Van Eps, who was able to make the case for the seventh string as eloquently as anyone ever has—see our FAQ section. I still use Joe Pass's chord on the word "till," and I think of him whenever I play or hear that stunning tune.

My brother Martin was there for Joe's visits and for every other occasion when my father's friends appeared at our home to sample my mother's cooking and to make music (usually in that order). A turning point in Martin's life as a musician came when he was twelve years old, before he had even picked up an instrument. Beginning in 1976, the bassist Slam Stewart would stay at our home while he and Bucky played engagements in the New York/New Jersey area, particularly a regular slot at Marty's on East Seventy-Third Street in Manhattan.

Born in Englewood, New Jersey, Slam had moved to upstate New York and was thrilled to be able to stay in our home instead of a hotel room for the week he was playing at the club (now a Dallas BBQ). The nightly routine was that after an early dinner, Slam would want to play our upright bass in our living room before he and my father left for their shows in Manhattan. Martin knew enough to sit close by and take in Slam's every move. Half of the famous "Slim & Slam" duo with guitarist and pianist Slim Gaillard in the late thirties and early forties, Slam actually had a couple of songs that hit the pop charts in those days—the catchy novelty numbers "Flat Foot Floogie (With a Floy Floy)" and "Cement Mixer (Putti Putti)." Over his illustrious and prolific career Slam had shared stages and recording studios with Fats Waller, Lester Young, Benny Goodman, Lionel Hampton, Coleman Hawkins, Red Norvo, Teddy Wilson, Errol Garner, and Art Tatum. And as if that weren't enough, he was the bass player on the Dizzy Gillespie session with Charlie Parker from February of 1945 that produced "Groovin' High," "Dizzy Atmosphere," and "All the Things You Are."

When you watched Slam, you were watching the history of jazz and the history of his instrument, the jazz bass—he was one of the essential bassists who created the bridge from swing to bebop. And Slam did it all while humming exactly an octave above where he played while using the bow and just the tips of his fingers for his walking bass line. For my money he is up there with Ray Brown, Charles Mingus, Milt Hinton, and Charlie Haden among the most versatile and talented bassists who have ever played. Martin and I treasured our time with Slam; we even joined him at the kitchen table for his late-night, post-gig glasses of Ovaltine with cookies. He loved to remind us that Zoot called Ovaltine "knockout drops," the perfect drink to mix before bedtime or an afternoon nap.

Slam's approach to singing extended to his unorthodox spoken-word conversations as well. He had famously toured with Slim Gaillard (again, they were Slim & Slam), a man who claimed to be fluent in eight languages. But during his days with Slam, Slim didn't speak French or Spanish or Italian—he spoke Vout, a form of Jive.

There were hundreds of other strange words flying around during those weeks. We all found ourselves mumbling a lot and speaking unintelligible "Slam-ese" for about a week following his visits. Even my mother got into the act. "Here's your food-a-rooni," she'd say at dinnertime.

Martin was a lucky fellow to have spent time with Slam, Ray Brown, Milt Hinton, George Duvivier, and Major Holley, just as I was to have heard George Barnes, Les Paul, and Joe Pass play guitar in our living room. Having shared so many musical influences over many years, Martin and I not only have common ground on what works, but we have enough trust to challenge each other to make the best possible music at any given time. Zoot absolutely had it right when he nicknamed Martin "the Keeper of the Flame"; I only wish Zoot had stayed around with us long enough to know Martin as he evolved into "the Keeper of the Time."

While I was absorbing all genres of music at home, my formal academic training took place at Don Bosco Prep in Ramsey, New Jersey.

Bucky with bassist and Ovaltine fan Slam Stewart. Taken at Gulliver's in New Jersey.

It is a Catholic institution of higher learning—with the emphasis on "Catholic" and "institution." The school's rich tradition in sports filled the air back when I roamed the halls. Music—well, not so much. During our annual grudge match against Bergen Catholic, the Don Bosco band began a version of "The Horse" in 1977 that didn't end until 1981.

The proudest moment of my high school days (besides surviving the wrath of Coach Pfanner after cutting his gym class) was the five minutes of being measured for my varsity jacket during my sophomore year. Once clad in the maroon jacket with white leather arms, I would be able to go to the Bergen Mall, the Garden State Plaza, the Fireplace, to the Stanley Warner movie theater—and it would signal to the girls of Bergen County that I was an essential cog in the Don Bosco machine.

The only issue with the jacket was that while football players had footballs on the backs of their jackets and basketball players had basketballs, the jackets given to band members had oversized (the real estate of at least two footballs) G-clefs. As things played out, I might as well have been wearing a giant bull's-eye on my back for the negative and downright unfriendly attention my beloved jacket heaped upon me. For a student body collectively on the hunt for defenseless targets with distinguishing characteristics that could be identified, mocked, exploited, then mocked again, the telltale G-clef was almost too good to be true.

On his classic *Child of the Fifties* album Robert Klein made the observation that upon turning thirty-five, he realized that his lifelong dream of playing center for the New York Knicks had probably eluded him. I was beginning to arrive at a similar realization about my pro baseball career during my high school days. After all, I hadn't played a game that didn't involve a Wiffle Ball in almost four years. I was still ready to play, to be sure, but how would the scouts even know where to find me?

Then I thought—possibly the G-clef could be my ticket to a big-time college. If I couldn't attend a school with Wrigley-like ivy growing from its residence halls (and I *couldn't*—my guidance counselor dove for cover whenever I approached his office), perhaps I'd be awarded a scholarship to a school where a hundred thousand fans gathered for football games—where the marching band formed complex sentences on the field. Schools where drum majors and F-minors alike were awarded scholarships. After all, the guidance counselor was fond of pointing out to me that colleges took "other stuff" into consideration, not just grades and SAT scores. Well, here I was—an eighteen-year-old musician who hung out with Doc Severinsen, Clark Terry, and Zoot Sims. And if ever something counted as "other stuff," it had to be living in a home where Slam Stewart drank Ovaltine and where Les Paul stopped by to try out his latest guitars and amps.

Well, my message to youngsters is that grades and SAT scores must count for more than the guidance counselors are letting on. I wish I could describe a more complex and sophisticated decision-making process for my choice of the University of Tampa besides—*they accepted me*! It was no accident that Don Bosco had kept me isolated from two-thirds of the student body for as long as they could, at least until the calamitous clerical error in junior year that resulted in my being placed in an honors section of algebra/trigonometry. I looked around and didn't recognize a single classmate. It was as though I'd been sent to an alternative school, and the segregated honors kids probably thought the same thing when they saw me. At the height of his powers Ted Williams became a baseball immortal for achieving success only two out of five times. The same success rate at Don Bosco Prep and on the SATs found me packing my bags for the University of Tampa and its renowned music program.

But my heart was still back in Jersey. With each holiday trip home and each concert or club date when I'd accompany my dad, I started to see myself as a professional guitarist rather than as a curious student and college-trained trumpet player. Actually, I had begun to feel that way right before I left for Tampa, when I served as the emergency substitute for my father at the annual Ridgewood Bandshell concert in front of thousands of people—and millions of mosquitoes. (And I thought it was the crowd that was abuzz.) Just prior to taking the stage, I noticed Victor's House of Music, where it had all started with Uncle Bobby, directly across the street. For the record, that night I played "Slambow," "Don't Let Me Be Lonely Tonight," "Yes Sir, That's My Baby" (on banjo!), and threw in a guitar instrumental of Chuck Mangione's "Feels So Good." And as further proof that I had what it took to be an authentic, card-carrying jazz musician, I broke up with my girlfriend after the gig that night during a torrential rainstorm.

Speaking of breakups, it didn't take long before I negotiated one that allowed me to put Tampa in the rearview mirror. After three semesters at the University of Tampa and extended philosophical discussions with my mom and dad about the value of formal education versus beginning a career as a professional musician, I promised to finish my college education at William Paterson College in Wayne, New Jersey—*a promise I fully intend to keep*.

Before checking out of Tampa I immediately flew to New Orleans, the Birthplace of Jazz, on spring break, where I was to meet my father and Zoot Sims for my first professional gig on the road. But in carefully weighing the pros and cons of leaving school to become a full-time musician, I hadn't counted on *this*.

"Higher, higher! Too high."

The situation was fast becoming a nightmare. And to make matters worse, I was under strict orders from my dad to wake him for breakfast with Zoot no later than ten o'clock in the morning, an hour that was fast approaching. I didn't want to muck up the first wake-up call of my professional career, but I was also afraid to look over to his side of the room. As much as I wanted to know what was going on, I was physically unable to turn my head in that direction. Even factoring in code-of-the-road considerations and the laissez-faire reputation of the city where we happened to wake up that morning, I was dealing with a crisis here. This was my father. Jeez, with me right there in the room. How could I look him in the eye again? Did the AF of M handbook have a chapter about behavior on the road? Did I bring the handbook? WWBHD? (What would Buddy Hackett do? What would *Bobby Hackett* do?)

"Higher! There you go."

"Higher, higher!" he said again.

"No! Lower, lower!"

Finally, I could take it no longer. And it was time for his ten o'clock wake-up call, and we didn't want to keep Zoot waiting. We couldn't miss breakfast. Expecting the worst, I slowly turned over to see Bucky—alone in bed—with the covers pulled up to his nose. He was watching *The Price Is Right* on mute.

"Higher, higher."

Yes, this was show business—and now I was a part of it.

3

Travels with Bucky

The hardest years in life are those between ten and seventy.
—Helen Hayes

While standing in the wings one Saturday night in Jazz at Lincoln Center's visually stunning Allen Room back in 2009, I found myself experiencing a flood of emotions. My quartet had been invited to perform as part of Lincoln Center's acclaimed "American Songbook" series, and we had reached the point in the program where it was time to concede the stage to the evening's special guest. In his usual understated manner the distinguished musician entered from the right, plugged his Benedetto archtop seven-string guitar into the amp, and took a seat. Wild, enthusiastic, and sustained applause had greeted the announcement of his arrival. Okay, it was an ovation that far exceeded the one accorded the headliner ninety minutes earlier. Smiling, because that's what he's usually doing, the evening's featured guest, *my father*, began his performance with a solo guitar rendition of an old favorite from the Benny Goodman days, Eubie Blake and Andy Razaf's "Memories of You."

The first thing I noticed as Bucky began playing was the undivided attention of the audience—at stage right I was in a perfect position to

29

see that every eye was on my father. Such focus from the people who come to see us is not something performers take for granted anymore. At some point in the not-too-distant past, performers reluctantly had to accept the reality of both the audience's inane and intrusive conversations (for example, "That's the son—Buzzy Jr.") and their undying need to light up their gadgets to send texts and e-mails of national importance ("Voice not great. Hope it's over soon. WTF!"). Dad's old boss during the Carson years, Skitch Henderson, often joked that he noticed audiences paying extra-close attention to his conducting after he had reached a certain age because "they don't want to miss the part where I go out with my boots on." Even though Bucky was in his eighties, he's never thought of himself as an old-timer. "My knees are only seven," my father often says, which makes an odd sort of sense coming from a man who's spent his entire career sitting down. And I like to remind audiences that for the past five years Bucky has been performing without a gallbladder, gaining him the nickname (at least from Martin) "Les Gall."

Meanwhile, framed by the sweeping floor-to-ceiling windows of the Allen Room, strategically placed six floors above Columbus Circle and Central Park with a view of the traffic lights of Fifty-Ninth Street that seemed to stretch east to Portugal, my father continued playing a song that was written when he was four years old and that has followed him around for his entire life. Taught the song in the early thirties by his Uncle Pete, he grew up listening to Benny Goodman play it on the radio and on records; he played it as part of bands and small groups through the fifties and sixties, then spent fifteen years in the seventies and eighties playing "Memories of You" alongside Benny as they performed concerts together around the world. The tune had been a good friend to him for nearly all of his lifetime, and now, in this glorious setting, Bucky was returning the friendship. "Memories of You" took just four minutes to play, but the version he played in the Allen Room that night had taken him seventy years to learn.

It would hit me later that same evening while walking out of the building that the Jazz at Lincoln Center space was a shrine—not only to jazz music as an art form, but also to generations of musicians who devoted their lives to practicing scales, learning tunes, showing up for their gigs and sessions, and packing up the instruments at the end of the night. JALC is a miracle made possible by the vision of Wynton Marsalis, the leadership at Lincoln Center, the help of forward-thinking corporations—and the musicians, club owners, and fans who kept the religion of jazz alive in New York City until someone could build its cathedral.

Emotions also ran high in early January 2011 when the 92nd Street Y generously honored my father's eighty-fifth birthday with five concerts that were built around songs on which Bucky had accompanied singers over the years. The show took the audience on a tour of American popular music—from Del Shannon's "Runaway" to Ben E. King's "Stand by Me"; from Roberta Flack's "First Time Ever I Saw Your Face" to the entire catalog of Dion and the Belmonts. (Dion DiMucci's touching letter about making records with Bucky was read aloud at each show.) My father has also played on recordings and in live performances backing Frank Sinatra, Tony Bennett, Peggy Lee, Sir Paul McCartney, Nat Cole, Rosemary Clooney, and Bobby Short. And Joe Mooney, Perry Como, Lee Wiley, Daryl Sherman, Barbara Lea, Barbara Carroll, Roberta Peters, Janis Ian, Teresa Brewer, Michael Franks, Chris Connor, Tony DeSare, Tony Martin, George Segal, Rebecca Kilgore, Susannah McCorkle, Helen Ward, Carmen McRae, Maxine Sullivan, Marlene Ver Planck, Solomon Burke, and Vaughn Monroe. Not to mention Jessica Molaskey and some itinerant string-plucker named John Pizzarelli. Of course, this is not a complete list of vocalists he's accompanied. And the above list and the shows at the Y didn't even touch on Bucky's work on instrumental recordings (Benny Goodman, Stéphane Grappelli, Wes Montgomery, Toots Thielemans, Stanley Turrentine, Dexter Gordon, Lionel Hampton, Kenny Davern, and Ruby Braff); commercials; film credits (including Stephen Sondheim's *Reds* soundtrack); Broadway shows (*Bye-Bye Birdie*); and television work (*The Tonight Show*, *The Dick Cavett Show*, *The Year Without a Santa Claus*, and the theme from *The Odd Couple*).

Those names evoke the atmosphere inside the Kaufman Auditorium on those evenings and afternoons at the Y in January 2011, when a continuous stream of vintage photos of my father and many of his vocalist collaborators were shown on an enormous screen as the corresponding songs were sung onstage by several Broadway singers (including Jessica, Judy Kuhn, and Darius de Haas) and a house band that featured my quartet, plus Aaron Weinstein on violin and Ken Peplowski on clarinet. As someone who is working to build and maintain a career in music, I was simply blown away by the quality and sheer enormity of my father's career as it was presented that night. Sure, I've been around for a lot of it, but until that celebration I hadn't truly absorbed it all. The sheer number of his album and CD credits, along with the hundreds of artists he has accompanied during live concerts, serves as a quantifiable (though not adequate) tribute to the elegance and greatness of his work.

As a young boy, I vividly recall my dad rushing home from afternoon recording and jingle sessions to have dinner with Mom, Anne, Mary, Martin, and me, then heading back to work at clubs in Manhattan. But I had never before seen his sixty-eight-year (!) body of work as a professional musician assembled and presented in this way. The crowd at the 92nd Street Y show opened their arms and hearts to him that night as audiences do everywhere he plugs in his Bucky Pizzarelli model Benedetto guitar—from the fabled stage of Carnegie Hall to Godfrey Daniels—a coffeehouse in Bethlehem, Pennsylvania—from a week of sold-out shows in a club in São Paulo, Brazil, to the basement of a converted church (near a good Chinese restaurant) in Albany, New York.

Truth be told, the loud ovations at Lincoln Center and at the five sold-out shows at the 92nd Street Y were out of the ordinary for a low-key guy who was the only son of a Paterson, New Jersey, grocer. According to his mother's accounts, young Bucky would deliver eggs to people's homes, then immediately return to the store to practice his guitar. Seventy years after his final egg delivery Dad continues to, in the words of Louis Armstrong, "practice, practice, practice." I recall my son Johnny being blown away by Bucky's work ethic while staying in New Jersey with his grandparents. *"Do U know that the first thing he does every morning is play the guitar?"* read one of Johnny's text messages that I saved. I should explain that Johnny's frame of reference could have been the wake-up rituals of his own guitar-playing father, whose immediate priorities each morning include (a) securing coffee and (b) checking on the West Coast baseball and/or hockey scores. Tough to move up in the BCS guitar rankings when there's someone with sixty-eight years of experience in front of you who is teaching himself solos from Fritz Kreisler's violin pieces before the clock strikes eight in the morning.

What helped our egg-delivering hero of this chapter in no small way was that Paterson in the thirties and forties was a hotbed of music, and home to a large population of talented musicians. Another natural advantage for Paterson's aspiring musicians was that the local schools all had dedicated teachers and orchestras, while most organized groups (fire and police departments, fraternal organizations, clubs) also had bands. As if this weren't enough, two of the more talented musicians and teachers in town were Bucky's uncles on his mother's side, the Domenicks—Uncle Pete and Uncle Bobby. As I said earlier, Bobby couldn't wait to come off the road and share what he'd learned musically with my father and Uncle Pete. In fact, it was Bobby who taught us the versions of "Honeysuckle Rose" and "Lady Be Good" that my dad and I continue to play to this day.

When Bucky talks about his early days, he always has stories about the most famous Paterson musician of that time, a guy named Joe Mooney (1911–75). A blind accordion and piano player who made some records on organ late in life, including one with Bucky on guitar, Joe also had a unique singing style that landed him on Paul Whiteman's national radio show, which was big stuff in those days. The Whiteman appearances and Mooney's top spots in *DownBeat* polls resulted in big-name musicians' making the trek to Paterson to sit in with Joe at Sandy's Hollywood Grill. A basement club with the stage built behind the bar, Sandy's attracted its share of well-known national acts, including (many times, according to dad) Nat Cole killing the room on piano in his early trio days. Paterson's most famous celebrity, Lou Costello, would often be in the audience. My father still reminisces about taking in a Joe Mooney set on a Sunday afternoon, sipping a Coke, and feeling on top of the world. This was all happening in 1941, when Bucky was fifteen. Just ten years later Dad would be Mooney's guitarist on some of Joe's biggest NYC gigs. But let's not get ahead of ourselves....

Arguably my father's biggest break came two years later, when he was invited to join Vaughn Monroe and his band in a late December 1943 tour that began in Scranton, Pennsylvania, and continued to

Binghamton, New York, and then two nights in Rochester, including New Year's Eve. Singer/trumpeter/bandleader Monroe had been tapped on the shoulder by Uncle Sam and "disbanded his ork [*sic*] in readying himself for induction" (according to *Billboard*). But when he was classified 4-F after failing his Coast Guard physical ("Never told us why," said Bucky. "I think it might have been a hernia."), he was back in business and did what bandleaders do—he immediately booked gigs. Only problem was that now he didn't have a band. A large number of his musicians had already moved on after Monroe had called it quits, including the guitar player. Calls went out—

Q: "I saw this kid sit in with Joe Mooney. Does he have a union card?"
A: "AF of M 248, since February."

Q: "Can he play with us this weekend?"
A: "Can you have him back to high school on Monday?"

Q: "How does he feel about an all-night train ride?"
A: "No problem."

—and that was that. Young Bucky, then a high school senior, was hired to play a three-city tour conveniently scheduled during the week of holiday vacation between Christmas and New Year's. And thanks to the sleeper train, he made it back to Paterson just in time to make his Monday classes at Central High School.

Monroe extended an invitation for Bucky to stay with the band full-time, but January 1944 was the height of World War II, and my father was turning eighteen and draft-eligible a week later on January 9. Central High School gave my dad his diploma in a private ceremony that month, and since he hadn't yet been formally drafted, he was able to continue working with Vaughn Monroe and the band. He got a taste of the road, toured some American League cities (Boston, Cleveland, Detroit), made a stop in Philadelphia, then got to come home for an extended engagement with the band at the Commodore Hotel in New York City—gutted down to its steel frames and rebuilt as the Grand Hyatt in 1980—located adjacent to Grand Central Terminal.

If you'd taken the points on Bucky becoming anonymous and falling off of Uncle Sam's radar during his time with Monroe's band, you'd have lost that bet. It wasn't long before my dad received his draft letter, instructing him to report on April 22, 1944, to Paterson's School #5, where he was shown to the same room in which he'd attended the third grade. After a week at Fort Dix in New Jersey, he took a train to Mineral Wells, Texas, for sixteen weeks of infantry replacement training camp at Camp Walters, which Bucky remembers for its "red clay, watermelon patches, and mosquitoes—*big* mosquitoes." Infantry replacement training was no picnic—he had to train to take the place of any one of twelve positions in the squad, which meant knowing how to handle every kind of gun, not just the basic .30-caliber M1 rifle. When it came time for his unit to head overseas, the Eighty-Sixth traveled from southern California on a circuitous train ride to Boston. The army forced them to ride in shirtsleeves so that the German spies wouldn't know that their large group was about to be shipped to Germany.

Armed with a .30 caliber six-string, Bucky (seated and smiling in the second row) poses with his army pals—a photo he carries in his wallet at all times.

I was surprised to learn many of the details of his war experiences, because for the longest time I had assumed that my father had essentially played rhythm guitar during his war days. Like many veterans of that time, he played down the physical and mental hardships of training, as well as his various roles (guard duty, receiving and registering the POWs, generally being shot at) in the concluding battles of the European theater that took place in Germany following the Battle of the Bulge.

And what happens after a war is over? As Bucky described it, "You watch a movie about how you're supposed to get home." There was a point system set up based on time served, and according to Bucky, "I didn't have many points," having been in Europe for only six months. But the army decided to ship the Eighty-Sixth Infantry home as a unit. The Eighty-Sixth had plenty of points, so Bucky was one of the first soldiers to make it home from Germany, arriving to a hero's welcome of "big bands and dancing girls" on ships waiting to greet them on the Hudson River.

Yet after just a few weeks at home, my father's unit was sent by train to San Francisco, where the Eighty-Sixth was scheduled to reassemble before sailing to join the war in the Pacific. This was in early August 1945. The unit received news as they were en route to Japan that the United States had dropped atomic bombs on Hiroshima and Nagasaki, and that the end of the war was near.

At that point the Eighty-Sixth made a detour from the Japanese theater to the outskirts of Manila in the Philippines, "where all we did was play basketball." Well, not *just* basketball. He also played baseball, running into future major league catcher and broadcaster Joe Garagiola. And of course, Bucky had his guitar with him, which somehow helped to bring him together with Frank Rosolino, a trombone player who would go on to play with Stan Kenton, Shelley Manne, *The Steve Allen Show*, and the Jones Brothers (Elvin, Thad, and Hank) in Rosolino's native Detroit. And Bucky became a first-call West Coast studio musician who played with everybody. What were the odds that two nineteen-year-olds playing a few Officers Club gigs in the Philippines would both later accompany Frank Sinatra, Peggy Lee, Tony Bennett, and Quincy Jones? Along with a Lieutenant Williams on bass and "the Captain of the Medics" on trumpet, Bucky and Frank found gigs all over the island. "We had a nice little group," he recalls. In contrast with the harsh conditions of Germany, my dad's tour of the Philippines was more like an episode of *McHale's Navy*. Bucky pulls no punches about his nine months in Manila—"The Philippines was glorious."

After hearing my father recount his experiences of 1944–46, I spent many hours in front of "World War II in HD" to check his chronologies, in addition to looking for his unmistakable face in the hours of enhanced footage. Hard as it might be to believe, I have found many similarities between my father's senior year at Central High School in Paterson (worthy of its own episode on the History Channel) and my own heroic victory lap that was senior year at Don Bosco Prep in Ramsey, New Jersey. For instance:

BUCKY PIZZARELLI'S SENIOR YEAR	JOHN PIZZARELLI'S SENIOR YEAR
Graduates early	Graduates barely
Boot camp in Texas	Day camp counselor in New Jersey
Lands on shores of France	Lands on shores of Jersey after prom
Stood around fire outside hut for warmth	Gathered at The Fireplace on Rt. 17
Able to shoot ten different kinds of guns	Able to play guitar and trumpet
Dodged bullets as Temporary MP	Dodged bullet, passed Physics
Fought battles at Cologne	Fought losing battle with Aramis cologne
Marched into Austria	Marched onto gridiron with Don Bosco Marching Band
Shells "dropping all around" in Germany	Ate Mom's stuffed shells
Returns to dancing girls on Hudson River	Sees refrigerator float by in Hudson
Atomic bombs change his assignment	Atomic Basie album changed his life
Honorable discharge from Pacific	Tasteless joke edited out

Meanwhile, a certain 4-F bandleader was keeping up on his current events, probably from watching the newsreels during his theater gigs. Vaughn Monroe just "happened" to call my grandmother to check on the status of my father's return about a week before he was due to arrive back from the Pacific. He repeated the message he always left with Bucky's mom: "Tell him the job is still his." When it was confirmed that Dad would return home in late May 1946, Monroe left a message at home to have Bucky join the band in Providence, Rhode Island, on June 6, 1946. It was Bucky's own D-Day.

After two weeks of home cooking following his discharge from the army, my father joined the Vaughn Monroe Band full-time. "Full-time" turned into a life of constant travel all over the country, including a stop each week at a different college for the *Camel Caravan* radio show. And no one was knocking Camels or cigarettes in those days—my father's pay at that time was about $160 a week, with $60 of it coming from the two broadcasts of the weekly radio show (an East Coast show, and another three hours later for the West). And in 1946, when the average weekly salary in the United States was $50, that was great money. Bucky often says that he learned a lot in those days watching the guest stars. Benny Goodman, the Basie rhythm section, including Freddie Green on guitar, and the otherworldly pianist Art Tatum were just a few of the musical stars who appeared with Monroe on the radio.

Good stories follow my father around, and the Vaughn Monroe era might have been the start of this phenomenon. We hadn't heard many specific stories about this time in my dad's life until some photos appeared in the mail, thanks to one of the women in the Moonmaids, the singing group in the Monroe entourage. Mixed in among the images of musicians and bandstands and Monroe playing, singing, and leading, appeared a photograph of a burning bus. Hmm—said my father. Seems there were a couple of stories about bus mishaps. Which one did we want to hear?

In the first instance the brand-new bus was making its way over the steep hills of Morgantown, West Virginia, when the card players in the band noticed heavy smoke accumulating in the back of the bus. Bucky said that the traveling party—singers, musicians, the

Moonmaids—alerted the driver, who stopped the bus, allowing the passengers to quickly file out and onto the road . . . just in time to watch the gas tank explode and the bus go up in flames. Not a total loss, in that all of the instruments were packed on a second bus that arrived at the hotel without exploding. But everyone's clothes and personal items were destroyed. In the ensuing court case the musicians were their own worst enemies, with some claiming to have been traveling with ten suits, several expensive watches, three pens, and two MacBook Pros.

"We lost the case," said Bucky. "Not a penny."

My father's second bus incident was self-inflicted and no less spectacular than the West Virginia bus explosion. It was a hot summer day in the upper Midwest, and Bucky had decided to surprise the band during their stop in Wisconsin by purchasing an industrial-sized quantity of Kaukauna cheese, which he intended to share with everyone at some point along the bus ride. After hiding his purchase among his own clothes in the luggage pit of the bus to better maintain the "surprise" element, he planned to retrieve the famous spreadable cheese at the first stop and pass it around with crackers. Big band bonding would occur, and it would be another happy night on the Vaughn Monroe Band's home on wheels.

I know what you're thinking—that under the best of circumstances mixing cheese and clothes would ensure that Bucky and his clothes would smell like the inside of a fifteen-year-old's hockey bag for at least a week. But these were not the best of circumstances. The extreme heat of the Wisconsin summer, combined with the lack of ventilation in the bus's storage compartment, caused a scientific event I am unable to explain based on just one year of C-minus chemistry (and two years of French) at Don Bosco Prep. Opening his bags at the next rest stop, Bucky realized something that should have occurred to him earlier in the day—that placing tubs of spreadable Kaukauna cheese among his clothing inside his suitcases was a flawed plan from the start. After what must have been a significant explosion, muffled by the bus's engine, my father found himself having to replace his entire wardrobe, including the blue suit and brown shoes he wore on the bandstand, for the second time in a little over a year. It was a tribute to the sheer strength of 1940s-era luggage that the overheated product from Wisconsin's finest dairy cows remained confined to the inside of Bucky's suitcases.

My father stayed with the Monroe band until its ultimate breakup in late 1951, an almost six-year run during which the band (according to a set of itineraries Bucky never threw out) played 1,023 separate venues, including the weekly *Camel Caravan* radio shows. It was also during this period (1950) that he met my mother, Saint Ruth Litchult, daughter of Russell Litchult (Pop was German, born in Jersey City) and Anna (Nannie came from Budapest as a young girl, and grew up in Waldwick, New Jersey). My parents met when Bucky stopped by St. Joseph's Hospital in Paterson to pick up his sister. Ruth and Aunt Marie both happened to work as nurses on the same floor at St. Joseph's. Marie's version of things is that upon setting eyes on Ruth, Bucky announced at that moment that he would one day marry her. But first they needed to be introduced—they were, and even managed to arrange a date, which was deemed a success by both sides. Within a few days, however, my father found himself back on the EBT (Exploding

Bucky playing guitar with his first boss, Vaughn Monroe (to Bucky's left in suit), at RCA Victor's Studio One on East Twenty-Fourth Street in Manhattan. Joined by Jack Fay (bass), Mike Shelby (piano), and Eddie Julian (drums).

Bus Tour) with Monroe, while his heart stayed behind in Paterson. To stoke the home fires (the computer asked if I meant to say "home fries"), our favorite guitar player unleashed a steady stream of postal correspondence from the road that piqued my mother's attention. No one besides my mother has ever seen the letters, though their existence is part of our family lore, right up there with Benny Goodman's surprise visits and the guitar in the center of the Pizzarelli coat of arms.

Author's note: Despite good-faith negotiations by lawyers for both my parents and my publisher, "Bucky's Letters to Ruth: 1950–52" were not made available for this book. I am hopeful of having them included in the director's cut of the DVD.

By this time my father had traded in the bus rides and one-nighters of Vaughn Monroe's band for a steady gig on television in 1953 and 1954 with the NBC Orchestra at the Hudson Theatre on West Forty-Fourth Street, backing *The Kate Smith Show*. The band's personnel included ace arranger Dean Kincaid, a number of alumni from Glen Gray's band, and first trumpet player and future *Tonight Show* leader Doc Severinsen, who, as we know, dressed like a Princeton student in those days.

For those not familiar with Kate Smith, the rugged soprano—and what else to call a popular singer who carried more heft than the NFL's star linebacker from the fifties and sixties, Sam Huff—introduced the country to Irving Berlin's "God Bless America" in 1938, hosted successful radio shows from the thirties into the fifties, and enjoyed a recording career that spanned five decades.

She was discovered all over again when her recorded version of "God Bless America," played prior to important games, inspired the Philadelphia Flyers hockey team to regrettable (for all fans of the New York Rangers) back-to-back Stanley Cup championships in the mid-seventies. The team's motto during those years was "The game can't start until the fat lady sings." I think I read somewhere that over the years the Flyers have won four times as many games as they have lost with either the recorded voice of Kate Smith—or, on a couple of occasions during the Stanley Cup days, Kate herself—belting out the Irving Berlin classic.

Dad's good luck continued while he was on staff at NBC with Kate Smith. A popular instrumental group at the time, the Three

Suns, needed a replacement guitar player when founding member and guitarist Al Nevins decided to retire. Bucky sat in on guitar in Nevins's chair when they came on Ms. Smith's show, and he was immediately hired by the group for an engagement at the rooftop nightclub of the long-gone Astor Hotel (now the site of the Minskoff Theater and an unsightly office tower, One Astor Plaza).

As Bucky remembers, "I'd leave the Hudson Theatre on West Forty-Fourth Street up near Times Square at six o'clock, walk home to clean up and change clothes on West Forty-Fifth between Eighth and Ninth. Then I'd walk back to the Astor Hotel on Forty-Fourth Street and be eating there by seven. It was great."

My father and mother were married in Waldwick, New Jersey, on January 9, 1954. That date was also Bucky's twenty-eighth birthday, which family statisticians agree prevented him from forgetting his anniversary at least five fewer times over the years than he actually did. When *The Kate Smith Show* hit the end of its run in June 1954, it freed him to take Ruth to Las Vegas, where the Three Suns were booked for the summer. The following year, 1955, also worked well for the newlyweds—a one-year engagement for the Three Suns at the Henry Hudson Hotel on West Fifty-Seventh Street. But when 1956 turned into a string of one-nighters, Bucky bid his good-byes to the Three Suns.

My dad and mom lived in Clifton, New Jersey, for much of the late fifties, with Bucky making the relatively easy commute by car to New York City to back studio bands, support and headline in concert settings, and answer the increasing number of calls for jingle dates. When he met Benny Goodman for the first time in 1958, he was working on a radio spot for Rheingold.

"The violin players were all contractors," Bucky recalls. "It was 'You hire me, I'll hire you.' And they always needed guitar players who could read, sometimes three or four guitars per session." Bucky says that three recordings a day was pretty typical for him between about 1956 and 1971.

Music scholars who have followed Bucky's career agree nearly unanimously that things began to fall into place for my father in 1960. First of all, certainly in order of importance, I was born on April 6.

Energized by the arrival of a newborn son who hit the ground crack-
ing wise (after two daughters, Anne and Mary), Bucky's career took
off. Don't believe me? Just check out all the work he did that year
on record—Doc Severinsen, George Barnes, Al Caiola, an album of
Hawaiian music, and a session with the Drifters ("Save the Last Dance
for Me" featured Bucky), not to mention many uncredited sessions he
did for early rock 'n' roll bands on some of the biggest hits of that time.

The early sixties were the golden days of studio and session work,
with Bucky sometimes working on four or five projects in a day, the
final one sometimes kicking off as late as one o'clock in the morning
or so. The New York music scene teemed with opportunity in those
days, and Bucky told me that it was definitely the heyday for a reliable
guitarist who could read arrangements and play a wide variety of styles.
On one magical day (October 27, 1960) he played guitar behind Ben
E. King on the singer's first hit, "Spanish Harlem," and when some studio time remained, he was called back to play on a quick arrangement
Mike Stoller had put together for a song King had played for them on
the piano that afternoon—"Stand by Me."

When Gene Bertoncini left *The Tonight Show* band in 1966 ("He
told me he wanted to do solo work," according to my dad), Bucky
was hired into the guitar chair by Skitch Henderson, who was slowly
putting together a team of jazz all-stars (Clark Terry, Walt Levinsky,
Al Klink, Tommy Newsom, Bob Haggart, Doc Severinsen—all with
experience in bands) after having initially inherited union-protected
players from the Jack Paar days. The hangouts back then were Hurley's
in Rockefeller Center—only an elevator ride away from Studio 6-B—
and Jim & Andy's across the street, apparently *the* gathering place for
jazz musicians in New York City at that time. Phil Ramone, now a
legend in the music industry as a producer/engineer, had a studio a
few floors directly upstairs from Jim & Andy's. He would often have
the bartenders make announcements when he needed specific players
on short notice.

Bucky also fondly remembers the group dinners at Pearl's, the
favored Chinese food hangout among musicians. When Skitch gave
them the word that there would be no rehearsal for a singer, seven

or eight of the guys would descend on the long, skinny restaurant in a Forty-Eighth Street brownstone for the ritual of the preshow meal. "We ate family style," remembers Bucky. "And no matter how many people we had or what we ate, the bill was always $7.50 a man. Always $7.50."

In 1969, during his years with NBC in New York, Bucky joined up with the first of his significant collaborators, George Barnes, the dynamic single-note guitar player from Chicago. For two months of every year readers get to listen to his distinctive introduction on Bobby Helms's "Jingle Bell Rock." George had been in New York since the early fifties and had been a regular on radio and TV gigs almost from the moment he arrived in town. In 1961 he formed a critically acclaimed guitar duo with an old-time rhythm guitar master, Carl Kress, whom Barnes had successfully coaxed out of retirement. After five years of terrific recordings and solid international bookings, Kress died of a sudden heart attack in 1966. A few years later Barnes invited Bucky up to his studio to test-drive Bucky's seven-string guitar, which Bucky had begun playing around that time, learning by listening to seven-string master George Van Eps. Barnes and Bucky liked what they heard, and the result was a critically and commercially success-ful partnership from 1969 to 1972, during which, according to Bucky, they played at local clubs almost every night. Since my father had not been playing the seven-string guitar for long when they initially got together, the early format was to allow George to take the single-note melodies while Bucky played full-chords behind him in the style of George Van Eps and Carl Kress. By the time George and my dad made *Guitars Pure and Honest* in 1971, however, two years and six hundred gigs into playing together, they had created a duo style that came across to listeners as one guitar voice. In a blind review of the record in *Down-Beat*, the critic Leonard Feather was undecided as to whether to guess that it was Herb Ellis and Joe Pass playing together, or one guitarist overdubbed.

Bucky always spoke highly of Barnes as being not only a skilled gui-tarist but also a genuinely fun-loving guy. (Catch his version of "Meet the Flintstones" on YouTube.) Barnes was also easy to spot in a crowd—he was about five six, weighed three hundred pounds, and, in the words of his wife, was shaped like an egg. George, obviously, liked to eat. He was also no stranger to adult beverages and I'm not talkin' Fresca.

A story that I love, and that musicians still tell each other, involved a serious fan of Barnes/Pizzarelli—a man who so enjoyed their music that the terms of his will directed that a substantial sum be set aside to hire Bucky and George to play at his graveside. In 1971 Bucky and George got the call to play this most unusual gig.

There was reportedly little conversation at eight o'clock in the morning between Bucky (behind the wheel) and George on the way to the Long Island cemetery, the guys having played a late set into the wee hours of the morning. When they arrived at the graveside, they were surprised to see that there were two caskets. (Bucky found out later that his fan and his son had died in an accident on the Long Island Expressway.) Next to the deceased were two chairs reserved for the guitarists who, upon cue, immediately began playing solemn music. Ah, but there would be none of that. Reverend John Garcia Gensel, the "Jazz Pastor" from St. Peter's Church in Manhattan, leaned over and demanded that they stop playing immediately. "He specifically wanted the music to be upbeat," announced the padre. "So play your jazziest up-tempo song."

So after what I imagine was a grunt from my father and probably a similarly primitive reply from Barnes, they broke into a song that was the big hit at their current gig at the St. Regis hotel and one that was even receiving radio airplay in those rock-heavy days—an especially peppy rendition of the Jerome Kern–Dorothy Fields song "Pick Yourself Up." Instructive message, to be sure—just not appropriate for this particular situation. I ask Bucky to retell this story on special occasions, and my dad just cringes. "The two bodies are right there, and I realize about halfway in that we're playing 'Pick Yourself Up.' What a thing to do!"

And it wasn't just at gravesides. Barnes took the same direction with album and song choices. His final album, released two months before he died in 1977 when he was only fifty-six, was titled *Don't Get Around Much Anymore.*

The Barnes/Pizzarelli duo would set the tone for many of my father's two- and three-man collaborations in the years that followed—with Slam Stewart, Zoot Sims, the various Hotel Pierre trios, Bunch and Leonhart, Howard Alden, Benny Green, Jerry Bruno, Ed Laub—and me. For all the solid gold, boldfaced names and music industry icons who have appeared next to his name, the pursuit of excellence in the duos and trios has always turned him on the most. I love that about him.

As I often joke, the smaller the place, the better he'll play. My dad has often insisted that the best he'd ever heard Zoot play was during a late set of theirs on a weeknight at Zoot's favorite jazz club and hangout, the Half Note on Spring Street—for an audience of exactly two people. In telling the story about Zoot and the nearly empty late set at the Half Note, my father made it clear that *this is the way things are done* and that we honor Zoot's spirit by playing our best for the two people who are sacrificing their sleep to hear music so late on a Tuesday night that it's Wednesday morning.

The thought of Zoot brought me back to a Sunday afternoon in August 1984. Our family was still reeling from the awful news we'd received a day earlier that Zoot had been diagnosed with incurable lung cancer, when the phone rang in the middle of the afternoon. It was Zoot, asking if it would be okay if he came over to our home in a little while and played a few tunes with Bucky on our back porch.

Things must have been pretty emotional with Mom that day because Bucky and I were left to fend for ourselves for dinner—it was just the two of us with Mom at home that day. But what Mom finally did put out on the refreshment table makes more sense as I've thought about it over the years: about a gallon of freshly squeezed orange juice and a large bottle of vodka. As Bobby Troup wrote about its sister, the lemon, the orange is "a highly healthful citrus fruit."

Zoot and his wife Louise arrived around five thirty, with Joe Cosgriff arriving shortly thereafter, with an overcooked story that left no doubt that he'd been tipped off. The six of us in the room talked about everything but the eight-hundred-pound gorilla—the brutal diagnosis Zoot had received two days earlier from his oncologist. For ten minutes or so, I found myself looking at Zoot and believing there must be a mistake. He looked a little tired, but he certainly didn't look like a man with just months to live. And he was only fifty-nine years old. It was while I was sneaking one of those glances at Zoot that I saw his eyes meet Bucky's, followed by a grunt and a head shake from each of them. It was time for them to get out their axes and play some tunes.

I sometimes wish I had recorded and taped every note of the five *hours* of ridiculous music Zoot and Bucky played that night. Then again, it might have made small one of the great nights of my life—reducing the songs to a mere setlist, and the music to a scratchy recording that would lose its significance when played out of context. "Emily," "The Very Thought of You," "Dream Dancing," "I Got Rhythm"—they played everything. In my mind and heart, for that night and forever, every lick they played swung like nothing I have ever heard before or since. I recall sitting in on "Lover Man" and "Sweet Lorraine," a song Zoot stopped to appreciate after we played it. After playing the song

Bucky is still at the top of his game at age eighty-six-plus. Great shot by Russ Titelman.

so frequently and for so many years on dates and on recordings, Zoot had given the tune a rest over the past few years, and he spoke about how much he liked hearing it again. And Zoot's ballad playing, always bordering on the otherworldly to start with, had somehow risen to another level in his final years.

The rest of the audience of four in the room that night sat in stunned amazement, helped along by the vodka and orange juice, which flowed in abundance. Zoot, who wasn't supposed to be drinking, slipped out several times to the kitchen, where we learned later he'd set up a minibar of his own inside one of the cabinets. I was honored and amazed to watch Zoot deal with his death sentence by affirming life with every note that his body and his tenor sax could produce. Now, almost thirty years after that August night, I count myself fortunate indeed to have been on the porch to witness my dad and Zoot that night and to experience from ten feet away the raw, deep, and emotional love of musicians for their music.

With that we head back to the Allen Room. Bucky has completed two solo numbers—including a flawless "This Nearly Was Mine"—and soon it's time for me to join him onstage. The duo number we have planned is "Honeysuckle Rose," the song that each of us learned to play at the age of ten, thirty-four years apart, from my dad's Uncle Bobby. Bucky is smiling ear-to-ear, and I realize my sister Anne had it right all those years ago. When asked as a first-grader to describe our dad's occupation, she gave the best of all answers—"He's a magician."

How I Met My Mother

A Freudian slip is when you say one thing but mean your mother.

—Author Unknown

It was the fall of 1972, and Johnny Carson and *The Tonight Show* had packed their bags and moved to Burbank earlier in the year. My father was busy trying to replace the steady employment that he had enjoyed as a member of a full-time studio band for six years.

During those days a lopsided amount of the day-to-day family responsibilities fell to my mom, who filled the roles of school picker-upper, executive chef, head of operations, homework supervisor, resident psychologist, and chief medical officer for Anne, Mary, Martin, and me. I write all of this from the perspective of 2012 because my mother didn't make a big deal about any of this back in those days—she gracefully fulfilled all of the commitments demanded of her (these and hundreds of others), as well as providing encouragement to my father and making it clear to us that his being away from home occasionally was essential to supporting our family.

My parents' unconventional courtship had prepared my mom for life with a working musician. Following their letter-writing period while he was crossing the country with Vaughn Monroe's band, my dad came back to live in New Jersey in the early fifties and joined the NBC television studio band on *The Kate Smith Show* at the Hudson Theatre. Mom recalls that the first time Dad left her side to play a TV remote with trumpeter Ralph Marterie at the Meadowbrook in Cedar Grove, New Jersey, she worried that he would turn into a TV star and that it would be the last time she would see him. But that night after she spotted him in the band on TV, he managed to climb out of the television and knock at the door in his spiffy gray flannel suit from Filene's. And he's still knocking—I hear he was knocking on the front door for fifteen minutes at three o'clock in the morning a few months ago after forgetting his keys.

Despite the various responsibilities and multiple hats she needed to wear at Pizzarelli, Inc., Mom could be counted on to be in her main office—the kitchen—in the half hour or so leading up to our five o'clock dinnertime. (We ate early and went to bed early in those days.) My regular banjo and guitar teacher, Uncle Bobby, had passed away suddenly a couple of months earlier, and with the transition to Uncle Pete, I had to make the jump to his system of intricate tablatures for chord fingering and strumming. Still sad about losing Uncle Bobby and frustrated at the new method and at not knowing the melodies (or at least the exact ones) for the songs I was trying to play, I would head to the kitchen and lay all of these emotions at the feet of my mother.

"I just don't get it," I would complain.

"What donchya get?" she'd ask.

"The *melody*," I'd say.

More than a few times we played out this scene, with my mom telling me to play the song, and within a few notes she'd begin to sing what I was playing, which would lead to an "Aha" moment. "That's it!" I would shout, channeling Lucy after Schroeder played the two-finger version of "Jingle Bells."

Over the years I have come to realize how much music my mom really knows. On a van trip from Sarasota to Palm Beach, Florida, with Mom, Bucky, Martin, and pianist Ray Kennedy, we put on a "Music of Your Life" station to pass the time. My mother was sitting next to me, and I'll be damned if she didn't identify every band or singer within the first five notes. Not just the Bobby Darin and Tony Bennett stuff—she nailed Ray Eberly, Dick Haymes, and Connie Boswell, too—all without hesitation. It suddenly occurred to me that she loved this music as much as, or more than, we did.

There was a moment at the Carlyle in November 2010 that also comes to mind. My mom and dad had come in to hear Jess's and my show at the Café, and at the end of the evening I called Bucky up to the stage to play two numbers with the quartet. The small room was packed, but I wanted to cede the stage completely to Bucky, so I sat next to my mother in the seat that my dad had just vacated. As my father played a gorgeous "Body and Soul," Mom leaned in and confided to me, "You know, he can be difficult and hardheaded at times—but who isn't? And listening to him play—it's amazing!"

What a cool thing to hear her say—a month or so from their fifty-seventh wedding anniversary. My mom wore all the hats and raised four kids, adjusted to my dad's absences and unconventional schedule, continues to unlock the front door for him at three in the morning, and awakens on most days to the strumming of chord solos coming from the porch. She has seen it all and heard it all. And she is still in love with that lug. Fortunately for all of us, she also loves the music. In my head I'll always hear her singing in the kitchen as she helped me learn melodies; shouting, "Jimmy Rushing!" as we drove across Florida; or simply whispering, "It's amazing!" as she listened to my father play "Body and Soul" for the 8,284th time. I know what a kick it is to see her enjoying my shows, and I can only imagine what it has meant to my father to be blessed with a loving partner and companion who is still crazy about his work after all these years.

4

Sing, Sing, Sing

We don't want to be playing guitar solos all night . . . why don't you sing one?

—John Paul "Bucky" Pizzarelli, 1980

That request came from my father. It happened one night back in July 1980 at the Café in New York City's historic Hotel Pierre, where Bucky had booked our duo act as the summer replacement for—*himself.*

Let's take a step back—for several years Bucky had been leading a piano/bass/guitar trio from September through Memorial Day. Mike Renzi, Tony Monte, and Russ Kassoff alternated on piano, while Ron Naspo and the indefatigable (a word borrowed from a song on Jess's setlist) Jerry Bruno were the two-man platoon on bass—with Jerry playing primarily against right-handed pitchers. Talk about a strong bench. As individuals and as a group they were in such demand that they usually took summers off to book themselves as headliners, as a trio, or as sidemen at high-paying outdoor jazz festivals all over the world. But in early May 1980, the room's manager mentioned he'd like to continue the success of the Café's in-season music program and asked Bucky for the name of a reliable musician he knew well who could serve as a substitute for the summer months. My father proceeded to recommend the most trusted name in the union book, someone he could vouch for without hesitation.

"I'll do it," he told them. There is disagreement among jazz historians, Bucky's biographers, and the *Congressional Record* as to whether his next words were "*with my kid.*"

Now I needed to learn songs. Thanks to my then-girlfriend, my go-to album around that time had been Frank Weber's *As Time Flies*, which included what I had assumed to be another Weber original, "Straighten Up and Fly Right." When I put it on for my father, he clearly knew the song, nodding and smiling as it played. "Find the Nat Cole Trio records," said Bucky. As if by wizardry, Capitol had just released *The Best of the Nat "King" Cole Trio—Volumes 1 and 2*. It was as though they knew I was coming. "Learn from the source" was my father's constant advice in those days.

Immersion in Nat Cole's records was a game-changer for my career. I recall a period of time when the radio station of my youth, WABC ("WA-Beatle-C"), regularly played Nat's "Those Lazy, Hazy, Crazy Days of Summer," with an occasional "Mona Lisa" thrown in as an "oldie" no. 1 hit. But I was hooked on the brilliant simplicity of the piano/guitar/bass trio cuts. The easy tempo Nat achieved on "For Sentimental Reasons" and "Route 66" sounded every bit as rock 'n' roll to me as *Led Zeppelin II*. The trio tracks were almost entirely made up of standards I had heard my father and his friends play on a loop over the years, sprinkled with a few lesser-known tunes that played to the strengths of Nat's voice and his personnel. By the time my ninety-nine-dollar stereo had worn out the grooves of those records (and it didn't take long), I had joined my father as a true believer in the genius of everything Nat's ever played.

My jazz vocal selections—once a few songs I'd cherry-picked from Kenny Rankin, Joe Mooney, Bobby Troup, Nat Cole, and João Gilberto records—increased exponentially that summer as the Café Pierre's regulars requested songs they insisted on paying to hear. Even as Bucky shook his head that incentives weren't necessary, they'd fill his hand and jacket pocket with both written requests for songs and accompanying twenty-dollar bills. In the spirit of capitalism, I spent my off-hours during the day furiously learning the favorites of our most generous customers. Although I was still playing rock 'n' roll and weddings with a few local bands back in Jersey, the Bucky gigs brought in most of my income, especially our five nights at the Hotel Pierre.

Those eight weeks represented a decisive bonding experience for my father and me, commuting into Manhattan each day from northern Bergen County, New Jersey, in the ovenlike, un-air-conditioned splendor of my Datsun 210. Did I mention we were wearing tuxedos? Truly an old-school disciple on many fronts, Bucky (1980 version) was a staunch opponent of automotive climate control in those days, preferring instead to rely on the "cross breeze" effect—a rumored "instant and gratifying cooling gust of air" resulting from opening the windows on both sides of a car. Two sweltering summer months later we were still patiently awaiting that first "cooling gust."

My father was an even-tempered and accommodating teacher during the summer gig at the Hotel Pierre—that's my story, and I am sticking to it. With a repertoire of songs going in that wouldn't have lasted through the first half of a short set, I will now describe the Bucky Pizzarelli teaching method during this time—"*Play this!!*" And he'd quietly begin a standard, such as Rodgers and Hart's "Isn't It Romantic?" And when I wouldn't pick up on the chords within seven or eight seconds, he'd begin playing *louder*. Think "Isn't It Romantic?" with vigorous, emphatic strumming and a menacing glare.

In a summer when almost every night brought brand-new adventures, one particular evening stands apart from the others. At about ten forty on a weekday night on which every employee (Pizzarelli and Pizzarelli included) was trying to will the time to be eleven o'clock, a lively group of about twelve people entered the Café—thus tripling the audience. (How many people were in the room before the large group entered? Solve for x. Further proof that I took honors algebra/trig at Don Bosco.) My dad immediately recognized one member of the party as Van Cliburn, the classical piano virtuoso from Texas, winner of the first International Tchaikovsky Piano Competition, defeater of Cold

War Russian pianists, and the only musician for whom a ticker-tape parade has ever been held in New York City. But the bartender had already announced "last call" a few minutes before they had arrived, and the permanently angry maître d' began pointing at his watch, universal signals for musicians to think about the closing song. But the Cliburn party wanted music and certainly helped their cause when one of the happy Texans shook hands with my father, told him that they wanted us to continue playing, and held up two crisp one-hundred-dollar bills, which my father made disappear in a New York second. It was great to see my dad in such high spirits, both to be in the presence of the celebrated piano prodigy—and for the unexpected financial bump. We were soon introduced to the great Cliburn, who asked how Bucky and I happened to know each other. Bucky told him.

"*Mother*," called out the keyboard master whom *Time* had once dubbed the Texan Who Conquered Russia on its cover. *"They're father and son!"*

The final obstacle would be selling the union guys—the hard-boiled maître d', a sour bartender, and a cranky waiter or two—on putting off closing time for a half hour or so. Somehow Bucky worked his magic, a series of shrugs, grunts, and possibly the words "ticker tape" convincing the staff that the hotel should not insult a man of Cliburn's stature, not to mention his entourage of talkative and anything-but-teetotaling Texans. And even more impressively, he did it without spending a dime of our overtime bonus. With the late closing assured, my dad and I proceeded to produce a rousing set that tore the cover off the ball—the collected works of Julian Bream, all three movements of the Rodrigo Guitar Concerto, the score of *Oklahoma*—you name it. Applause broke out, there were handshakes all around, e-mails were exchanged—even though it was 1980, and e-mail hadn't yet been invented. Like Carlton Fisk blocking the plate, Cliburn's mother stopped my father's beeline to the exit with a protracted hug and several minutes of gracious words. When we finally all managed to call it a day, Cliburn led his mother and the Texans from the Café, bound for "one more stop." Bucky was finally able to exhale.

As I carried the guitars and amp to the car, Bucky walked about ten feet behind me, roaring with laughter the entire time. "All right, Dad, what's going on? You've been laughing nonstop for the past fifteen minutes. What's up?" He just kept up with the snickering. At one point he tried to speak but couldn't get out the words.

"C'mon, Pop,… out with it."

Dramatic pause . . .

"The mother gave me another hundred!"

In addition to learning about two hundred songs that summer, I picked up a PhD in "Bucky Math"—an alternate universe in which half of three hundred is one hundred.

After eight weeks the summer master class with my father at the Pierre came to an end on the Saturday of Labor Day weekend. For his part, Bucky took two days off, dove into the pool, cooked up some steaks, then returned on Tuesday to his familiar chair at the Café Pierre with his trio. I, on the other hand, now had fewer outlets for playing the music I had absorbed over the

Dad and I playing on one of our first road trips together at a jazz party in Odessa, Texas.

previous sixty-five working nights with my dad. So with Nat Cole, Chick Corea, Duke Ellington, Harold Arlen, Cole Porter, and Joe Mooney swimming around my brain, I went back to a schedule where half of my gigs were with rock bands. Every so often there would be a duo gig with Bucky—"Jazz at Noon" once a month in Manhattan; a gig at DeFemio's in Yonkers, where tradition dictated that the owner play the drums; St. Peter's Church in NYC; or Gulliver's Jazz Club in West Paterson. My regular gigs were the Magnificent Crepe (an oxymoron) on Fridays and Giulio's on Mondays. As Bucky had suggested, I played mostly instrumentals, mixing in about three to four vocal numbers per set, usually the Nat Cole classics "Route 66," "Straighten Up and Fly Right," and "(I Love You) For Sentimental Reasons"—along with a song Nat never got to sing, "I Like Jersey Best." (More on "Jersey Best" later.)

Not for a minute do I wish to be dismissive of my nonjazz bands, in which I played from age fifteen until I was in my midtwenties. And while sometimes we embellished and categorized our bands' music as "rock 'n' roll," we knew then and know now that we weren't the Clash. Or even the Cars. The Cars, by the way, remain a significantly underrated group, the pop music equivalent of Brian Doyle of the 1978 Yankees (back when it was possible for the words "Yankees" and "underrated" to coexist in the same paragraph).

Since I played in rock bands for over ten years and have played "Smoke on the Water" more often than I've strummed "Smoke Gets in Your Eyes," it might be a good idea at this point to document the rock years. For starters, rather than actually trying to remember the bands' names, I went with the "I Feel Lucky" Google search for "Pizzarelli Rock Bands." And talk about lucky . . . I stumbled across a series of quizzes about—ME! Never one to pass on a test of knowledge that gives me a fighting chance, I looked forward to answering questions from two twenty-four-question tests for which my life had uniquely prepared me.

In a story reminiscent of the possibly dubious tale of Tom Waits-in-disguise finishing third in a Tom Waits soundalike contest in

Chicago, I scored 21 out of 24 in the first test, which was supposed to be the easier of the two. (Who knew my mother's name is Ruth?) The three hiccups can only be attributed to the lack of available time to concentrate on the subject and the subject matter. That and my habit of coasting on tests when I know I have the Gentleman's C-minus safely in the scorebook. For future trivia contestants, here is the definitive list of my bands' names and fun facts, offered here for the first time in one convenient location:

Emanon ("no name" backward. Yes, deep stuff). Mostly Beatles and Jim Croce songs on the setlists.

> ➤ PERSONNEL: Emanon featured Augie Sodora on drums, Steve Lafiosca on bass, John Pizzarelli on guitar. The main guitar at this time was my father's Fender Jazzmaster. Highlights: my mom hired us to play for my sister's high school yearbook party, a biggie. From there we played Glenn Hauenstein's backyard party, then tragically broke up during/after Paul Grosso's porch party. It was a big three and out for Emanon. Final tally: one hundred rehearsals and three gigs.

Omega ("The Last Word in Rock 'n' Roll"). Also, apparently the last band people considered for actual gigs. Highlights: This band actually rehearsed, mostly for the postrehearsal runs to the Barbecue House on Kinderkamack Road in Walter Whitney's van.

> ➤ PERSONNEL: Walt Whitney—van transportation and lead guitar; Mike O'Hara—bass; Eric Engber—drums; JP—rhythm guitar. Notes: after Whitney took his van and went home, Lafiosca (see Emanon) joined on rhythm guitar, and I was promoted to lead. Lots of gigs at Catholic and Jewish young people's centers. Bill Burke, who taught me to tie my shoes, joined on drums when Engber left for school. His main influence was Mickey Dolenz—he also began the band's tradition of wearing our grandmothers' hats during gigs. "Rock Me Baby" and "Johnny B. Goode" on the setlist. When Kathy Kelley joined on vocals during junior and senior years, we

added Linda Ronstadt, Fleetwood Mac, and Boston material to the sets. Guitar at the time was Guild's inexpensive line, the Madeira. Defining gig: the Bergen Mall.

The Phil Bernardi Band. Of the Rolling Stones, Bon Jovi, the Black Keys, and the Phil Bernardi Band, this was the only band named for a north Jersey high school teacher. Had first hit of "I Like Jersey Best" in 1981 on WNEW-FM's *Prisoners of Rock 'n' Roll* segment hosted by Vin Scelsa. Don't forget producer Kara Manning. PB Band given key to city of Seaside Heights, New Jersey, in 1983. Would come in handy when bandleader Bernardi was stopped for speeding while in Seaside Heights to accept the award. "Jersey Best" possibly the final actual 45 rpm record ever made. Trivia: B side is "Nice House, Nobody Home." Defining gig: Ocean County Mall. Celebrity hangers-on: Miss Ocean County.

> ➤ PERSONNEL: Phil Bernardi—guitar, lead vocals; no one— keyboards; Martin Pizzarelli—bass; John Pizzarelli—guitar; Mark Horst—drums

The Phil Bernardi Band—me (top center) and Martin (to my left), along with Phil (bottom) and drummer Mark Horst at the recording session for "I Like Jersey Best" in 1981.

Sanpaku (the title of a Michael Franks song, probably named after an eye condition, also mentioned in John Lennon's "Mind Games"). Highlights: The band had its own touring jackets, not much else. Well, there were the two attractive blondes in the graphics store where we ordered the band jackets, the closest that *any* John Pizzarelli–led music organization would ever come to having its own groupies. Guitars: used the Stratocaster.

> ➤ PERSONNEL: Tommy Mintz—drums; Steve Lafiosca—guitar; Dave Thomason—saxophone; Martin Pizzarelli—bass; JP—guitar. Bonus tech guy: Dave Grill on sound and lights—Dave has since done lighting for several Democratic and Republican National Conventions, as well as the Super Bowl.

Johnny Pick & His Scabs. Highlights: Did jazz gigs at the Hotel Pierre or at J's with my dad, then ran across town to perform in NYC rock clubs as Johnny Pick. This curious arrangement inspired the famous (among the six of us) Bucky quote: "You're the only person in the history of music who plays jazz to support his rock 'n' roll habit." Guitars—Benedetto and Gretsch seven-strings for Bucky gigs, Fender Flame plugged into Mesa Boogie SOB amp for Johnny Pick engagements.

> ➤ PERSONNEL: Eddie Decker ("Eddie D")—guitar; Doug Sweet ("Dougy Blue")—keyboards; Don Gardner ("Donny Ram")—drums; Martin Pizzarelli ("Joey Regulatta")—bass; JP ("Johnny Pick")—vocals, guitar

Some bands I *wish* I had played for:
➤ New Squids on the Dock
➤ Kathleen Turner Overdrive
➤ Uncle Daddy and the Family Secret
➤ Agent Orange in Bite-Sized Tablets
➤ Afghanistan Banana Stand
➤ Jiggle the Handle
➤ The Hugh Beaumont Experience
➤ Mary Tyler Morphine
➤ Band Over

> ➤ Gig Canceled
> ➤ Not Drowning, Waving
> ➤ Cap'n Crunch and the Cereal Killers
> ➤ Smorgasborgnine

The most astute bands on the world stage, like the top-of-the-pack baseball teams, know that they must have a strong closer. For many years, the Yankees have entrusted the final inning of their games to their incomparable Zen master, Mariano Rivera. Both Benny Goodman and Bucky Pizzarelli would, together and separately, call in Gordon Jenkins's time-honored (and self-explanatory) "Goodbye" from their respective bullpens of music. When we toured with him, Sinatra wrapped up each show with "New York, New York," just as he had sung "My Way" at the end of shows during the early seventies. And for nearly all of my ten years of playing with pop/rock/other bands, our grand finale—*our* "Born to Run"—was the theme from *The Mary Tyler Moore Show*. ("Who can turn the world on with her smile / Who can take a nothing day, and suddenly make it all seem worthwhile?") At J's on the Upper West Side, Judy helped the song evolve into a more elaborate ritual—as you'd expect if you know anything about the establishment—imitating Mary's end-of-song hat toss, a practice soon picked up by the club's ready-for-anything regulars who were often up for an excuse to throw *anything*. At Nobody's Inn in Mahwah, New Jersey, the staff would dance around the club while singing along with the band, then shout "Oh, Mr. Grant!" at the end of the song while throwing their hats into the air. (Eventually, there were more hat-wearers in bars and clubs where we played than in the stands at the 1956 World Series.) And another early stop on the Pizzarelli caravan of entertainment, Rhyan's in New Brunswick, seized on the ritual and began selling headgear in the gift shop— hats that were animal heads. The club's two-tiered design made it ideal for throwing the hats high in the air. Although we didn't know it at the time, we have since learned that actor James Gandolfini and star chef Mario Batali's brother both worked at Rhyan's during the hat-throwing era. I know—hardly rock 'n' roll—but hey, we never promised you the Sex Pistols. And with so much headwear already on the floor at the end of our shows, it made it that much easier to pass the hat.

Yet as much as I loved being with my pals and playing covers of pop tunes, I couldn't shake the hundreds of new songs I had learned over the summer that continued to camp out in my brain. As I mentioned, my father did his best to work around his regular hours to pick up a surprisingly large number of outside gigs for our duo act. Because people trusted Bucky, I was able to accompany him all over the country to jazz festivals and jazz parties, the best of which were the ones Dick Gibson threw in various locations around Colorado every Labor Day weekend for about thirty years. An investment banker who formed the Water Pik company in the early sixties, Dick had the resources to invite all of his favorite musicians, whom he then assigned to play in unconventional groupings. The result was a spontaneous and happy atmosphere, both in terms of the music it brought out and the old friends his parties reunited.

In the spirit of throwing me into the ocean to teach me to swim, my dad didn't object as I was informally assigned to jam sessions made up entirely of Hall of Famers—Zoot Sims, Clark Terry, Harry "Sweets" Edison, John Bunch, Phil Bodner, Slam Stewart. It's one thing to be familiar with the notes and chords; it's quite another experience to try to keep up with the top echelon of world-class musicians who *inhabit* the songs they play. Sitting in for the first time with Sweets Edison was a graduate course in the Basie approach—Sweets took things in a less-is-more direction, with bursts of notes followed by prolonged, defined rests. He resumed my continuing education a few years later (in the late eighties) at the Fortune Garden Pavilion on East Forty-Ninth Street between Second and Third Avenues (now Pampano). With only three of us left in the room for a Tuesday night late set, Sweets sat at our table, muted trumpet in hand, and again demonstrated how to make one's notes count. He played four songs, then joined us for a gourmet Chinese dinner—now *there* was a New York City night out. Bucky embraces the Sweets Edison mind-set, often muttering under his breath "Lot of notes, lot of notes" when the must-be-getting-paid-by-the-note guys are taking solos.

I got even more of a peek behind another type of show business curtain later that year when I was hired to play a recurring character on the ABC soap opera *All My Children*. And the role was more of a stretch than it sounds—that of a *bass* player in the show's local band, the Valley Dukes. My struggles included (in reverse order): (a) suddenly having to read and play the bass lines of sheet music and (b) delivering my one or two spoken lines per show as though I were not made of wood. Or lead.

But not even my inept soap opera work could keep me off television. While I didn't fully comprehend it at the time, I passed through the Ellis Island of show business in 1980 and 1981 when I was invited to make a couple of appearances on *The Joe Franklin Show*. There was no disputing that Joe knew his stuff; his encyclopedic knowledge of vaudeville, silent films, and entertainment trivia has produced more than twenty books over the years. Not to mention a Times Square office that still looks like a bombed-out paper mill. The inherent greatness of his show cannot easily be described; one or two YouTube clips (To Marky Ramone: "How did you break into the show business game?") are not sufficient to adequately demonstrate Joe's complicated relationship with an interview. A representative panel over the years could have included Otto Preminger (155 appearances), an ex-wife of Robert Goulet's, and the lead singer of a Dave Clark Five tribute band. Joe's around-the-horn question for the panelists could well have been, "If Bob Goulet were on our panel today, what would he have to say about . . . synchronized swimming?" I often watched *The Tonight Show* with an expectation that wackiness could happen—within the framework of a Burbank, whipped-cream-in-the-pants, Johnny-said-*what*-to-Ed structure. On the other hand, one tuned in to *The Joe Franklin Show* because literally *anything* could happen.

Franklin was a democratic gatekeeper. Just as he provided the first-ever television appearances for Woody Allen, Barbra Streisand, Liza Minnelli, Dustin Hoffman, and Sammy Davis Jr., he also served as the final stop for character actors and comedians boarding the no. 86 express bus to obscurity. And Joe famously mispronounced names, once referring to Oscar winner (and star of *McHale's Navy* and *Marty*, not to mention Ethel Merman's husband for thirty-two days) Ernest Borgnine as "Borg-ninny." (Borgnine smiled, got up, and walked off.) There was no tune to rehearse or instruments to carry because the show's unconventional approach to presenting music was to play a cut from a record while the guests and the host shared awkward glances for about three or four minutes. Franklin would then come out of the song and usually ask the other guests what they had thought of the music. Or of the prospect of peace situation in the Middle East. There was no denying that he was one of a kind.

Because *The Joe Franklin Show* was all about quirkiness, you can understand how thrilled I was in my first appearance to share the program with a professor of behavioral sexuality from Syracuse University. What happened next is a blur—Joe might have mumbled something about Charlie Chaplin or held up a Mae Questel 78 rpm record. But at some point he asked the professor if his students ever sought advice in his chosen field. The professor took a deep breath. "Well," he said, "someone in the class left a note in the anonymous question box yesterday. The note asked if it was a good idea to wear a diaphragm and an IUD at the same time."

> Joe: That is an interesting one. And what was your answer, Professor?
> Professor: *My answer was that it was a little like designing a mousetrap; you have to leave some room for the mouse.*

Franklin didn't hesitate. "And what do you think of that answer, *John Pizzarelli?*" Um, John Pizzarelli was hoping the crew would stop laughing at some point during the one-hour show in time to cue his new record. W. C. Fields had famously recommended that entertainers never perform after children or animal acts. He could have easily added "and professors of behavioral sexuality with prepared material."

A joint appearance with Bucky on a later date saw us navigate the usual minefields, even working the nutritional benefits of pasta into an answer to Joe's non sequitur question about vitamins. But it was the chef in the show's second segment who elevated our show to cult status among students of *The Joe Franklin Show*. Looking back, I'll never understand how a production team that couldn't grasp the technology to broadcast music of any kind (when Bing Crosby actually sang shortly before his death, it was a cappella) believed it could somehow replicate a working kitchen on Joe's stage. After naming the steak dish after us ("Let's call it Steak Pizzarelli," Joe proclaimed), Franklin then mispronounced our family's last name fifteen times in a frantic two-minute play-by-play of the steak sizzling in a pan. With Bucky hoping to be the taste-tester for Steak Pizzarelli, we looked on in equal parts astonishment and horror as the folding table folded, sending the portable gas heater, the grill pan, the bowls of ingredients—liquids and spices, the Steak Pizzarelli—and the chef's book, to the floor. There were no injuries—except to the steak, which Bucky had been eyeing hard. Oh, there were a couple of localized small fires (the steak and the book), but so nimble and skilled was the staff member/firefighter who put them out that we concluded "Stand ready with a fire extinguisher every day" could have been the guy's complete job description.

I'll always be proud that I made twelve years of appearances on *The Joe Franklin Show*, and I am grateful to Joe and his staff for inviting me to be part of show business history.

In May 1983, on the heels of the artistic (limited) and commercial (laughable) success of the 1980 record *2 × 7 = Pizzarelli*—two seven-stringed guitarists playing heady instrumentals—my dad and the brain trust at Stash Records made a decision to give the record-buying public what they were clamoring for—an album of John Pizzarelli vocal selections. Stash Records had been so named by its founder, Bernie Brightman, after a compilation record called *Reefer Songs*. The stoner record had reportedly sold through about ten pressings, affording Bernie the luxury of house money to underwrite less profitable releases. That's where I come in. Before Stash had time to second-guess their green light, Bucky had driven me to Lobel Productions—the balcony of a converted movie house in West New York, New Jersey, where we found ourselves laying down the tracks to another album—*I'm Hip (Please Don't Tell My Father)*. My father had hired two terrific musicians from his Café Pierre Trio—Russ Kassoff on piano and, from the

Vaughn Monroe Band and a survivor of the famous Vaughn Monroe bus fire of 1949, Jerry Bruno on bass. Kassoff would go on to tour with Frank Sinatra in the late eighties, while Bruno's spoken lines in Woody Allen's *Broadway Danny Rose* did nothing to change his status as a full-time bass player. One of our favorite people (and now in his early nineties), Jerry was last seen at the Glen Rock Inn—examining his check in the middle of a bass solo, a musical sleight-of-hand that probably took him seventy years to perfect.

What I recall from my first session as a vocalist was that things moved along smoothly without the sense that anyone was rushing. The Dave Frishberg song ("I'm Hip") and the Nat Cole tunes from the resulting record have become staples of my live sets to this day. The album also includes the no-frills version of Joe Cosgriff's valentine to our native state, "I Like Jersey Best." Russ Kassoff's creative arrangement, in fact, adds a few thrills and frills, working in bits and pieces of "The Jersey Bounce" and "New York, New York," with close-listening musicologists claiming to hear traces of Dave Edmonds's "Get Out of Denver" and the late tenor Roger Ducet's version of "O Canada" when the record is played backward.

What amazes me still from that day was that we walked into the movie theater/recording studio at nine in the morning, departed at five in the afternoon, and I went home carrying a fully mixed cassette of the completed album. A glossary section in the back of the book will explain the word "cassette" to our younger readers. Just kidding.

My next record, *Hit That Jive, Jack*, benefited from a happy accident of scheduling that allowed the left-handed piano genius Dave McKenna to join us in the studio. We hadn't even considered bringing Dave in all the way down from Cape Cod and Boston where he spent most of his time, but we'd noticed an ad in the *Times* a couple of days before the session that put Dave at Hanratty's on the Upper East Side at night on the same day we would be making the record during the day. Once we reached him and made clear that we'd have him out in plenty of time to play the gig, Dave was in with both feet. There was no moving him from the piano bench. And while my singing on those original three Stash albums is sometimes cringe-worthy, the other talent on those records more than makes up for the singer's work—McKenna's and Bucky's harmonies on *Jive*, the tight rhythm of Kassoff and Bruno on the first record, and my own guys, Gary Haase (bass) and Steve Ferrera (drums), making solid contributions after getting lost and showing up ninety minutes late for the *Jive* session. They must have impressed people in a short time at that session because the producers invited them back about a year and a half later to play on my record in the same studio (with Kenny Levinsky, who played in my original road trio, on piano, Eddie Daniels on clarinet, and Amanda Homi on vocals)—*Sing, Sing, Sing*.

Barney Kessel might have oversimplified things when he said the hardest part about studio work is finding a parking place. (For my guys, it was finding the *studio*.) In making an album there is an almost infinite number of moving parts, in addition to hundreds of pages of notes that demand decisions. Do we play them as written? Tweak them? Scrap the arrangement? Lose the song? That I am invited to produce records for fellow artists today is a privilege I credit to the experiences of Bernie Brightman and the early Stash records, as well as guys like Kassoff, Bruno, Butch Miles, Dave McKenna, and Bucky, who were beyond patient and generous with their time, and most of all with their vision of how things are supposed to get done in a recording studio.

A happy result of making a vocal album was that my songs began to get airplay on a few local radio stations. Thanks to one of my dad's regular pianists, Tony Monte (as I will explain in the chapter on New York City radio), my music found its way to Jonathan Schwartz, already a radio personality for almost fifteen years in New York, first on WNEW-FM, playing free-form rock, then on WNEW-AM, which featured the Great American Songbook (with an emphasis on Sinatra) on Sunday mornings. And I can't express what a kick it was to hear my music played before, after, and between Sinatra, Tony Bennett, Bing Crosby, and Ella. When the management of WNEW-AM decided to try out a six-to-nine weekday evening show with live music called *New York Tonight*, Tony strong-armed Jonathan to hire me to play in a permanent small group that both played jazz and would accompany singers. Again, as I'll explain later, the show was an instant phenomenon with radio critics, entertainment columnists, and, according to Arbitron's questionable rating book, about twelve passionate listeners—hundreds of whom would come up to me at gigs to profess their love of that show.

My music on the Stash series of albums received generous airplay all over the country, but especially from WNEW and WBGO-FM in the New York area. And despite a live setlist and three albums that included songs from the greatest composers and lyricists to ever whistle a tune, the song that attracted the most enthusiasm was a cut from my first record, the three-chord (rounding up), tongue-in-cheek tour of the Garden State entitled "I Like Jersey Best." Written by my friend Cosgriff—music and lyrics—at work during a rainy lunch hour, the song was immediately embraced by both New Jersey residents and New Jerseyans at heart—WOBM-FM in Toms River might have jumped the gun a bit by naming "Jersey" the no. 42 Song of All Time, just ahead of Billy Joel's "Just the Way You Are." (I bet they want a mulligan on that one.) New Jersey's Senator Bill Bradley invited Joe to appear on his television show and, in a *Wall Street Journal* interview years later about politicians' use of television, told the reporter that Joe's segment (he'd brought along WNEW-FM's Jim Monaghan to sing "Jersey Best") had been the most popular interview in the show's history. That tells you something about the scintillating quality of the senator's other guests—wow. At least two books by Rutgers professors note the song's attitude toward New Jersey as being "Sometimes it's so bad, it's good." Not sure I buy all that analysis, but as I have tried to make clear in any previous discussions about academics—not my chosen field.

What I like most about the song is that it was obviously written with affection for New Jersey, warts and all. No purple mountain majesties or scenic byways—it's about the Turnpike, chemically enhanced sunsets, and a beach or two at the end of your schlep—with ascending chord changes and arranger Kassoff's nods to "The Jersey Bounce" and "New York, New York." The version of the song I recorded in 1983 on Stash came with scrubbed-down, audience-friendly lyrics about Newark Airport and sports teams, replacing the bribes, crooked politicians, and

Mafia rubouts that wove through the colorful 1981 original we played with the Bernardi Band on the bar circuit.

Lacking a state song, New Jersey residents, their leaders, and the media throughout the state have often come off as a bit trigger-happy to fill this musical vacuum. New Jersey politicians had been down this road with Springsteen's "Born to Run," nominating it as the state's Official Rock Anthem—whatever that means. When enough assemblymen/women played Bruce's iconic song and realized it was a song about getting *out* of New Jersey, the votes began to disappear. And let's face it—"I Like Jersey Best" is a blast for me to sing, even dethroning the theme from *The Mary Tyler Moore Show* as our group's closer for many years. But it shouldn't be the official *anything*. Kids, veterans, state leaders—no one—should take off a hat, raise a flag, and place one's hand over the heart while singing, "Fork-ed River ain't chopped liver."

This was the context in which Bucky and I gassed up the car in December 1985 and headed to Trenton, where I was invited to play "Jersey Best" before the State Assembly, prior to a vote on an actual bill ("I'm Just a Bill") that had sought to name the song the Official New Jersey State Jingle. Originally, we'd heard there had been a debate about nominating it for State Song, but cooler heads had prevailed. As the legislation chugged its way toward the voting process in the Assembly and the Senate, the song came under a level of scrutiny from television reporters, people on the street, humorless politicians, and newspaper editorial writers that our little song was never written to endure. "Had I known that poor Pizzarelli would have to sing it at the State House in front of so many serious people, I wouldn't have put in so much funny stuff," apologized songwriter Cosgriff to one of the hyperconcerned media outlets that harassed us 24/7 for the four days the song dominated New Jersey's news cycle.

Bucky was in rare form for our big day. We had been on the road for a half hour before I realized that we had no directions to Trenton or where we were to report once we arrived there. "We'll just follow the signs for Trenton, then park when we see the big dome," he said, repeating the questionable approach he had suggested for our Blues Alley gig in Washington, D.C., two weeks earlier. (With Blues Alley located in Georgetown, the "look-for-the-big-dome" strategy that had served us admirably on a trip to the center of the nation's capital didn't work as well for locating the jazz club.) Perhaps mindful of the recent D.C. experience, my dad punted as soon as he saw the first sign for Trenton—getting off the Turnpike at the distant Exit 9 rather than the more direct approach that would have resulted from using Exit 7A. We soon found ourselves on Route 1 South, a notorious stretch of the state highway system that allowed us to enjoy 74 percent of New Jersey's total number of traffic lights—all of them turning red for us on this particular evening.

Finally catching sight of the elusive dome, as well as a parking garage nearby, I suggested that we end the madness, park the car, and pay the nominal fee. (The price came to something like two dollars for a month of parking.) The only problem was that until recently, my father didn't believe in paying for a parking space—*under any circumstances.* The New Jersey State House is in the middle of an urban area, and there were simply no parking spaces on the streets of Trenton. We wound up parking the car in south Metuchen and walking a half hour back to the dome. (Joke will work best for readers from central New Jersey.)

After much ado we made our entrance into the General Assembly Chamber of the New Jersey State House. As was his practice, Bucky was in favor of our playing the music and departing—as soon as possible. But years of watching *Schoolhouse Rock* had taught me that politics will not be rushed, especially with the New Jersey State Assembly having scheduled vital legislation to ponder and debate on this night. Believe it or not, there seemed to be pending bills that sounded, at least to my untrained ear, more important than yea or nay on the State Jingle.

The order of things dictated a vote in the State Assembly that night and, if we passed the audition, another vote by the State Senate in mid-January. Even without a scorecard, we sensed that the evening's important issues had been discharged when one of the lawmakers rose and, in a solemn and stately voice, introduced us to his colleagues—pointing first at Bucky seated in the upper reaches of the balcony, while I stood poised in front of the Speaker's podium, ready to sing in front of what I knew would be the definition of a tough audience.

"Before John performs a song nominated for State Jingle, I would like to introduce his father, the famous jazz guitarist, Rocky Pizzarelli . . ."

High above the proceedings, Bucky waved and smiled, but he later confided, "I didn't have a good feeling." An uncanny bellwether when it came to these situations, Bucky had seen lawmakers with their coats on leaving the building as he came out of the State House men's room shortly before they announced us. Sure enough, when I played the song shortly thereafter, the number of assembly members remaining in the State House had dwindled to a precious few—it felt like a Mets game after a two-hour rain delay. Yet even with a sparse crowd remaining, the conversations of the politicians bordered on boisterous, to the extent that the Speaker or the sergeant at arms cracked his gavel during the second verse of the song. I immediately looked around, hoping no one had been shot. And this is not a gratuitous attempt at a lame Jersey joke; it genuinely sounded like a gunshot.

There would be no 1776-like Broadway musical to celebrate the courage shown by the New Jersey Legislature on this December evening in Trenton—especially not the three assemblymen I met who were hiding *in* the bathroom while the official vote was taking place. Not wanting to be on the wrong side of this landmark legislation, these and other members of the State Assembly didn't want to be on *any* side of it and simply sat out the vote. Still, the song somehow passed the Assembly with barely enough votes to move on.

Several weeks later, Bucky and I were in Switzerland, unable to perform the song at the State Senate session when the vote would take place. The final reckoning in the Senate was in the neighborhood of 13–3 in favor. But as those of you who attend New York City co-op board meetings know well, sixteen votes doesn't represent a quorum when there are forty voters. Having run into assembly members hiding all over the State House while those votes were being tallied, we had a theory about what might have occurred in the State Senate, only with a larger gathering in the men's room. As Yogi Berra once said, "If they don't want to come, nobody's going to stop them." The bill to make "I Like Jersey Best" the State Jingle of New Jersey officially died on the Senate floor. It would be the best-case result for everyone.

Without the pressure of official designations, "I Like Jersey Best" took on a relaxed life of its own after we returned from the historic session of New Jersey lawmaking. There were Trenton stories to tell, imitations/versions to sprinkle throughout the song (Billie Holiday, Paul Simon, the Beach Boys, Bob Dylan, Frank Sinatra), and many new components I could add on the fly. My steady Thursday gig at J's Jazz Club on Broadway between Ninety-Seventh and Ninety-Eighth Streets in Manhattan provided me with the perfect venue to allow my performing style to spread its wings. Owned by MAC Award–winning singer (and full-time Yankees fan) Judy Barnett, J's gave me a New York City platform. By interrupting my shows after almost every song in order to announce (a) updates on that night's Yankees score or (b) a complete major league scoreboard of games in progress, Judy played to my love of baseball and encouraged me to mix humor with the music, something I've tried to do ever since.

One night I recall playing a particularly swinging set, interrupted as always by Judy's updates of the Yankees game (sample—Judy: "Mattingly has doubled to drive in Rickey Henderson. Henderson, it was reported today, has not paid his rent in Fort Lee for the past two seasons. Yankees lead, 5–1. Jack Morris on the ropes. Back to you, John") and I would continue singing "These Foolish Things."

After working all day in Manhattan, my father had uncharacteristically found himself with a Thursday night off, so he had stopped by on the way home and sat alone at a table next to the stage. After the set had finished up, he motioned me over, most likely, I assumed, to go over some of my chord selections or fingering choices on some of the solos. Or maybe to compliment my ever-evolving stage presence. But when I got to him, his request was brief and to the point—"Get the scores!"

J's was also the home to one of my great triumphs. (I try not to think about how sad I was when J's closed—to be replaced by a Sleepy's mattress store.) After releasing an instrumental album with Bucky and Johnny Frigo, I heard that because of the success of Harry Connick Jr., the Chesky label was looking for a male vocalist to add to its roster. One night David Chesky showed up at J's to hear one of my sets there. After a representative set that included "Jersey Best," "I'm Hip," a lot of baseball scores, some Gershwin, and more baseball scores, the Chesky people offered me a recording contract during the break between my sets.

By the way, the Chesky folks added, you ought to think about hiring a full-time trio and management to promote the records we are going to make together. Agents, managers, full-time musicians on the payroll, a record deal with a label that was handling some of the biggest names in jazz. I'll be eternally grateful to Judy and the J's community for giving me a New York stage, constant encouragement, and some of the happiest, most entertaining nights of my life. It had been a whirlwind couple of hours that I'd relive for years to come. I'd played a gig and was offered a record deal between sets. Just about every musician on earth has dreamed that dream—and mine had come true.

5

The King of Swing

BENNY

I came dressed as I would in Hollywood, in a pair of corduroys, sweatshirt, and loafers, with probably no socks, and he said, "Where are you going, fishing?" I said, "No, I'm coming to rehearsal," and he replied, "Go home and put a suit on. This is New York."
— Jimmy Maxwell, trumpeter, on Benny Goodman

This is the second time I have written about Benny Goodman. The first attempt took place over thirty-six years ago, back in Mr. Hughes's sophomore English class at Don Bosco in Jersey. Our class had been assigned to write "a persuasive argument" on a subject of each student's choosing. So less than two years after Richard Nixon resigned the presidency in disgrace (and moved to our hometown), with the United States finally out of Vietnam, and shortly after the headlines in the New York *Daily News* announced that President Ford had told fiscally strapped New York City to "drop dead," I took pen to paper to unleash the rage that was coursing through my veins. It was my time to argue the case for one of the fundamental tenets of my generation—*Why Benny Goodman was the* true *"King of Swing."*

Of course, I realize now it might have been more of a fair fight had I not kept Fletcher Henderson, Count Basie, and Woody Herman out of the paper while shooting holes in the other bands of the time. (I used Eddie Condon's line about Stan Kenton's band: sometimes it sounded as though they'd called three hundred musicians for the gig, and all three hundred had shown up on time.) Duke Snyder would have been the best center fielder in New York back in the mid-fifties—had baseball fans left Willie Mays's and Mickey Mantle's names out of the discussion. And I might have been a little hasty to dismiss the immensely talented clarinetist and bandleader Artie Shaw, who, despite the frequency with which he proposed marriage, was voted "King of Swing" by *DownBeat*'s listeners in 1938—as well as embodying the unlikely juxtaposition of "matinee idol" and "clarinet player." But Shaw, Herman, and, arguably, Basie never were part of anything as historic as the concert by the Goodman band on January 16, 1938, at Carnegie Hall. With all due respect to the *DownBeat* voters, once Benny Goodman walked into the September night following his three-week engagement at the Palomar Ballroom (its floor could accommodate *four thousand* couples) in Los Angeles in 1935, he would be the then and forever "King of Swing."

Speaking of votes, when they were all counted, I came home with a B+ on the Benny Goodman paper. As I used to say to Mr. Buck at the pork store, "Wrap it up—I'll take it." This was rarefied air compared to the grades teachers had been writing on the top of my non-KOS assignments for the first two years of high school. (KOS = "King of Swing"—one of two acronyms I use to represent actual people.) You'd think this might have been an "aha" moment, but no such luck. Far from kicking my butt in a scholarly direction, the B+ on the Benny Goodman paper served to deprive me of my no. 1 excuse for mediocre English grades—"Mr. Hughes doesn't give anything higher than a C."

Before we go on, in case you're wondering why a high school sophomore in the spring of 1976 would feel so strongly on the subject of Benny Goodman—*I knew the man*. After my dad played a glorious guitar instrumental of Jimmy Van Heusen's "Deep in a Dream" on *The Tonight Show* on Monday, May 30, 1966—we still have the scratchy acetate—he claims I took a phone call a day or two later (I was six, might have been the first time I ever answered the phone) from Benny Goodman, who asked that my dad return the call when he got home from working. To paraphrase Updike—gods don't leave callback numbers. Benny later told my dad that he'd seen him on Carson, had always loved his playing, and wanted him to join a small group for an engagement at the Waldorf-Astoria Hotel in New York City. It would mark the beginning of a mutually rewarding twenty-year working relationship between Benny Goodman and my father that took them on American and European tours, included small group recordings, and continued through the final concert performances of the KOS's life. Bucky liked to point out to Benny that they had previously worked together on a 1958 commercial jingle for Rheingold Beer. My dad recalls everyone on the date receiving a case of "the extra dry beer" to take home.

Although Benny and my dad got on famously for the two decades they worked together, their first professional meeting nearly went up in smoke—literally. And, as could often be the case, the situation was lost

Benny Goodman and Bucky, with Nancy Adams (Huddleston) at the microphone. Maury Feld (back left) is on drums, and the great Doc Cheatham is on trumpet.

on Benny. Wanting to sound his best for the KOS at that first rehearsal (which could well have been a tryout in disguise), my father had borrowed Uncle Pete's prized 1959 Fender Vibrolux Tweed amp to use at the Waldorf. Dad said later that his playing and his sound were on the money and that things had come off without a hitch—until Benny absentmindedly left his lit cigarette on the tweed amp, burning a large and visible black hole through the top of the case. Although it was Bucky's first day on the job with Benny, he'd picked up enough information about the KOS over the years to understand that he wouldn't be filing a claim for the damages. And Benny wouldn't be volunteering restitution. The next day Bucky apologized profusely to Uncle Pete and bought the scarred amp from him. Along with the first house in Saddle River, it was to become one of the best investments of my father's life.

The Vibrolux with the telltale Goodman cigarette burn survived a more harrowing brush with the scrap heap a few years later when my father backed over it in our driveway. How does one drive over an amp, you ask? More easily than you'd think, it turns out. With Bucky in the process of packing the amp into the trunk, my mom called him back to the house for an important phone call. Running late for his gig, Bucky ran back to the car, closed the trunk, backed up to leave, but didn't notice the amp—or driving over it. It must have occurred to my dad that he might have missed a step in the process because he called from a pay phone (remember those, kids?) about fifteen minutes later.

"Is the amp out there in the driveway?"

I looked out in the driveway, and there it was. Uh-oh—one large piece and a few scattered body parts.

"Make sure it still works."

Not unlike Darren McGavin in the shattered lamp/leg scene we'd see a few years later in A Christmas Story ("Not a finger!"), I gingerly cradled the amp, along with what was hanging from it, and carried it all into the house. But then something miraculous occurred—after I brushed off the asphalt and reinstalled some tubes that had dislodged, it *worked*. That Vibrolux turned out to be such a survivor that after riding out my father's entire *career* with Benny Goodman, it became my primary amp for my New York City gigs in the 1990s. My dad finally put it out to pasture (okay, to the curb) about five years ago—after forty years on the job and thousands of gigs. It should have gone to the Smithsonian.

By remaining back in New Jersey when the Carson band headed to California in 1972, my dad could continue working with Benny when their schedules permitted. Uncle Pete and Uncle Bobby had been telling my dad since the 1930s that the three "dream" jobs to which a rhythm guitar player should aspire were the Basie, Ellington, and Goodman bands—and here was Bucky in the guitar chair once occupied by Charlie Christian, George Van Eps (the father of the seven-string guitar), and Allan Reuss, three of my dad's heroes. To give you an idea of how big Benny was in his heyday, the teenage girls used to go crazy for him, dancing in the aisles at his shows, and lining up around the block to get in. Before they swooned over Frank Sinatra (also at Times Square's Paramount Theater, where Benny preceded him), went crazy for Elvis, or fainted over the Beatles, twelve thousand screaming women entered the Paramount on March 3, 1937 (first set: eight thirty in the morning), and flipped over Benny. He was the original teen idol!

Even when he reached his sixties and seventies, Benny could still play a mean Buffet R13 clarinet and still pack a concert hall. In May 1975 Dad saw that he was scheduled to play a series of small group shows with Benny at the Nanuet Star Theater in nearby Nanuet, New York (Zoot, Slam, Urbie Green, and Hank Jones were among those in the band), and had the idea to invite Benny to come to dinner at our home after the final show of the run, a Sunday matinee. Just prior to the start of that Sunday show, Benny *accepted*. Given the KOS's reputation for having a short fuse and a famous glare, my mother took no chances, issuing strict orders that Anne, Mary, Martin, and I were not to even *look* at Benny, much less engage him in conversation. To further eliminate any wild-card variables from the Benny equation, we were told to stay away from the dinner area completely. For the record, my mom's first KOS dinner featured eggplant parmigiana as the main course, with rigatoni in a red sauce on the side—a traditional Italian dinner. The only complication was that Benny's last-minute acceptance hadn't left Mom enough time to make the red sauce from scratch, so she ran out to the local store and bought the only sauce they carried. Not only did Benny love the meal, he wanted to know exactly what ingredients had gone into making her sauce, calling our home a few days later to learn more about what my mom called "the secret recipe." She didn't dare tell him that the "homemade" sauce he'd been raving about had been a jar of Ragu.

The culinary success of that first visit led to a number of subsequent appearances at our home by Benny Goodman, who made it a point to stop by for lunch and, weather permitting, a swim whenever our home happened to be "on the way" between his Stamford, Connecticut, home and that night's concert destination—usually in Pennsylvania or New Jersey. When he'd come back into the house after a few laps in the pool, he'd invariably end up taking a nap on our parents' bed. It wasn't unusual in those days for Martin and me to come home from school and run upstairs, only to do a double-take at the sight of the King of Swing on his back—asleep on the bed—in his boxers, socks, shirt, and tie. (Where's *that* photo? If only . . .) Yes, a shirt and tie while napping! I later learned that Frank Sinatra would nap this way as well. It was all about not wrinkling the pants.

Around 1980 Bucky talked Benny into having our duo act open about six or seven shows for the KOS in various parts of the country, with my dad informally sitting in on rhythm guitar about half the time during Benny's sets. The first of these shows was scheduled to take place at El Camino Community College in Torrance, California, whose notable alumni include Chet Baker, Brian Wilson of the Beach Boys, Bo Derek, and Frank Zappa. Still, it was my first trip to Los Angeles, and the city was, as Stevie Wonder famously said, "just like I pictured it." The first-day highlights were Grauman's Chinese Theatre and those great footprints (the Marx Brothers, Lassie) and the corner of Hollywood and Vine, the location of the iconic Capitol Records tower. The recording studios inside were originally designed by Les Paul, with the concrete walls ten inches thick and a component of cork and rubber ensuring complete sound insulation. It is impossible to overstate what Frank Sinatra and Nelson Riddle accomplished there after 1956 in Studio A. This was the same studio where I joined

Paul McCartney, producer Tommy LiPuma, and a Diana Krall–led small group in 2011 to record an album of standard songs that Paul and John Lennon played in their early days and used as structural models for their own classics.

We moved on to Phoenix, then to Iowa, and back to the East Coast. Benny's setlist varied from show to show on that trip, but the core components were "Avalon," Horace Henderson's "Big John Special," "South Rampart Street Parade," "Memories of You," a playful version of Scott Joplin's "The Entertainer," and two selections from a Broadway musical Benny loved, Stephen Sondheim's *A Little Night Music*: "You Must Meet My Wife" and "Send in the Clowns."

For all the cautionary tales I had heard about Benny, the King seemed to be on his best behavior for the 1980 shows. One of my favorite trips was the Piedmont Airlines flight from New York to Wilmington, North Carolina, for a concert at UNC Wilmington that same night. Since there was no first-class section on the small plane, Benny sat directly in front of us, joined by a flight attendant who plunked herself next to the King of Swing for 90 percent of our time in the air. At some point, she began to tell him jokes—bad ones but well told. Following the first one (probably her best), Benny's laugh followed the punchline by a second or two and took the form of sucking in air a few times. It was clear by the fourth or fifth joke—all drawn-out stories with no payoff—that Benny was having a ball. Bucky and I had some laughs, too, appreciating the enthusiasm of the joke-telling in the face of such second-rate material. I wished she'd been able to combine her delivery and timing with Bucky's joke inventory. But it didn't matter—Benny was howling.

In what seemed to be no time, we'd landed in Wilmington, at which time the flight attendant brought the merriment to an end and instructed Benny, "Wait here!" Evidently, the cockpit had received word that Benny Goodman's trip to Wilmington had created a scene not unlike the Beatles' landing at JFK on February 7, 1964—reporters and photographers were mobbing the area where we would be descending the stairway to exit the plane. Meanwhile, Bucky informed me, "I gotta take a leak," at which point he ran to the back of the plane.

The plan was for everyone to get off of the plane, after which the King of Swing would pose at the plane's exit, as the rich and famous have done since the advent of air travel, then descend the stairs to the snapping of flashbulbs and shutters and the calling of his name. ("Hey, King of Swing! Over here . . . ")

All went well—I made it to the bottom of the stairs—and now it was Benny's moment. He majestically took each step as though being the King of Swing and all, he had obviously done this before. Flashbulbs were popping, reporters were screaming—man, this was an *event*. Then, all of a sudden, Bucky appeared at the top of the steps, having finished his meeting with a man about a horse. Not wanting to break celebrity protocol and deplane after Benny, my father decided to run down the steps into the sea of flashbulbs, darting around the slow-moving, regal Benny about halfway down, and dashing through the pack of assembled media until he was well clear of the hoopla. It was hilarious. I wonder if one of the photographers assigned to Benny Goodman's historic arrival in Wilmington returned to the darkroom only to discover that the only shots of the waving KOS in his camera also included Bucky practically pushing Benny out of the way so he could slide by him and continue down the stairs.

Immediately after we returned from those shows, Bucky and I were headed to somewhere in Connecticut to do a benefit gig where a long lineup of performers would each do a song or two. At this point in the book you will not be surprised to learn that twenty minutes into the ride we established that my father once again had no idea where that night's show would be taking place. "Make a left where the old tree used to be" and "I got it" were his two most common responses to my question, and a recurring theme of our travels together, *"Do you have any idea where we are going?"*

As we were crossing the border out of New York State, Bucky said, "I think we can get Benny to come with us." Yes, we didn't know where we were going, and now we would have the King of Swing in the car with us. So, we stopped at Benny's (Bucky *and* his car always knew the way to Benny's house), knocked at the door, and walked in to see Benny with a female friend, seated in a palatial living room befitting the King of Swing. Almost immediately Benny mentioned that he had a new supply of reeds he wanted to try out (because ten minutes never passed without Benny testing reeds), and the next thing I knew we were playing an extended version of "Avalon." Benny and Bucky swung as though their lives were hanging in the balance—for an audience of one. And I even got to play a solo. Soon, there were more reeds to test, and when we finally looked at a clock, hours had passed. In the end, our lack of directions was a moot point. We didn't make it to the benefit.

In the late summer of 1983, almost ten years to the day before my dad and I played our memorable set as the supporting act for Frank Sinatra at the then Garden State Arts Center—now PNC Bank Arts Center—in Holmdel, New Jersey, we had the opportunity to open for Benny Goodman on the same stage. Books and the blogosphere are rife with lengthy accounts of Benny's eccentricities, and the intent is not to pile on here. After having read the accounts of his unfortunate tour with Louis Armstrong—Benny left the sold-out tour after two weeks of being upstaged by Armstrong, citing health issues—as well as the expanded play-by-play of his trip to the Soviet Union in 1962 (Q: Zoot, what was it like to play with Benny in Russia? Zoot: "Every gig with Benny is like playing in Russia"), I was expecting far more erratic behavior than he displayed during the time I knew him (1975–86). That said, we did have a wild and zany ride one day at the amphitheater just off Exit 116 of the Garden State Parkway.

For me this was a story of three concerts—the one witnessed by the audience, the account submitted by the reviewer for the Newark Star-Ledger, and, finally, what was actually transpiring backstage and onstage. The day began innocently enough, with Benny calling Bucky on the morning of the gig, asking if he would run the sound check. It was a solid band: Scott Hamilton—tenor sax, Spanky Davis—trumpet, Chuck Riggs—drums, Phil Flanigan—bass, Chris Flory—guitar, Joel Helleny—trombone, and Gentleman John Bunch—piano, with Bucky and me to open. They set up the way they always had with Benny—a mic in front and pretty much nothing else. Benny had built-in radar for locating stray microphones, and he didn't much like stage monitors either. Dad and I weren't terribly sophisticated about sound checks back then; we figured that as long as *we* heard the band, it was okay with us. Scott Hamilton went out of his way to compliment Bucky on how fast things went, asking if it were possible for him to run *all* the sound checks.

It seemed like an eternity waiting for the show to begin. And the curious thing was—*no Benny.* At two in the afternoon my father and I went out and played the usual set we played for the KOS—"Love for Sale," some Ellington, "Straighten Up and Fly Right" (sung), a couple more instrumentals—then declared victory. It went well. As we came off the stage, someone mentioned that Benny had just arrived, so Bucky said to Martin and me, "Let's go say hello."

We knocked on the dressing room door, were waved in, and came upon the King of Swing, his back to us, eating a hot dog. Benny never really turned his body our way, but I recall his acknowledging our presence and, between bites of the hot dog, letting me know that he liked my "Route 66." (My mom had sent him my new record—at least he'd listened to the first song.) With the hot dog eaten, Benny began to tell us the story of his radiantly gold Mercedes-Benz, which we had noticed parked near his dressing room. (As we walked by the car, I said to Martin in my best Johnny Carson—"King of Swing drive nice car!") As he always insisted about his clarinets and reeds, Benny believed that if someone looked hard enough, that person would find something out of order inside this jewel of a Mercedes. With two separate service specialists from the Northeast unable to flesh out a single defect, Benny called Germany to insist they send an expert from Stuttgart to pretty much take the Mercedes apart. They did—again, nothing. Still, he insisted, *something* had to be wrong with the car.

In the meantime twenty-five minutes had passed since we had left the stage, and the Jersey audience of about ten thousand began to collectively rumble—as Jersey audiences are wont to do. The people clapped in unison, and it didn't seem to be happy clapping. After all, it was a matinee in late August, and their summer was slipping away while they continued to behold an empty stage. At this point Benny stood up and asked my dad to help him straighten his suspenders, grumbling all the while about his back pain, which had alternated between chronic and acute throughout his entire career. With the mood of the crowd officially crossing the "impatient" threshold, Benny proceeded to lie down on the floor of his dressing room and request that we turn off the fluorescent lights. As Bucky gave me the "Let's get out of here *now!*" look, I glanced back to see the King of Swing with one leg in the air as he also began to clear his throat repeatedly. Before the door completely closed behind me, I heard the sound of Benny's leg hitting the floor. "The King might be dead," I thought to myself, as I turned back and opened the door slightly. I heard Benny continuing to clear his throat (Good, he's alive!), still agitated, however, and still on the floor. The audience began clapping more loudly and in perfect rhythm now, making me recall Albert Brooks's line about such an audience in San Antonio—"How did they get organized so quickly?"

With the audience's irritation being communicated in no uncertain terms, Bucky mobilized the troops. He was clearheaded and demanding—"Scott, you play this . . . then John plays this, then we all play this. I'll get Benny." Everyone was in agreement that the show needed to kick off, and the plan of action was about to be implemented when—a gust of wind and a man in a suit holding a clarinet flew past them and onto the stage. The audience roared with delight. The band was so stunned that it took the guys about ten seconds to realize their leader was in place and that they should follow him out there—*now!*

I watched the show from the side of the stage and saw it all. Make no mistake about it—*Benny was a terror that day*—whistling melodies when they weren't being played 100 percent correctly, stopping and starting the band if the tempos seemed off, searching the stage for stray mics, and I think he found one on the bass that shouldn't have been there. I was white with fear that afternoon—and I wasn't even on the stage. Bucky accompanied Benny on certain tunes, and when he came offstage, he did his classic laugh ("Heh, heh, heh"—deep and gruff) and kept asking, "So you want to play for Benny? Heh, heh, heh. You think it's easy? Heh, heh, heh."

We thought for sure they'd kill us in the review, but it was apparently a far different show from the audience's perspective. They loved it. And with sufficient distance between her seat and the curious behavior taking place on the stage, the reviewer for the Newark *Star-Ledger* found the whole thing charming. "Benny toyed with the band for tempo," she observed. She even added, "Benny was in great spirits whistling along."

Whistling along? I thought. Man, if she only knew . . .

Benny didn't do a lot of playing in public after he had a pacemaker implanted in 1984, but he had committed well in advance of the surgery to playing a wedding. As the story goes, the father of the bride asked how much to get Benny Goodman to play his daughter's wedding, the response was "Lots and lots," and the proud papa answered, "Okay, see you there."

My dad had just started working with tenor sax whiz Harry Allen back then, and he thought Harry's sound would be perfect for Benny. What my father didn't know about Harry was that in those days it took him forever to get things set up. Soak the reeds, wipe down the sax, test the reeds, wash, rinse, repeat—each *step* took at least ten minutes—until finally, you wanted to hit him in the back and shout, "Norton, get on with it!"

When it came time to play the wedding, Benny needed a band, so Bucky got a call, as did Urbie Green (trombone), Bill Crow (bass), Chuck Riggs (drums), and the impeccable John Bunch on piano. Because the King of Swing wasn't big on springing for rehearsal space, the run-through took place at the proud papa-of-the-bride's apartment on East Fifty-Seventh Street in Manhattan. Harry came with us and sat on the sidelines at first, just watching the rehearsal. I recall the bride's father stopping the music and asking the band to play "Daddy's Little Girl," so they went over that one a few times. (When you have Benny Goodman for a wedding, I think you forget about "Daddy's Little Girl" and ask him to re-create the Carnegie Hall concert. But that's me. . . .)

Harry sat patiently while Benny and just about the tightest band you'd ever find rehearsed for a good forty minutes before taking a break. After our host sprinkled the infield with generous pours of Pouilly-Fuissé, the band started off with "Avalon," and while Benny was blowing, he pointed his clarinet as a signal for Harry to take out his sax. It was the only time I have ever seen Harry unpack his sax, skip the preliminaries, and be ready to play in seconds flat. Benny had that power.

My father always had a genuine admiration for Benny and truly loved his playing. For jazz academics, Goodman critics, and Artie Shaw, Benny might have reached his peak in 1938 at Carnegie Hall; perhaps it extended another couple of years while Charlie Christian was still with the band. But I shared my father's capacity to be moved by the enduring, swinging power of what Benny brought to music.

For all the wackiness that surrounded Benny, both real and exaggerated, Bucky remained his friend until the day Benny died while playing Mozart in the guest bedroom of his New York City apartment. They found him still holding his clarinet.

Did I tell you that Benny Goodman read my high school paper? My mom thought it might be amusing to bring my paper to a party she and my dad attended at the Goodman home in Stamford. According to Goodman scholars (okay, my father), a sizable group gathered around Benny while he critically reviewed my symphony of prose (with an oversized red "B+" at the top of it) and rendered the final word on my masterpiece.

"B-plus??? Only a B-plus? This paper deserves an A."

My Mother's Eggplant

Maybe it's the way she grates her cheese,
Or just the freckles on her knees.
Maybe it's the scallions. Maybe she's Italian.
I can't reveal her name but eggplant is her game.

—Michael Franks, "Eggplant," from The Art of Tea
(Reprise—1976)

Eggplant has become as revered and central to the Pizzarelli family narrative as the story of the loaves and fishes is to the Bible. And the similarities don't end there. Dozens of people have greeted me over the years, claiming to have sampled my mother's never-ending eggplant from just two small Tupperware containers she brought to a tailgate for a Bruce Springsteen concert over Labor Day weekend of 1985. All this while the rest of our family was attending Dick Gibson's jazz party in Colorado. As the story goes, word of mouth spread rapidly throughout the Giants Stadium parking lot, until half of New Jersey had come by Parking Area 1C to sample my mom's specialty. There was even a rumor that a fracas ensued over the assignment of leftovers.

From tailgates and picnics to weddings and formal dinner parties—eggplant is a dish that never fails to present itself in varied settings with a sense of aplomb and self-confidence. "Don't worry," you can almost hear the eggplant reassuring you. "Everybody likes me."

Just as everyone in our family who plays an instrument has learned "Honeysuckle Rose," everyone in the family has mastered the eggplant recipe (that is, except Martin, who, however, must be considered among the dish's most highly evolved consumers). And by now, each family member has a story of how eggplant saved the day—surprise dinner guests . . . stores closed . . . Benny Goodman shows up . . . late plane, home at two in the morning. I'd even speculate that had Mary Richards served our family's eggplant recipe instead of the Veal Prince Orloff, it would have bailed out her dinner party (and Mr. Grant wouldn't have gone home starving).

It is a straight-ahead recipe made even simpler by the addition of traditional ragu (recipes for which are available all over the Internet). Sure, purists can scoff—but it all works. More important, it holds up well to short-term refrigeration or freezing. It worked for years served cold on rye bread after late-night gigs at Nobody's Inn. It sustained my guitar maker and his friends during the week following 9/11 in the old jazz apartments in Saint Louis. And like those 3 a.m. Black Friday shoppers you see in the news clips, our dinner guests nearly trampled me one Christmas Eve at our Lexington Avenue apartment as I walked two platters of eggplant to the table without police protection.

In a world where the "sure thing" often finishes fifth at Santa Anita, eggplant with red sauce is the absolute truth. Bet on it. Always. It is nonnegotiable.

Knowledge is knowing that eggplant is a fruit; wisdom is not using it in fruit salad.

—Old Joke

MAMA PIZZARELLI'S EGGPLANT RECIPE

ABOUT SIX SERVINGS

2 eggplants
¼ cup flour
3 eggs, beaten in a dish
1¼ cups Italian-style breadcrumbs
2 tablespoons olive oil, plus extra
1 tablespoon butter, plus extra
1 1-lb., 7.9 oz. jar Ragu Old World Style sauce, or a sauce
    of your choice
1 cup Parmigiano-Reggiano cheese, freshly grated

Thinly slice the eggplant into rounds (¼- to ⅓-inch thick). Flour the rounds, then dip into beaten eggs, then breadcrumbs.

Heat two tablespoons of olive oil in a skillet with a tablespoon of butter.

After the foam of the butter subsides, carefully fry each breaded round on both sides to a golden brown. Fry several rounds at a time. Repeat, adding more olive oil and butter as needed, until all rounds are fried.

When you are done with the frying, put a thin layer of olive oil and a layer of sauce in a baking dish.

Then layer in the fried eggplant. Put a dollop of sauce on each round and a bit of cheese and continue until the baking dish is full.

Bake at 425 degrees F for about 25 minutes or until it is bubbly.

I am not a licensed chef and, therefore, take no responsibility for details, ingredients, or the final result. Any publication, reproduction, or retransmission . . . If you want the real recipe, I refer you to my mother.

6

Raised on Radio

I like radio better than television because if you make a mistake on radio, they don't know. You can make up anything on the radio.

—Phil Rizzuto

It's mid-December 2010, and it's another day when I love my job. I am scheduled to tape *Radio Deluxe*, the weekly syndicated radio show I host with Jess from "the most deluxe living room from high atop Lexington Avenue." We get to have our friends join us as guests—Barbara Cook, Liza Minnelli, Kurt Elling, Mitch Albom, Ann Hampton Callaway, Steve Tyrell. It's all unscripted, and we sing and play the music that we love. What could be better? People actually like the show. Don't believe me? We found someone (Christopher Loudon) who even put it in writing (*Jazz Times,* August 2008). He wrote, and I quote:

> Among radio's greatest pleasures is each weekly installment of *Radio Deluxe,* two hours of great jazz and smart, sassy repartee from John Pizzarelli and Jessica Molaskey, the hippest husband-and-wife team since Louis Prima and Keely Smith.

Only on this day, Jess has an out-of-town singing gig, so I enlist our daughter Maddie, who was almost thirteen at that time, to do her best Joy Philbin (this reminds me—Regis was a great *RD* guest, too) by jumping in as the substitute cohost. Maddie has stolen our show more than a few times, most notably when she joined us one afternoon and shared some observations after visiting the Metropolitan Museum of Art for the first time. On this day I pick her up at school, and we walk home, deciding during our walk that we will be taping our holiday spectacular. Skipping rehearsals and preliminaries, we roll tape and immediately fall into a discussion about our concert schedule and our family's holiday plans.

Then, for some reason, I decide that we need to decorate a Christmas tree—only we have no tree. But it *is* radio, after all. So I begin to crumple some paper from a nearby gift box, which was close enough to the sound of moving branches. Maddie picked right up on what was going on and began describing each ornament she pretended to put on the tree, making just enough odd sound effects to sell the idea that we were actually trimming a tree. After we sprinkled in Nat Cole, Gene Autry, Burl Ives, and "I Saw Mommy Kissing Santa Claus," we wrapped up and declared victory. I was convinced we'd come up with the radio equivalent of an *Andy Williams Christmas Show*, minus the visuals. (Of course, we couldn't hope to compete with the blowout years when he'd have on the Osmonds). The dreamer in me imagined families in all 108 of our radio markets forming a circle around their vintage but lovingly restored Zenith 12-S-471 radios, drinking hot chocolate, and celebrating the holiday season with Maddie and me.

Such hopes and dreams are not unusual for someone like me who grew up at a time when radio was *everything*. Like so many of us who grew up in the New York metropolitan area during the Beatles' run in the sixties, Anne, Mary, Martin, and I were glued to the fifty-thousand-watt nondirectional signal of WABC, which had its transmitter just off Route 17 in Lodi, New Jersey. Fifty-thousand watts so close to our home meant that kids with a certain kind of dental filling could transmit WABC's signal through their teeth. We love talking with fans on the road about our respective radio roots, and it is a kick to hear that people from as far afield as Canada, Chicago, and the Carolinas also grew up listening to the music countdowns, the annoying chime, and the memorable deejays of WABC—Cousin Brucie, Harry Harrison, Ron Lundy, Chuck Leonard, and Dan Ingram. And "Howard Cosell, speaking of sports" at 5:25 p.m.

The station choices around our house began to change in the early seventies, as my sisters led the move to FM radio, mostly to WNEW-FM and WPLJ, stations that played several songs consecutively and ventured more deeply into album cuts than simply Top 40 tunes. The free-form programming of WNEW-FM was also driven by its radio personalities, but these were not the barreling baritones of WABC. Two of the WNEW-FM voices in particular, Alison Steele ("The Night-bird") and Jonathan Schwartz ("Jonathan Schwartz"), spoke softly and soothingly about the city they inhabited and the music they loved, often after playing forty-minute sets that introduced us to artists who remain an essential part of our lives over thirty years later—Joni Mitchell, Bob Dylan, the Mamas and the Papas, Jimi Hendrix (who wrote "Nightbird Flying" for Alison), Crosby, Stills & Nash, Judy Collins, Jackson Browne. And Alison's silky and smoky delivery of a nightly refrain (accompanied by an Andean flute) to begin her ten o'clock show had no trouble capturing the rapt attention of this New Jersey teenager. She exuded a quality of serene maturity and wisdom I wasn't finding in fifteen-year-old women at the Bergen Mall.

So come. Come fly with me, Alison Steele, the Nightbird.

And then more often than not, or at least on nights when I tuned in, she opened with "Nights in White Satin" by the Moody Blues—in E minor.

I previously mentioned Jonathan Schwartz, a WNEW-FM original who began there in 1967 following the station's failed experiment to have all-female disc jockeys (of whom Alison Steele was the only one to make a long-term trip to the new format). He is often cited as the quintessential voice for the late sixties–early seventies anything-goes/progressive rock format that put FM radio on the map. Projecting an image of someone who was perfectly at home behind a radio mic, knowledgeable about the music, and not bashful about sharing his personal passions—Hass avocados, the Boston Celtics and the Red Sox, Delaney and Bonnie, Count Basie, the station's food policies, and the music of Francis Albert Sinatra—Jonathan's was the perfect calming radio voice for people who were still in a hangover from the sixties and didn't need all the screaming. How can you not have hope, he seemed to say each night, when artists are able to produce such riveting and original music? Never did I dare to imagine as I listened to his show on WNEW-FM in the early and mid-seventies that Jonathan would be the driving force behind my own radio career.

It's fitting that the bond between us, two avid Red Sox fans, would find its origins in a production of *No, No, Nanette,* the 1925 musical long believed to be the catalyst for the sale of Babe Ruth from the Red Sox to the New York Yankees. Our modest production of *No, No, Nanette* was scheduled to be unveiled at Michael's Pub, located at 211 East Fifty-Fifth Street in Manhattan (Note: Now an Outback Steakhouse), and in its time, *the* cabaret room in town (along with the Café Carlyle). The bookings there represented the best of the new singers, well-known instrumentalists—Kenny Davern, Benny Carter, Ruby Braff—as well as the cream of the vintage jazz singers whose careers were again on an upswing (for example, Anita Ellis and, later, Mel Tormé), plus Woody Allen on Mondays, a gig he'd maintained with the New Orleans Funeral and Ragtime Orchestra since 1971. And in the late seventies and early eighties they experimented with several four-week runs, rain or shine, of stage adaptations, thus the booking of *No, No, Nanette* in 1979.

During our engagement in 1979 and until the day it closed in 2011, the owner of Michael's Pub was Gil Wiest, a character in every sense of the word. One of the lively debates about Gil, a rough-talking, spiffily attired, iron-fisted proprietor, centered on who received worse treatment—the musicians and singers or the customers. Gil didn't play favorites that way. A friend once shared that his formula for receiving occasional humane treatment from Gil involved greeting him with the words, "Give me the worst fucking table you have. And make it snappy."

So when I showed up late for the first rehearsal, which took place in the basement of the now-departed O'Neal's Balloon—so named due to a law carried forward from Prohibition that banned the use of the word "saloon"—I thought Gil would have my head. The musical director for these stage adaptations, a good friend of Jonathan's, a frequent accompanist of my dad's, and a man who would be on speed-dial for the rest of my life, Tony Monte, had gotten me the job (rhythm guitar), and his face communicated concern that Gil's other shoe was certain to drop—right on my throat. But for reasons that eluded Monte and me, as well as Wiest scholars for years to come, the seldom-forgiving Gil decided to give me a pass.

What I recall was an enjoyable engagement at Michael's Pub, with some top-notch musicians (Allan Hanlon on guitar, Jack Six on bass), a flawless Mary Mayo on vocals, and Bernie Knee on male vocals. Mary had a tendency to lock eye contact with male members of the audience when she sang, which certainly commanded the attention of my then girlfriend's father. Her performance also called for her to sing a series of birdcalls, which she executed perfectly, although Tony and I struggled each night to keep from losing our professional composure during this part of the show. When Tony's pal, the same Jonathan Schwartz who played all the cool FM tunes, came to our show, all composure went out the window during the birdcalls.

While it was great to have steady work at Michael's Pub, the highlight of that gig was being introduced to a very hip slice of New York City by a man who had taken on the role of my nightlife mentor, Tony Monte. On most nights we'd head off to a nightclub to hear music, after which Tony introduced me to what he believed to be proper Manhattan bars —P. J. Clarke's, Oggi, Café Divina, the King Cole Bar at the St. Regis. Among the musicians and singers we saw back then were Dizzy Gillespie at Fat Tuesday's (with a young John Faddis in the group), Helen Humes at the Cookery on University Place (best chocolate cake on Earth), and Barney Kessel and Anita O'Day at Marty's on Seventy-Third and Third (now a Dallas BBQ). Anita showed me what changing tempos and swinging was all about: the elegant playing and short sets by Ellis Larkins at the Carnegie Tavern, Dave McKenna and Dick Wellstood at Hanratty's on Second Avenue in the Nineties, and Daryl Sherman on piano at Jimmy Weston's on East Fifty-Fourth Street.

One night at Weston's I remember Daryl handing over her piano to Tony so he could accompany the singer Billy Daniels, who had dropped by and was looking to sing. At the time she didn't believe she could play the Arlen/Mercer tune "That Old Black Magic" as Daniels was asking for it to be played. (Daniels wasn't about to skip over "That Old Black Magic"; his 1950 recording for Mercury had sold nine million copies!) Or perhaps she just didn't want to accompany Daniels, who had been banned from playing New York nightclubs for three years (1956–59) by state liquor authorities for what was euphemistically termed "a shooting incident." Tony not only knew "That Old Black Magic," he also had the book on Billy Daniels, as he did on most musicians and singers who had spent any time in New York City. Mr. Daniels's colorful past, along with his career-long habit of gazing directly into the eyes of the most obviously spoken-for and hovered-over female members of the audience from the stage, had understandably placed him in the cross-hairs of an incident or two over the years—think Billy Martin at the Copacabana. None of this was lost on Tony, who could be seen that night plainly ducking his head low as he played, in an effort, he said later, to stay out of the line of fire.

After *No, No, Nanette* played its final birdcall (and chorus of "I Want to Be Happy" and "Tea for Two"), Tony and I remained close, primarily because he was, depending on whether you went with the AP or UPI poll, the no. 1 or no. 2 piano player in my father's Hotel Pierre trio. Occasionally I would sub for my dad in the guitar chair when he had an important concert in-town or out-of-town one-nighters—for example, when he had engagements at the White House or concerts with Benny Goodman—or both. And when I filled in for Bucky, it usually meant a night of continuing education with Tony.

As I discussed in a previous chapter, I spent much of the 1980–83 period alternating between a duo act with my dad (when he was not at the Hotel Pierre with his regular trio) and in small group combos with friends of mine from New Jersey. You might believe I'm joking when I say that my father pushed me to sing because "it'll mean we have to play fewer solos," but that was the prevailing reasoning for him at the time, at least when he first mentioned the idea.

During that period my dad and I made a couple of instrumental albums, most notably $2 \times 7 = Pizzarelli$ on Stash, that began to get airplay on WNEW-AM. And thanks to those records, my dad's reputation, and Tony Monte's getting the word out, the station occasionally mixed in cuts, usually "Route 66," from my 1983 vocal album *I'm Hip*. Besides being no small benefit to my career, and a significant attendance booster for my live performances, it was great fun to hear my singing voice on a station that was already part of radio history. The station's lineup of radio personalities back then was a 1927 Yankees Murderer's Row: Jim ("Mr. Broadway") Lowe, William B. Williams ("Hello, world!"), Ted Brown ("Got a smile on my face, not a frown"), Bob Fitzsimmons, Bob Jones, and Al "Jazzbeaux" Collins. Rich Conaty and the Big Broadcast filled in on weekends, and Jonathan Schwartz crossed the hallway from WNEW-FM on weekends to do his Sunday show. Airplay on WNEW-AM was also a big deal because both my mother and especially my Aunt Lynn listened to the station all day, every day, as did just about every person of a certain age (hmmm, about sixty-five or so) who lived in the New York metropolitan area in 1983.

Jonathan also had a nightly television show (*The Jonathan Schwartz Show*) on what was otherwise a sports station, MSG Cable (now the MSG Network), the "MSG" standing for Madison Square Garden. Madison Square Garden already produced concerts in its arena and theater, and its TV network was looking to expand into entertainment at the time (as was ESPN in the early days—the "E" standing for "entertainment"). A sophisticated music show with a decidedly New York City sensibility clearly must have fit into their plans back then. Had I been told at the age of eleven or twelve that there would one day be a TV network that televised the Knicks, Rangers, and Yankees and that I would be featured on that station, I would have guessed that it would have been as a big league outfielder. But as I have pointed out, when every sixth-grade pitcher turns you into an automatic out, it might be the voice of the baseball gods suggesting that you come up with a Plan B. Eleven years into Plan B I was thrilled when Jonathan Schwartz called and asked my dad and me to appear with him on the sports station to make music. And I suspect his piano player/partner in crime, my buddy Tony Monte, had something to do with it.

My first appearance on Jonathan's TV show was an eventful one. A few weeks before the show I had received a cassette of Blossom Dearie's record, *Blossom Dearie*, which featured Blossom on vocals and piano, the great Ray Brown on bass, Herb Ellis on guitar, and Jo Jones on drums. The cover of the cassette pictured her singing into an old microphone, looking like a librarian in tortoise shell frames. I must confess: I fell in love with that woman! The music was magical to me. "Tout Doucement," "It Might As Well Be Spring" (in French), "You for Me," "A Fine Spring Morning," "Deed I Do," and more. I played it so often in my old Datsun B-210 that I half-expected the car to spit it out one day on its own. I had just turned twenty-three, was getting ready to make my own record, and all aspects of the Blossom Dearie record were informing my musical sensibilities during that time.

So you can imagine my excitement and surprise when I showed up in a decidedly unglamorous studio downtown and saw that the show's other musical guest would be, of all people—Blossom Dearie!

First of all, I hadn't realized that *Blossom Dearie* had been recorded, for the most part, in September 1956, almost four years before I was born. Here we were twenty-seven years later, and she did not look or sound like the cassette. (But then who *does* look like a cassette?) I would later have audience members come up to me and voice similar complaints about my live singing compared to the studio versions ("I'm not saying the record was better. It was just *different*," they'd say), but this wasn't the same thing. I had fallen for Blossom—the distinctive glasses, the tiny voice, the humorous phrasing, the sophistication, her singing in French, figuring that when I met her, I would rescue her from the string of poor choices in men that had informed her lyrics.

I clearly wasn't prepared for the meeting; otherwise, I might have run the numbers on the recording date and spared my aching heart a trip to the floor. With future crushes based on visual images—Ava Gardner, Barbara Stanwyck, Sophia Loren, Catherine Deneuve (b. 1943)—I was always careful to run the calculator on their actual ages, as well as living or dead status, in order not to be ambushed as I was by Blossom.

A postscript on Blossom—in her later years at Danny's Hideaway on West Forty-Sixth Street, I thought she'd regained many of the vocal qualities I had so admired on *Blossom Dearie*. And she was always extremely friendly to me, a function of my not having come clean about my crush on her 1956 self.

As he was the TV show's producer, Tony Monte was good at making sure I always had a moment of my own, whether it was in a live show at Michael's or on television. He gave me a slot on the show to sing, and Bucky decided the tune would be Joe Mooney's "Have Another One, Not Me." Neither of us knew why I did that song, but it would not be the last time we would have no rational explanation for song choices. I have since received a videocassette of our performance on that show, and while not my best stuff, no animals were harmed during those three minutes either.

All went well with the appearance, and to quote Lindsey Nelson doing Notre Dame football highlights, "We move ahead to further action." Fast forward to 1984, and I learn that WNEW-AM has given Jonathan, assisted by Tony and Rich Conaty, a six-to-nine-o'clock slot on week-nights, hosting a show called *New York Tonight*. It would feature live music, banter among the show's participants, and occasional calls from listeners. I knew it would be more than okay. But soon *New York Tonight* became, and this is with apologies to Bob & Ray, Jean Shepherd, and Phil Rizzuto talking about non-baseball subjects on Yankees broadcasts, the best thing I had ever heard on radio. And with a corollary of the Bucky Pizzarelli Theorem again in play—"Anything that good is going to be gone in a hurry." I made sure I listened to the show faithfully every night. It featured a little bit of everything, including live

performances by singers with engagements in town. And as if by wizardry, just as had occurred with the TV show on the sports channel,
Tony and Jonathan enlisted me to join them, most often on Fridays.
But things were different on the radio show. We quickly planned musical arrangements—sometimes I'd sing, other times Jonathan would,
maybe there'd be an instrumental with Tony. But apart from the music,
the show had taken on a free-form life of its own, as we talked among
ourselves about any subject that happened to come to mind. And the
final half hour was particularly wacky, usually highlighted by phone calls
on no particular subject. Often it would be musician friends on their
way to gigs, asking for the best directions to out-of-the-way places—
remember, there was no GPS back in the mid-eighties—followed by
five or six callers arguing about the best shortcuts to the club. One night
a caller simply said, "David Bowie is God," then hung up. Jonathan,
who had essentially been doing radio since broadcasting into an inter-
com microphone in his family's apartment back in the 1940s, was
ready with a response: "A man has decided to call this station and
declare that David Bowie is God. Thank you, sir."

And lest I neglect to mention, scotch was usually poured at about
eight thirty, giving us a kick-start for our first stop at the old Pen & Pen-
cil on East Forty-Fifth Street, followed by a tour of Manhattan saloons
and music establishments. Tony and Jonathan were ideal drinking
companions, bringing expertise to the worlds of both cocktails and
music. Tony was the first person to lecture me (and several bartenders)
on the quality and temperature of ice in cocktails. Cheap imported
commercial ice machines, he'd complain, generated ice that was barely
below the freezing point (thirty-two degrees Fahrenheit, according to
my sources). "No shards" was his mantra, insisting on the largest and
coldest available cubes, even recommending his ice machine of choice
(a Scotsman). He wanted a cold cocktail, he'd remind them, not a
watered-down one.

During one of my guest appearances Jonathan asked how much
money it would take to secure me as a regular cast member of *New
York Tonight*. Jonno has never been what you'd call reckless with the
purse strings, so the speed with which he accepted my number left

no doubt that I'd left money on the table. It was no matter, because what he didn't know was that I'd have done the show for free. Or maybe for parking money—this was Manhattan, after all. It was two or three days a month (at least two Fridays). Incredibly, I was being paid to be a guest on my favorite radio show of all time, and I was having a blast.

I got to play behind some remarkable performers on those shows. Alongside Tony Monte (who could have been a famous French painter had someone thought to reverse the last two letters of his last name), we were fortunate enough to accompany Tony Bennett—the master himself and the beloved pride of Astoria—singing live on the station. WNEW, by the way, was the same station that had figured out a way to broadcast a young Frank Sinatra live from the Rustic Cabin in New Jersey in 1935. Tony Bennett sang the opening line to a Schwartz and Dietz standard—"By Myself"—and given his habit of responding to applauding audiences at that point in that song, Mr. Bennett shouted out, "Thank you!" even though there was no audience in the studio. I remember telling Monte afterward that I can only pray that the day arrives in my career when the first words of my songs are interrupted so often by applause that I need to build "Thank you" into the lyrics.

With the full support of Jonathan and Tony, I also had the opportunity to play behind Mel Tormé, Barbara Cook, Margaret Whiting, Nancy Lamott, Mandy Patinkin, and Michael Feinstein, as well as Jule Styne, Burton Lane, Cy Coleman, and Sammy Cahn when they received their songwriting awards and posters from WNEW. One Monday night I played for Lionel Hampton on Nineteenth Street for a Ted Brown Monday night special. I have to say—Monte put me in some pretty interesting situations for a guy my age (early twenties).

What I particularly loved was that the show used my talents for laughs as much as for my singing and playing. As I got my feet wet in radio and as we all grew more comfortable in the freewheeling format, Jonathan and Tony encouraged me to stretch our usual boundaries. My Bob Dylan impersonation became a staple of the show, both taking part in conversations with the guys and in singing decidedly non-Dylan material. Their nightly feature with Rich Conaty, called "Conaty Tonight," was *unscripted mayhem* (fluff for his Wikipedia page) that involved phone bits spliced together as a soap opera. Trust me—it was funnier than it sounds. Conaty himself is a bit of an outlier, having hosted a form of *The Big Broadcast*, songs of the twenties and thirties, for over forty years at WNEW-AM and WQEW-AM, sandwiched around two extended stints at WFUV-FM, the public radio station of his alma mater (and my son's), Fordham University. *The Big Broadcast* has become something of a New York City institution. In addition to driving a 1950 Nash Ambassador Custom, Conaty also owns a fifties-era television that he hooks up to a player of some kind so he can watch *Superman*, his favorite show, on an authentic black-and-white set that was around when the show first aired. I'm a fan of the show, too ("Great Caesar's ghost, Kent!"), but Rich takes it to another level.

After two years of creating what one of our fans called "appointment radio" each night between six and nine, WNEW's station management and some MBA bean counters canceled *New York Tonight* in 1986. Instead of relying on research and statistics to program the show, they had handed the keys to Jonathan and trusted him to produce a show that was as authentic as it was entertaining. But in the end, it became all about the ratings, and the show's Arbitron ratings didn't hit the magic metrics. From where I stood, there was no way to compare those who ignored us—attention-deficit audience members hitting buttons and jumping from Top 40 station to Top 40 station in their cars—to our emotionally invested listeners who told us they took earlier buses home from New York City so that they would be home for the beginning of *New York Tonight* at six o'clock. As I would feel years later when my favorite television show, *Arrested Development*, was similarly taken off the air due to low ratings (and years earlier, when it was *Adam-12*), this was the cruel reality of Bucky Pizzarelli's Theorem in action—"It's too good; it won't last."

I could write about it for hours (okay, at least thirty minutes), but you would get a much better sense of *New York Tonight* by hearing a few of the shows. We are in the process of borrowing some tapes that friends recorded, reviewing our legal rights, and if all checks out, making some of the *New York Tonight* shows available free of charge through a website and a Facebook site that we set up for the book. Some of the cultural references might be dated, but I agreed with our former bosses on this one—ours was not always humor with broad appeal. But we always succeeded in making one another laugh, and that was always the highest standard to which we could hold the show. And that's why it is not surprising to me that people continue to come up to Jonathan, Tony, and me over twenty-five years since we were axed—and go on . . . and on . . . and on . . . about how they still miss *New York Tonight*. Good luck even finding the music of Tony Bennett on nonsubscription radio, much less stumbling across a show that has him dropping by to hang with old friends and sing live in a studio.

The demise of *New York Tonight* was crushing to our spirits, because it represented everything that could be great about radio in New York City. But as I picked myself up and dusted myself off, I found that there was still opportunity for me in radio. Jonathan must have put in a good word for me at WNEW because I soon received a job offer from the station manager, Quincy McCoy, to work weekends and fill-in slots. He told me that it would be weekend shifts as needed, with six to nine on Saturday nights being my more-or-less regular time slot.

Even in the tightly programmed *Swinging Saturday Night* slot, radio started to be fun again. It wasn't *New York Tonight* fun, but it wasn't bad. And as you'd expect, after I'd been on the air for a little while and had drawn some weekend assignments whose formats weren't as etched in stone as *SSN*, I was able to spread my wings a bit. Friends called in with weather forecasts, sports reports, from fake (chest-pounding) helicopters with traffic—things were starting to go off the rails again, and I felt more comfortable with the show. One Saturday afternoon ("five o'clock in the East") I interrupted in progress the daily cocktail ritual of Bobby Troup and Julie London ("two o'clock in the West") for an extended interview about both their music and television careers.

I even revived our old *New York Tonight* call-in bit, with musicians again feeling welcome to phone in to our show if they needed directions to gigs. But the best calls I received during my solo radio years took place off the air—no, it's not what you think. It was a deep, menacing voice in a gangster's New York accent. The calls began with:

>Caller: When are you gonna play Shirley Bassey?
>Me: Um, sure. Let me see what I can do.

The next week . . .

>Caller: Are you listenin' to me? I wanna hear Shirley Bassey.

I was on a short leash at WNEW when it came to venturing outside the music format. And Shirley's big hit was "Goldfinger," from the Bond film, and it was definitely not on the station's approved list of songs, at least not in 1988. The station had played "Goldfinger" 1,429,834 times during the sixties, and someone had exiled it to WNEW's equivalent of Siberia.

Behind the WNEW microphone in 1988.

While I was deciding if there was a Shirley Bassey song I could play and still remain employed, the phone rang again, and my friend sounded more annoyed than ever.

Caller: You didn't play any Shirley Bassey, cocksucker.

I'll remind us all at this point that it was 1988, the calls were coming in on the station's private line, and caller ID had not yet been made available to the masses (or even to radio stations) to screen out unpleasantness. But the calls were becoming more, um, aggressive. I either had to notify someone at the station or call the police. Or go with Plan C—actually play a Shirley Bassey song. After conferring with someone who knew Ms. Bassey's stuff, I almost went with "Don't Rain on My Parade," then went with her version of "All of Me," and that was that. And I waited for the phone call. It didn't take long to come . . .

Caller: Man, you played Shirley Bassey. Wasn't that great! Isn't she the greatest?

No longer a gangster, no longer menacing, and no longer profane—and all it took was playing one record. Maybe there is a lesson here for world peace; it seems so elusive, but perhaps it is as close as one Shirley Bassey record.

Another entertaining WNEW-related evening took place in September 1987, and it began with my attending a Frank Sinatra concert with Jonathan Schwartz. This was a point of détente in Jonathan's complicated personal relationship with a singer whose body of work he revered above nearly everything. (Although on any given day, his family, the Red Sox, and Arnold "Red" Auerbach might provide worthy competition.) His emotional connection with Sinatra's music was such that he hated more than most of us, or perhaps more than anyone who has ever lived, to see the singer make a calculated misstep. And this is exactly what he believed the third record (*The Future*) of Sinatra's long-awaited *Trilogy* set to be when he previewed it in 1980 and why he referred to it as "a shocking embarrassment" during an airing of the entire album on his Sunday show. Two short days later, Jonathan was off the air and sent to the penalty box for a three-month "sabbatical" by station management, although neither Jonathan nor his listeners initially knew the length of the suspension or even whether he would ever be permitted back on WNEW's airwaves.

We were now seven years down the road, and Jonathan had clearly survived the incident. And when he returned, he was certainly fit and extremely tan. The *People* magazine stories immediately following the sabbatical, as well as later articles about either party that cited the suspension incident, seemed to cast Jonathan as the more sympathetic figure in the imbroglio. Our tickets for this evening at Carnegie Hall came courtesy of Sinatra's camp and were in the third row. During Lionel Hampton's opening set, a gentleman of considerable heft tapped Jonathan on the shoulder, telling him that he was wanted backstage by the evening's headliner. Jonathan returned just before Hamp's finale, a large grin on his face.

As though this were not enough, Sinatra introduced Jonathan from the stage between songs during the concert. "I want to introduce a man who knows more about me than I do"—"And he's right," Jonathan pointed out later—began Mr. Sinatra's generous introduction. He eventually gestured for Jonathan to stand up, and a roar went up from Carnegie Hall that almost rivaled the one that greeted the Man himself. It might have been Sinatra's audience, but these were Jonathan's people. Indeed, I would venture to say that many in this crowd found their way to Sinatra's music after hearing it presented in the flattering context of Jonathan's weekly Sunday show. Schwartz was bathed in Sinatra's own spotlight and did a 360-degree turn in waving to the crowd. Having played over six hundred cabaret shows during the eighties, Jonathan is no slouch at playing to an audience. The cheering continued. There is some dispute about the exact wording, but we could swear we heard Sinatra say over the applause, "That's right, that's right. You don't mess with Jonno." Sometimes, there *are* second acts. What a perfect night for Jonathan.

For me, however, the night quickly deteriorated into a variation on Martin Scorsese's *After Hours*. Jonathan, basking in the Sinatra intro and the resulting cheers from a packed Carnegie Hall, started the drinking portion of the evening with enough adrenaline working to supply every ER in the city. But a few drinks into the postgame, he asked that we call it quits. He'd had enough and was going home. Perhaps he planned to phone everyone he knew to tell them what had happened on this night at Carnegie Hall—I know that's what I would have done. Or maybe he really was going to bed, happy that after seven long years, his issues with Frank Sinatra had come to a satisfying and public resolution. It was about one o'clock in the morning, and it was time to drive back to Jersey. But I was not prepared for what greeted me after my walk over to Fifty-Sixth Street.

The indoor parking garage was closed. Bolted shut.

I had assumed, incorrectly, that I had parked in a twenty-four hour lot; c'mon, this is the city that never sleeps! Sinatra himself had just sung these very words four hours ago. Oddly, the first thing that came into my mind was the Steven Wright punch line as to why a place with an "Open 24 Hrs." sign had closed. "Sure it's open twenty-four hours," said the clerk when he eventually returned. "But not in a *row*." Believe me, I was exhausting all on-site options: (please excuse the passive voice) buttons were pressed, bells were rung, emergency phone numbers listed on the garage's door were called. Nothing, nothing, nothing. Then I spotted a tiny sign with the header "Hours of Operation." It read "Open—8:00 a.m. to 12:00 midnight." It was about 1:45 a.m. I was SOL.

At this point I needed to make a phone call, but to whom? My personal Rolodex began spinning in my head. I couldn't call Jonathan; no sense ruining what had been a perfect evening with him. Girlfriend . . . best guy friends . . . my father . . . my high school algebra teacher? At two in the morning, it was now too late to call any of them. What's a guy to do when late night begins turning into early morning in the Naked City, you're at the end of your rope, you're far from home, the buses or trains have stopped running, you don't have a credit card with you, and the alternative is sleeping on the sidewalk?

Not a moment too soon, I realized that you do what anyone with his private phone number would do—you call Al "Jazzbeaux" Collins!

There is not much I can say about the mythical Jazzbeaux that hasn't been said already or that could do justice to the man or his career in radio. Nearing the age of seventy—plus or minus ten, and these were *hard* miles—he was back at WNEW for an encore run on the overnight shift after having worked there in the early fifties prior to his abrupt departure for Pittsburgh, the Bay Area, and points west. (He told me he'd been fired the first time around by WNEW for spending one entire overnight playing one song fifty-five times in a row—"Mr. Sandman" by the Cordettes.) The "theater of the mind" world he described to his listeners included his personal work-space, the Purple Grotto, replete with mushrooms, stalactites, and a 176-year-old Tasmanian owl named Harrison. When he read dog food commercials, he made it clear that he was reading them directly to the dogs. His collection of Slim Gaillard records was impressive, as was his wardrobe, which seemed to consist almost entirely of purple jump-suits that had been hand-knit by his wife. Along with WFAN's Steve Somers ("The Schmoozer") and perhaps WOR's Joey Reynolds in the early 2000s, Jazzbeaux's run in the eighties was the last frontier of the overnight cult favorite on New York City radio. Working musicians, who often find themselves driving home during radio's overnight shift, are well acquainted with the voices in the night and are particularly thankful when the one-to-six-o'clock jocks can entertain us (and keep us awake) along the way. That's why we'll always be grateful to guys like Somers and Reynolds, to Ken Dashow on the old WNEW-FM, to Fred Hornby at the editor's desk at WINS, and to Jazzbeaux, for providing us with the mix of engaging radio and good company that helped us get home safely on so many evenings after we'd finished playing.

Speaking of Jazzbeaux, I quickly realized that reaching out to him was the perfect call—he was a man of the world (and then some!). *He* would know what to do. So I called the Purple Grotto on the private line, and Collins immediately picked up. And as with most calls he received in the studio, he immediately put the call on the air. Skeptical that it was me, or at least pretending to be, he asked, "How do I know this is John Pizzarelli?" "Jazzbeaux, I swear it's me," I answered him. "Okay, caller—if you're really John Pizzarelli, then sing a song for us. How about 'Route 66'?" So I sang "Route 66" (without guitar and trio but pretty damn well), after which Collins asked, "So, Pizzarelli, how can I help you? Where are you?" All of this occurred over the fifty-thousand-watt airwaves of WNEW-AM! My wild night was probably making news among insomniacs up in Bangor, Maine.

Jazzbeaux then put out a call over the air that I needed a ride from Fifty-Sixth and Seventh Avenue back to the WNEW studio on Forty-First and Third Avenue. How can I definitively state that Jazzbeaux was an overnight cult favorite? Because within about a minute of his broadcasting my location, I was descended upon by at least fifteen cabs, all opening the window and giving me at least ten different pronunciations of the evening's password—"Jazzbeaux." The cab driver who drove me to WNEW's studios would not think of taking either a fare or a tip for the ride. "I do for Jazzbeaux," were the cabby's parting words.

After taking the elevator up to the station I knew immediately that there was no early departure in the cards for me that night. Jazzbeaux welcomed my companionship, and between songs he pleaded with me not to go home, promising that he'd make sure I had a ride at some point. We laughed, I sang a few songs, I took over while the host left his post to stretch . . . and the next thing I knew, it was four thirty in the morning. It was still another three and a half hours until the garage opened, and I was completely exhausted. And not wanting to see the morning team or the management suits when they arrived, I wanted out. So Jazzbeaux put out another call over the air: "Does anyone want to drive Pizzarelli to New Jersey?" Jazzbeaux immediately received a call from one of his regulars, a character nicknamed "Turnpike Dan." He was a New Jersey Turnpike toll collector, thus the nickname. Dan drove a hard bargain; he would drive me home only if I would play a guitar duet on the air with him. Twenty minutes later he appeared in the studio—with both guitars. And about forty minutes after that, I was home in my bed in New Jersey, taken there by the second WNEW enthusiast in three hours who would not take a dime of compensation for his troubles. Man, Jazzbeaux had fans!

The curtain came down on my first shot at a career behind a radio microphone after an overnight shift during the summer of 1988. Asked so many times by the WNEW-AM program director to stick to the playlist, or at least the outline of it, I rolled the dice one morning at around four thirty that no one in station management would be tuned in when I played a set of Carly Simon, Kenny Rankin, and James Taylor. Not exactly a Ratt, Poison, and Iron Maiden heavy-metal trifecta, but for the Sinatra-centric brand that WNEW-AM stood for in 1988, my rogue set was enough to finish me as an employee. Kaput. For those scoring at home, James Taylor's "Baby Boom Baby" is likely the song that did the trick. A short time later Jazzbeaux was also gone, replaced by Larry King and a syndicated call-in show.

Although I'd find myself back on the radio and decorating make-believe Christmas trees about twenty years later, I still miss the WNEW days—a lot. Jonathan is still very much a force, both at WNYC in New York City and on Sirius/XM. But for every Jonathan Schwartz, Rich Conaty, David Kenney, Max Schmid (WBAI in New York on Sunday nights), and the KMOX crew, there are hundreds of computers playing exactly the quality of insipid music you'd expect to be chosen for you by a collection of wires and circuits that has been fed flawed surveyed results of focus groups recruited at a mall.

At least for me, the demise of WNEW (with due respect to its well-meaning successor, WQEW) meant the end of a shared experience for many of us who love the American Songbook and the singers and musicians who interpret it. The end of the eighties also seemed to mark the end of a time when the characters who presented the music and conversation could unite these unusual subcultures (cab drivers willing to give free rides, Jean Shepherd's listeners screaming out their windows) with the message that we are all in this together. It would be another twenty years before I figured out what I was going to do about it.

7

On the Road

There will come a time when you believe everything is finished. Yet that will be the beginning.

—Louis L'Amour

I would expect most readers of this book to know the voice of William Conrad (possibly dubbed in a recording studio) as the voice behind the memorable introduction of the start of the brilliant 1966 album, *Sinatra at the Sands*:

> The Sands is proud to present a wonderful new show, "A Man and His Music." Featuring the music of Count Basie and his great band (*cue Basie and band vamping "All of Me"*) and the man . . . is Frank Sinatra!

Mr. Conrad, who had a successful career in radio, TV, and the movies, also played the karate-chopping private detective in *Cannon*. The eight-hundred-pound gorilla on this show (well, not quite) was why anyone would ever allow the super-slow-motion Cannon to get close enough to employ his signature chop. Maybe not the ideal visual as you're taking in the intro of *Sinatra at the Sands*, but welcome to my world. My perspective is often a funhouse mirror colored by watching reruns by the dozen on my iPad and in hotel rooms, then asking the hard questions during airline flights. Which brings us back to 1990 and a series of decisions that set the stage for a life spent on airplanes, inside hotel rooms, and in search of the perfect late-night club sandwich. (Hilton, by the way, gets major club sandwich points for their consistency throughout their properties.)

In 1990, I'd been offered a record deal following a soaring set at J's on upper Broadway (still a Sleepy's). I was thirty years old. I still remember how I felt that night—as though I were a grizzled veteran of the music business who had paid his dues and was now about to collect his well-deserved pot of gold. With a recording contract in hand I believed I'd crossed some kind of finish line. But as I would find out soon enough, my career still had its feet in the starting blocks. Or hadn't even made it out of the locker room on the way to the track.

The record deal with Chesky also represented security in my life, as I was about to be married to Maria Traversa. From the time I met her back in 1987, Maria had impressed me with her well-developed mind, a passion for politics and the arts, and her deep love of Brazilian music. Music tapes she shared when we first met, mixes that included Toninho Horta, Elis Regina, and other major figures from Brazil, exposed me to these wonderful artists for the first time. (Bucky had started my Brazilian education with Gilberto/Getz and all things Jobim.) My relationship with Maria challenged me to expand my narrow view of the world, both culturally and intellectually. We married early in the summer of 1990 and welcomed our son Johnny in September 1991.

My professional life up to that time as a guitarist and singer consisted mainly of local gigs—playing jazz dates with my dad, working weddings with Martin and pals of mine, and performing at local New Jersey bars, where we often passed the hat (or a large bottle) for tips. There was also a series of albums on Stash Records during that time, as well as a few prestigious out-of-town jazz events that Dad and I were invited to play as a duo. And I picked up shifts of weekend work at WNEW. But in terms of building a sustainable, long-term career, I hadn't advanced the ball very far up the field.

I soon followed the recommendations the Cheskys had shared with me upon my signing the record deal with them, so (a) I put together a full-time touring group and (b) I hired a manager to oversee the "big picture" and overall direction of my career. Let's talk first about the more pleasant of the two—the trio, which I decided to model on the piano/bass/guitar configuration of the early Nat King Cole Trio. The first pianist I ever hired was Ken Levinsky, and I cannot say enough good things about his time with us. He came from a musical family like ours—his father being a first-call player on clarinet, alto sax, and flute who played with Tom Dorsey, Sinatra, Tony Bennett, and Benny Goodman. Ken and I are roughly the same age and had a blast rehearsing, and his playing was essential to our getting on everyone's radar as quickly as we did. The highlight for us was probably the two weeks at the 1992 Montreal Jazz Festival, playing with Nat Rader's band at the Club Soda for two weeks in front of wildly enthusiastic audiences. Today, Kenny tells me he's proud and thankful that he got to record with his father twice (Walt passed away in 1999)—on *All of Me* (1990) and *Naturally* (recorded in 1992, released in 1993). It was the only time Kenny and

With Martin, the only Pizzarelli never to receive a guitar for Christmas.

Walt had ever worked in the studio together, and they seemed to enjoy each other's company immensely on both projects.

Martin Pizzarelli was my first and only choice to be the trio's bass player, as long as he was comfortable traveling, playing music, and existing in a benevolent dictatorship with his brother. As I mentioned in the chapter about his and my musical influences, I know where Martin has been, especially musically, and this is immensely valuable when it comes to dealing in the daily shorthand of a working band.

Given that my brother is my bass player, people must laugh when they hear that there is no room for nepotism in my music or in my career. Sure, all ties go to Martin (ask Bucky—all his good ones from Brooks Brothers seem to disappear), but it doesn't serve Martin, me, the music, the gig, or my mental health to have one-third of a three-person group struggling to play the music. In Martin's case, it's the complete opposite—he has an incredible beat. The late Jake Hanna, a Woody Herman alum and a swinging drummer in all situations, once told me of a jazz party where he'd been working harder than he would have liked on what he assumed would be an informal jam session. As can sometimes occur, there were as many tempos on the stage as there were musicians. But then, for a reason he couldn't immediately explain, he felt his shoulders begin to relax and the rest of his body become loose. He looked next to him and saw that Martin had taken over on bass.

The first important lesson I came to realize about life on the other side of the record deal was that everything involved on the periphery and in support of the music—managers, sidemen, travel, amps, sound quality, aisle seats on planes, scheduling, attorneys, insurance, booking agents, the marketing of records—needed to remain a distant second to the high standard to which we held every note of music we played or sang. But what I didn't know early on was that an important component of that commitment is making musicians feel comfortable and putting them in positions to do what they do best. That sounds intuitive, but it was a concept I stumbled upon by trial and error.

With a can't-miss, dream-team lineup of Dave McKenna—piano, Clark Terry—trumpet, Connie Kay—drums, Milt Hinton—bass, and Bucky—rhythm guitar for my first Chesky record date (*My Blue Heaven*), my misguided plan was to hand them stacks of foolproof charts and then watch them tear up the recording session. Soon afterward I realized I should have selected tunes we all knew, given the guys a gnarly road map, counted it off, then stepped back and allowed the whole thing to breathe. Instead of tying their hands and making five jazz legends play a lot of written-out sheet music, I should have trusted the (better, more swinging) arrangements they carry around in their heads. Or I could have simply given them song titles—they knew how to do it. The Hall of Fame manager Sparky Anderson once said about his Big Red Machine teams of the seventies that the best thing he did on most days was stay out of his team's way. It would have been a sound approach for me on this session.

Even after I left Chesky Records after two years and moved to RCA in 1992, I still had a lot to learn. The first two RCA records featured big bands, humongous budgets, and plenty of management types whose jobs were to keep the trains running on time. And while that is going on, you hope your manager doesn't insult a musician friend, a recording studio owner, or a club owner along the way. Musically, I was beginning to get the hang of it, but too much of my time began to be filled by issues that had nothing at all to do with music. There were far more distractions than I thought possible. As the Grinch famously said, "One thing I can't stand is the noise, noise, noise, noise!" And too much of the new landscape was cluttered with noise.

To be sure, there were some early wins—no relation to Early Wynn—and I give our manager full marks for helping us find our way to the Oak Room at the Algonquin. It was a lovely room to play, a true singer's room, made more special by the rich tradition of both the Roundtable and the hotel. But the timing of this engagement, which none of us could control, wasn't the best, occurring as it did during the aerial (and most television-friendly) portion of the Gulf War in January 1991. We thank everyone's favorite mother, Florence Henderson, for supporting us at one of three occupied tables on the first night of the air strikes. And thanks to Donald Pleasence for coming in for a show and asking us to join him at the bar after, and to Kelsey Grammer for making it on closing night. Speaking of celebs, in 1997 the room's maître d', Arthur Pomposello, put the entire staff on high alert one night when George Clooney had called to make a reservation for a weekend late show. I called my sister and Jessica to tell them, and they just "happened" to be in the room that night. It was like the *Fawlty Towers* episode where the entire hotel was in a tizzy over the impending arrival of a hotel inspector. Finally, ten minutes before showtime and under the watchful eyes of many, Clooney entered the front door—*Nick Clooney*, that is, accompanied by his wife, Nina. (They are George's parents and people I would see many times during the years when I performed with Rosemary Clooney, who was Nick's sister.)

My goal in that first year was to get us to where we were as good as a trio as Bucky and I had been as a duo. Kenny, Martin, and I sometimes got ahead of ourselves, and I felt myself dialing us back to the same sense of simplicity and organization I had experienced with my dad. This meant cutting back on the complicated arrangements and adding ones that would keep us from getting hurt. And when I realized we couldn't sustain three sets of simply blowing jazz, we added material like "Three Little Words," "Jamboree Jones," and "Rhode Island Is Famous for You." The more we were able to offset the jazz with accessible vocal material, the more popular we became. Often we'd hear the comment, "I don't like jazz, but I like you guys." The balance between jazz and near-jazz made our solos and pure jazz runs better for us; the less-is-more approach has helped keep our audiences more receptive when we do send it around for extended solos. By the time we were invited to larger stages in Montreal, in Brazil, and with Sinatra in 1992–93, our trio and our sets were better structured to play to our group's strengths.

We returned to the Algonquin in 1992, this time with a string of sold-out shows, and also had highly successful long-run engagements at the old Ballroom on West Twenty-Seventh Street in New York City (for a month of Sundays) and with Nat Rader's big band for two weeks at the old Club Soda (Avenue du Parc) in our first trip to the Montreal Jazz Festival. Friends who came up to Montreal told us that the local buzz by the end of our run was that Club Soda was the hottest place in town. We came home on a high after the Ballroom and Montreal and made the studio album *Naturally* with many of the large band arrange-ments that had worked so well in our live playing.

Meanwhile, the managerial experience, specifically what it was taking to *manage the manager*, was adding to the stress of dealing with so many new challenges in all aspects of my life. Rather than taking things from my plate, the manager seemed to thrive on constant chaos, starting fires that he then needed to put out.

The manager's decisions seemed to be rooted in those he'd made for a well-known singing couple back in the mid-sixties. To hear him tell it, the defining professional move of his career was holding back the pair from appearing on *The Ed Sullivan Show* until they were given twenty minutes at the start of the show. My position was that of a "We are on the low rung at the moment and ought to take what we can get" kind of guy. And besides, I had always loved Rosemary Clooney's story of her first appearance on the *Sullivan Show*—right after performing seals had opened the show.

A highlight from the road—singing the national anthem at Boston's Fenway Park on Carl Yastrzemski's birthday. Loved hearing myself on five-second delay from the giant speaker in centerfield.

While I was still adjusting to the concept of working with a manager, a series of questionable incidents and decisions that didn't pass my "smell test" began to accumulate over a short time. There was odd behavior during the June 1992 wedding of one of the Bronfmans in Montreal, for which the trio had been hired to provide musical entertainment for the wedding reception. Our manager succeeded in blindsiding the mother of the bride at the reception with the unexpected announcement that there would be "no dancing allowed during the John Pizzarelli Trio's performance." Anyone who witnessed the manager-mother exchange (and given the stature of the Bronfmans) would agree that this moment probably represented the height of diplomatic tensions between the United States and Canada. The head of the aforementioned eponymous trio, however, defused things quickly by playing a nondancing opener ("Three Little Words"), and then following it with an invitation for all guests to dance for the remainder of the reception. I wasn't about to go down (or up) with *that* ship.

Another incident involved my compensation for serving as the opening act on the U.S. leg of the 1993 Sinatra World Tour. (We had already opened in Europe.) Even though the first offer to play was obviously a lowball, "Mr. Hardball" (in all other situations, believe me) insisted that we accept it. We didn't. Then, after all parties finally agreed upon a more workable number, there was an elaborate network of agents, brokers, and contractors, each of whom was demanding to be paid a percentage of my fee. If only purchased by people who were in line to receive a commission on my fee for the second half of the Sinatra tour, our book will be a best seller. It got to be like *The Producers* at one point, when I calculated that over 150 percent of my compensation was flying out the door in various commissions. And that was before I paid Kenny, Martin, and Tony Corbiscello, the drummer we took with us to play with Sinatra's large orchestra.

All of this was on top of the first managerial order upon my signing: to indefinitely ban me from playing professionally with my dad. We *did* play a disproportionate amount of golf during those years, which apparently was acceptable. Something about "breaking out of his shadow," "forging your own identity," and similar mumbo-jumbo.

The two-year ban on playing gigs with Bucky was lifted in 1993.

Not great when I'd be asked about performing with my father, which occurred about ten times a night, and I would hear my hollow voice offering the lame explanation: "We don't play together anymore—I'm 'forging my own identity.'"

Looking back now at the early nineties, I realize how unprepared I was for it all. I know that no one wants to hear the whining—about being handed a record deal, about making our way as a family, or about having to suddenly spend so much of my life in airplanes and hotel rooms. Understandably, people without record contracts might think these deals represent "money for nothing." Without refuting that notion for five pages, let's just say that large corporations are not intrinsically altruistic. Also, people who don't travel for a living associate their happiest memories with the ten or twelve days a year when they get to board an airplane, check into a hotel, have a few days off from work, and get to hit the minibar. Though I am far more of a road warrior these days, the first year or two of four thirty in the morning wake-up calls sprinkled throughout an extended multiple-city trip makes clear to you in stark terms that the life you have chosen will not always be a glamorous one.

The lightbulb came on one day when I recall saying to myself—*Hold on a minute—I'm not going anywhere. I am still going to be doing this in twenty years and should be performing and making my decisions accordingly.* You arrive at such a place once you slowly begin to lose the fear and the "what-ifs"—what if I don't sell tickets, what if I screw up a solo, what if the new record is a bust, what if I get bad reviews, what if, what if, what if—and you realize that it's all about creating a special evening for the people in the audience. They have made the reservations, put down their money, found the parking, and finished the salmon. Other people have done all the hard work—especially catching the salmon. All that's left to do is give them reasons to laugh, cry, tap their feet, hum to the music, clap their hands, and text their friends.

Under siege during his first six months as an unknown, untested, and unconventional talk-show host, Conan O'Brien used to joke that NBC was measuring his career with an egg timer. I watched and empathized with Conan during those days and learned from him, particularly how he seemed to take the long view—carrying himself and delivering his material as though at least *he* believed that he'd be around in twenty years.

When I finally made the inevitable break with my first manager during the summer of 1993, it enabled my dad and me to have one of the most fulfilling experiences of our professional lives, our time onstage together at the then Garden State Arts Center as I opened for Frank Sinatra. Starting with that concert, my father and I have since joined forces for some of the coolest gigs on earth (for example, Paul McCartney's album, Bucky's and my quartet at the Café Carlyle, the Allen Room at Jazz at Lincoln Center, Jonathan Schwartz's Christmas parties, *Radio Deluxe*, Bucky's cowboy record, Shanghai Jazz, the tribute to Bucky at the 92nd Street Y, every year at the Ridgewood bandshell).

As good as *Naturally* had turned out and as much as we looked forward to hitting the road in 1993 to support it, our momentum took a hit right after we made the record. Ken Levinsky, after the travel in 1992 and with the aggressive schedule we'd planned for 1993, decided he wanted to work closer to his New Jersey home. The travel and touring was what we had all signed up for, but in Kenny's defense and as I personally experienced, it's one thing to read the schedule on paper and quite another to wake up every morning to a hotel wake-up call, knowing you're somewhere in the Midwest but you're not sure exactly where.

I have mentioned that I was probably not ready either musically or personally for the life changes associated with heading a working, traveling band and combining it all with a new family. In early 1993 Kenny Levinsky had played his final gigs with our trio. By the end of May the manager was gone, as was Chesky Records when the manager found a contractual loophole and higher bidder for which he would receive a percentage. And far worse than any of the above, my marriage ended in 1994. Fortunately, from the vantage point of 2012, Maria and I find great joy and satisfaction in everything our son Johnny is and in what he has accomplished.

Those first four years on the road represented a time of significant wins, but I also believe we were taking at least one step back for every two we took forward. It might sound inaccurate to describe this period of time—when we sold out the Oak Room of the Algonquin to great reviews, made a knockout debut at the Montreal Jazz Festival, recorded three terrific records, and opened a tour for Frank Sinatra—as the professional equivalent of playing .500 ball, but it was.

It occurred to me around this time that it would be as important for me to find my personal voice as my musical one. I also believe I needed to own up to my decisions—both my musical ones and my personal ones—and that was a difficult task for me during 1990–94. I had conceded too many musical decisions to my manager and outsourced my emotional life to the all-purpose "I'm too busy, let's pack the suitcase—no time to deal with this right now." There are no explanations or excuses for my decisions and for my behavior except that I had a ton of growing up to do and was forced to do it on stages and in front of a lot of people.

A series of developments toward the end of 1993 and in 1994 gave us optimism about the future. Kenny's replacement, Ray Kennedy (you'll read about him in the next "Road" chapter), quickly sent the musical message that Martin and I were going to have to raise our games. We loved playing with Kenny, but Ray was nudging us in different directions and demanding (without explicitly saying so) that we keep up. Also, the experience we took away from both the European and U.S. legs of the Frank Sinatra tour had given us tremendous confidence. Play a few nights in front of ten or twenty thousand people, and you know you can do this. You become eager to play in front of large audiences all the time. Our early years on the road had been a combination of wins and losses, but here we were—still standing— and convinced that the trio was becoming less about short-term chaos and more about being part of a longer race. And, like Conan, we were going to keep playing as long as it took to get it right.

8

Counting My Blessings

LOVING ROSIE

Rosemary Clooney: An American treasure and one of the best friends a song ever had.
          —Inscription on Rosie's ASCAP Pied Piper Award

There are countless reasons why most men would like to be George Clooney. He was named/voted/anointed *People* magazine's "Sexiest Man Alive"—*twice*. He was nominated for acting and directing Oscars in the same year (2006). And it's not everyone who receives an apology from the bank on his ATM receipt for being able to fit only the last nine digits of his account balance.

Of course, George has never sat on eggshells at Town Hall, waiting to find out whether he's won a Nightlife Award. Or had two of his musical arrangements nominated for Grammy Awards (um, I didn't write the actual charts—that was Don Sebesky). Or had his arrangement of ESPN Sunday Night Baseball's theme music make the semifinals of the fans' vote—and lose by fifty thousand votes to three seven-year-olds who play feedback and air guitar. I am not even envious that George Clooney has houses in both Lake Como and Cabo.

For me there have always been two reasons and two reasons only to wish I'd grown up as George Clooney:

1. He was at one time the chauffeur for "4 Girls 4."
2. He is Rosemary Clooney's nephew.

While I have held some colorful jobs in my life, nothing in my past compares with having transported Rosie Clooney, Helen O'Connell, Margaret Whiting, and Rose Marie (with Martha Raye on standby) in the back seat of a rusted maroon Monte Carlo on a concert tour of the Midwest. *Nothing close.* There's a rumor that George even saved the tour by finding Ms. Raye's missing false teeth under a bed in his parents' home. The stories I heard from Margaret about those days make me wish that if there were only one reality show ever filmed (and that *is* my wish), it would have been *4 Girls 4*—24/7. But I do share with George the privilege of having had his Aunt Rosemary play a significant and essential role in my life and my career.

Rosemary Clooney first entered my life as she probably introduced herself to many of us—by way of radio and television. WNEW-AM in New York played "Hey, There!" from *The Pajama Game* in heavy rotation from the time of its 1954 release until the station signed off for the last time on December 11, 1992. And Rosie's 1951 novelty hit "Come On-a My House" was still getting radio airplay in our house fifteen or twenty years after it charted as the no. 1 song in the country (as was the Alvin and the Chipmunks songbook, written by the "Come On-a My House" cowriter Ross Bagdasarian, aka Dave Seville). The first time I recall setting eyes on Rosie on our TV was in her role of Betty in the 1954 classic *White Christmas*. It took a few Decembers of watching the film before I began identifying with Bing Crosby, both as an unpretentious, natural singer and as a man whose days were about to become merry and bright after straightening things out with Rosemary at the end of the picture. When I saw Bing subsequently wind up at the altar with the glorious

Grace Kelly at the whirlwind conclusion of *High Society*, the career path of crooner suddenly began appearing on my radar as a viable option.

As someone who grew up to be a fan of Rosemary's and her singing, it was gratifying to witness her second-act success. After meteoric early-career stardom with hit records and popular films, Rosemary's singing career was stopped in its tracks by rock 'n' roll, and her offstage life suffered from debilitating psychological issues, many brought on by heartbreaking life events. Her personal problems are well documented (mostly by Rosie herself), as she presented the unvarnished version of her life in two autobiographical works, *This for Remembrance* (1977), and *Girl Singer* (1999). Rosie had been on the cover of *Time* magazine in 1953, the star of one of the most beloved films ever made—then found herself begging for singing work in hotel lounges just fifteen years later.

In a return of good fortune, however, Rosemary received rave reviews as the supporting act on a 1975–77 tour that celebrated Bing Crosby's fiftieth anniversary in show business, a series of concerts in the United States and Europe that would mark the final tour for her pal Bing, but one that would define Rosemary's comeback. In 1977 Carl Jefferson and the highly regarded Concord Jazz label took notice of her work and signed her to a recording contract. To Rosemary's surprise, the label had the good sense to stand aside and allow her to choose the songs and have input on all artistic considerations related to the albums. It is no accident that the twenty-five albums that flowed from her relationship with Concord remain some of the best vocal albums made *by anyone* on the planet.

I became aware of Rosie's work with Concord when Jonathan Schwartz began including her Concord recordings on the setlists of his weekend shows on WNEW-AM in New York. He had always played her two collaborations with Nelson Riddle—*Rosie Solves the Swinging Riddle* (1961 on RCA) and *Love* (acquired by Sinatra and Reprise in 1962 when RCA would not release it). *Rosie Solves* is simply one of the best records of singing there is—Rosemary with a confident, effortless style, and Riddle in the artistic sweet spot of his career. From the opening brass notes of "Get Me to the Church on Time," you know you're in good hands.

The all-ballad *Love*, echoing Sinatra's concept albums (think "Wee, Small Hours of the Morning," also arranged by Nelson Riddle), was in production the following year, when a love affair between Rosie and the then-married Riddle was reaching an inevitable and unhappy conclusion. Just as theories abound that Sinatra's failed marriage to Ava Gardner informed his singing ("It was Ava who taught him how to sing a torch song," insisted Riddle), Rosemary's reading of the lyrics on *Love* is a revelation—the maturity she brought to the Concord records, but sung in a youthful voice that could sustain longer notes. Maybe the sound mix could have benefited from another set of ears, but let's not be greedy. We almost didn't have the record at all. Frank Sinatra's newly minted Reprise label, badly in need of content around this time, purchased the rights and distributed the record after RCA passed on it.

By the time the early nineties came around, my father had been recruited as the guitar player for Rosie's annual engagement at Rainbow & Stars, the exquisite cabaret room Joe and Charles Baum had opened in 1988 on the sixty-fifth floor of 30 Rock. And in early February 1992, I was wrapping up four months of singing and leading the big band down the hall at the historic Rainbow Room, so I looked forward to poking my head in the cabaret and sitting (or standing) near the door to see and hear the show. Standing where I did meant that I could observe the performance of the club's maître d', Bismark Irving, whose management style the *New York Times* once likened to that of Humphrey Bogart's Rick in *Casablanca*. There could be no higher compliment. And Rosie loved him.

Then one day I received a call from Bucky—he needed to be out of town for a couple of days during the extended engagement and wanted to know if I would be available to sub for him. That he was even asking me meant he'd already cleared it with the small group of brilliant musicians that John Oddo, the musical director, had assembled to accompany Rosie. It also meant that someone had run it past Rosie.

By all indications, my career as a singer/guitarist was about to take a major step forward. I had just signed with RCA Novus Records, and my first album with them, *All of Me*, was about to be released on February 14 (probably took a four-hour marketing department meeting to come up with that drop date). RCA had authorized a sizable budget for my first recording with the label, so I went into the studio with an aggregation of the most talented sidemen I knew. The contributing musicians included Jim Pugh and Michael Davis (from the Sinatra tour) on trombones, Walt Levinsky (father of the record's piano player, Kenny) on lead alto sax, Randy Sanke on trumpet, Scott Robinson and Phil Bodner on tenor, Joe Cocuzzo on drums, Bucky on rhythm guitar, Martin on bass, and straight-ahead, intelligent arrangements by Dick Lieb. Did I make it clear that we had a budget?

I mention the album and where my career stood in order to help you better understand the reaction of my manager at the time to what I believed was an FYI call to inform him that I'd be sitting in for my father with Rosie's band at Rainbow & Stars:

> What'd ya' mean you're gonna sit in? You're making your own albums now—you can't do this stuff. It's not proper for you to be a sideman anymore. Don't do it!

It was not a pleasant conversation. I'll always remember the words "not proper." But this wasn't a discussion, and it was not negotiable. I'd promised my dad I would cover for him, and besides, I was genuinely excited about sitting in with Rosie and her talented band of veteran musicians: John Oddo—piano, David Finck—bass, Scott Hamilton—alto sax, Warren Vaché—trumpet, and Joe Cocuzzo (who played on my record)—drums. In this engagement Rosie was singing just one song backed only by guitar (Rodgers and Hart's "Spring Is Here"), so my dad and I spent an afternoon going over the chord changes to that song, as well as the rhythm charts and half-chorus solos I would play on the full-band selections.

Bucky also clued me in that Rosemary might be more emotional than usual during this engagement, given the death of José Ferrer less than two weeks earlier. An Academy Award–winning actor (the first Hispanic actor to win an Oscar) and acclaimed director, Ferrer had married Rosie in 1953. They divorced in 1961—only to reconcile and remarry in 1964, then divorce again in 1967. He was the father of her five children. She became pregnant and had children in such rapid succession during the 1950s (having all five children between 1955 and 1960) that Tennessee Ernie Ford (look him up) once said to her, "You've got to find out what's causing this!" And Bing Crosby sent her a gift of track shoes.

Rosie used to tell a story during her shows about being pregnant with her daughter Maria, and being asked by Billie Holiday if she could be the godmother. And Billie asking to meet with Rosemary to review her role and what would be expected of her. A five-hour discussion took place at Rosie's house over gin, orange juice, and cigarettes, during which Billie presented her qualifications. "It takes a *baaadddd* woman to be a good godmother," Rosie recalled her saying. Billie got the job.

Any anxiety about Rosie's mental state and how it would affect her singing on this evening was put to rest in short order. From her first number, Antonio Carlos Jobim's "Wave," to her closer during this engagement, "The Best Is Yet to Come," she stopped swinging only to talk to the audience—and make asides to the musicians. She spoke of how Tom Adair and Matt Dennis's "Will You Still Be Mine?" evokes "New York City in the forties." When she sang "Hey, There!" she asked John Oddo, as she did on most nights, "Were you alive when I recorded this?" (Close call, but my money is on *no*.) And I was completely won over when she'd look out the floor-to-ceiling windows of the sixty-fifth floor during musicians' solos, facing away from the audience to the breathtaking view to the north, and drop asides to us about low-flying planes and the traffic on the distant George Washington Bridge. Rainbow & Stars was truly an enchanted place in those days, made more so because the woman who stood in the center and in the spotlight still saw the room through the eyes of a teenager from Maysville, Kentucky.

The best thing I can say about *my* first night behind Rosie is that there were no major injuries, despite hands that felt like twenty-pound oven mitts on the guitar. Still, what I remember more than my stiff playing was how the new guy was welcomed by the performers, particularly by John Oddo, the musical director, and by Rosemary herself.

I am happy to report that by the time I took my seat for the second night in Bucky's chair, the audience could no longer see my heart pounding through my tuxedo jacket.

"Hey," Rosie called out when I saw her before that second show. "You just had a record come out. And it's supposed to be *very* good." (*People* and *Entertainment Weekly* had just hit the newsstands with good reviews.) My hands went from weighing twenty pounds apiece in my debut to having fingers that could have almost been described as borderline nimble on night two. My guitar playing rode the learning curve on the second night, as I recovered my sea legs and felt more like myself. After the show Rosie could not have been nicer, going so far as to invite me to sing at "Singers' Salute to the Songwriter," the seventh annual benefit concert for the Betty Clooney Foundation that took place each April in Los Angeles. Rosemary's younger sister, Betty, who sang with Rosie in Tony Pastor's band in the late forties and continued performing throughout the fifties, had passed away all too soon as the result of an aneurysm and the resulting brain trauma in 1976 at the age of forty-five.

The "Singers' Salute to the Songwriter" event at the Dorothy Chandler Pavilion in April found me as the equivalent of the guy who bats eighth in the batting order and, unlike Jorge Posada, has no beef at all with that role. In the lineup on this night (a partial list) were Rosie Clooney, Bob and Dolores Hope, Barry Manilow, Bernadette Peters, Michael McDonald (perennial nominee for Nicest Famous Person), Dianne Reeves, Cleo Laine, and *Bea Arthur* (singing "When the World Was Young"—one of my life's "I was there when . . ." moments)—headliners all.

Given the choice between a song by Johnny Mercer and one by Holland/Dozier/Holland, I wanted to do Johnny Mercer's "Jamboree Jones." I figured I'd have no competition for the song, I love the Bobby Troup record, and I'd hit it out of the park. But my manager (remember him?) had different ideas. He envisioned a *"big numbah,"* where I'd begin as a ballad, the tempo would come in, the band would announce itself, I'd play a blazing guitar solo, back to original tempo, then brass, then juggling a chainsaw, then cue the American flag, a few rockets overhead, and all is right with the world. Rube Bloom and Johnny Mercer's "Day In, Day Out" was selected. Andy Williams's brother, Dick, wrote a special lyric about Mercer into the middle of the song, which did not make things easier on the singer. All things being equal, I did about a B-minus "Day In, Day Out," but there was Rosemary as I came off the stage, applauding and encouraging me as though I'd gotten an A-plus.

The excitement was in the dressing room, where my roommates were Joe Williams, Harry Crosby (from my soap opera days), and Michael McDonald. We stared a lot at Joe Williams—what a regal presence he was. Steven Bishop stopped by to see Michael, mentioning a book project that had him collecting original drafts of famous songs. Michael mentioned that he had the initial draft of "Taking It to the Streets" on an airline cocktail napkin somewhere in his home. Also (not sure I told him in all the excitement that night), Michael's selection of "You Can't Hurry Love," sung as a ballad, was an inspired choice.

The lasting recollection I took away from that event was the sincere and generous hospitality I received (and have always received) from the Clooneys. Including the cousins and everyone's kids, that's a *lot* of hospitality. Also, the entire evening overflowed with affection, both backstage and in the three-thousand-seat hall, for the true star of the evening, Rosemary Clooney, a woman who never failed to make audiences and friends—and even substitute guitar players—feel as though they were members of her family.

I'd be remiss here if I didn't take a minute and introduce you to Dante DiPaolo, the man who made so much possible. He was Rosemary's rock of support, source of strength, and main confidant, at least from where I stood. And he was low-key, quickly appearing in the clubs and at concerts to grab Rosie's arm, put out a chair for her, or make a quick joke. She'd jokingly call him "the best road manager anyone could wish for," and she was right. And he loved to cook pasta.

The story of how Dante and Rosie met, or more accurately, how they got back together, goes beyond implausible to another category entirely. "Unbelievable?" You'll believe it. But I wouldn't recommend trying this at home.

The shortish version is that Dante, said to be a dapper hoofer in his day, had been assigned to give Rosie dancing lessons for the film *Here Come the Girls* (1953), which was filmed on the Paramount lot. But Dante had to quit the set of Rosie's next film, *White Christmas*, for Idaho and the set of a film that offered him a performing role, *Seven Brides for Seven Brothers*. For reasons best explained by Rosie in *Girl Singer*, she wound up eloping with José Ferrer in the summer of 1953. Dante was crushed. The next twenty years was a dormant period for Dante and Rosie as a couple—until 1973, when Dante's 1956 Thunderbird stopped for a red light in Beverly Hills beside Rosemary's Corvette. He called out his nickname for her: "Rosella." She shouted out a phone number, he wrote it in the dust on his dashboard, he called the number soon thereafter, and he didn't leave her side for twenty-eight years. After years of both of them insisting to anyone who would listen that there was no need for them to be married, they tied the knot ("for the grandchildren") in Rosie's hometown, Maysville, Kentucky, in November 1997. As someone pointed out, the courtship first took flight during the Eisenhower administration—as I said, don't try this at home.

My next collaboration with Rosie would be a few months later, a recorded duet of "It's Only a Paper Moon," the Harold Arlen–Yip Harburg (and perhaps Billy Rose) chestnut from *The Great Magoo*, a 1932 comedy with just this one (fantastic) song. In his 1982 review of the revival in Hartford, Mel Gussow of the *New York Times* called *Magoo* "as insubstantial as cotton candy." But he liked "Paper Moon." So did Rosie. And so did Dolores Hope, a close friend of Rosie's. The official story is that Bob Hope became so captivated while listening to Dolores sing "It's Only a Paper Moon" at the Vogue nightclub in 1933 that he made up his mind at that moment that he would someday marry her.

I haven't yet mentioned Allen Sviridoff, the man who had the idea of recording the "Paper Moon" duet. He was also Rosemary Clooney's manager for the final twenty-three years of her life and, from where I stood, one of the true heroes (along with Dante) of Rosie's second act and critical acclaim. Clearly I am biased because of the considerable role Allen played in giving me a more prominent role on Team Clooney after the initial Rainbow & Stars cameos as a sub for my father *and* for his enthusiastic support of Jessica's singing career. For all of you who have enjoyed the concerts and Carlyle engagements Jess and I have performed together—note that Allen Sviridoff is the person who first strongly suggested that Jess and I perform and sing together (back in 2000 at Feinstein's). Up until then she and I had only considered it—but Jess speculated that it might be like Lucy Ricardo sneaking down to the bandstand and ruining her husband's show. And were that the case, she'd have some "'splainin'" to do.

Allen's association with Rosie began in 1979 when he was called in from Buenos Aires ("I was there with Ginger Rogers") to Phoenix for an interview for the job of road manager for the "4 Girls 4," who at the time were handling their own travel, luggage, bookings, schedules, and lighting—as well as all ground transportation not being handled by twenty-year-old George Clooney. And they all had to manage their individual managers, who all wanted to be involved. Margaret told us that before Allen came aboard, there was a side act called "4 Managers 4," which was just as entertaining as the stage act—just behind the scenes. Rose Marie had been the first of the women to reach the boiling point first on the DIY approach and sold her pals on the benefits of a full-time road manager, leading to a call from a Broadway pal of hers to Allen in South America.

By all accounts, Sviridoff brought order to the chaos, no small feat given the personalities and the sheer amount of baggage involved (no pun). Then, with Rosemary having exactly one concert (a charity engagement) in the books for 1979, Allen took over as her personal manager and producer.

Thirteen years later Allen Sviridoff stood in the Skyline Recording Studios in Manhattan to oversee the vocal duet of "It's Only a Paper Moon" that Rosie and I were about to sing. The album on which it would appear was *Do You Miss New York?*—my favorite Rosemary Clooney album of the Concord set—with a version of the title track (with words and music, as with "Sideman" and "Sweet Kentucky Ham," by Rosemary's frequent contributor, Dave Frishberg) that often makes me cry, punctuated by the spoken "Me, too" that finally answers the song's musical question. The format was old-school for this one—Rosie singing live with the band, and her vocals were strong all day. I joined Rosie, Dante, Allen, musical arranger John Oddo, vocal arranger Earl Brown, engineer Michael McDonald (*not* the "What a Fool Believes" Michael McDonald), and a cast of dozens to cut the final track for the album. I wish I had engaging stories to dish from this session, but after going over the vocal parts with Earl, Rosie and I sang along with the guys (Oddo, Hamilton, Vaché, Bucky, Finck, and Cocuzzo—same lineup as at Rainbow & Stars). Rosemary completed all of her tracks on Wednesday. And because my father needed to leave the session early to make a nightclub when I was already there to sing "Paper Moon," that's me (uncredited) playing rhythm guitar on "May I Come In?"

At the conclusion of the first take of "Paper Moon," my boss had heard enough.

"Well, *we* were perfect," said Rosemary Clooney.

Happily for me, my father's booking agent (who is also my father) would inexplicably book him elsewhere for four or five nights each February during Rosie's annual visit to Rainbow & Stars. This allowed me to continue my musical relationship with Rosemary, as well as experiencing the honor and sheer joy of playing with *those* guys in *that* room, for seven years. I'd have done it for free; oops—upon further review, I think I did. (Memo to self: call Dad!)

Besides her ability to sing the songs the right way, I loved Rosemary's sense of humor. At the last show of the week on Saturday night, she'd continually call out, "We're going over the wall—we're going over the wall tonight," a throwback to what she remembered "Bing and Bob" calling out on film sets late on Friday afternoons when the cast had the weekend off. And when she wasn't commenting on the grand views of Manhattan during the musicians' solos, she'd sometimes walk among the first row of tables near the stage and toss out one-liners ("Is that a scotch?") to patrons. She needed to occupy herself while the guys blew their solos, and what she decided to do during those times was consistently, wickedly funny.

One of the traditions on the final night of the Rainbow & Stars engagements that did involve adult beverages was the gathering of Rosie's entourage at a large table by the window in the Rainbow Grill for a night of storytelling. John Oddo told a few of us about a good-natured disagreement one night between Rosemary Clooney and Dolores Hope concerning the song "Thanks for the Memory"—the beloved Ralph Rainger–Leo Robin classic, an Academy Award winner, and Bob Hope's signature song for over fifty years.

Dolores Hope hated the song.

"No, it's a great song," countered Rosie, who then proceeded to sing/speak the final verses of the song a cappella, which took the group of musicians who were there and nearly reduced them to a puddle. John said that even after having heard Rosie perfectly land for so many years, her accompanists were stunned speechless after what they'd just heard.

There was dead silence for exactly three beats. (John said the comic timing was perfect.) Dolores replied, *"It's still a shit song!"*

In 1998 Rosemary Clooney's fans, friends, and family found themselves anticipating the ambitious schedule that had been put in place to celebrate Rosie's seventieth birthday. First, there would be a Carnegie Hall concert on February 11 to celebrate her remarkable career—the cover of *Time* in 1953 at the age of twenty-five, singing at Holiday Inns on weekends after being released from a mental institution, then back to headlining at Carnegie Hall (for the fourth time in her career) as she ended her seventh decade. I guess she was okay with the trade-off between the frigid, raw February weather in New York versus the sheer exhilaration of performing her songs on the great stage on West Fifty-Seventh Street. Back in May of the previous year Rosie had made clear for us her reason for switching the monthlong Rainbow & Stars gig out of the winter season: "I can't stand freezing my ass off in February in New York anymore." Her May 1998 engagement at Rainbow & Stars would then serve as an extended celebration of her seventieth birthday, with stars aligning so that the big day fell squarely on the final night of the engagement, May 23.

But she became ill after she'd arrived in New York for the Carnegie show. What had seemed to be a minor illness and was characterized in the local New York papers as "the flu" soon became viral meningitis and a 107-degree fever, with the disease soon spreading to her brain (encephalitis). Her family members, many of whom stayed with her around the clock, were told that her chances of survival were 50–50 at best.

When Rosie finally woke up, she had been in a coma for three days. When she was asked by a doctor if she had seen a light and a tunnel on "the other side" (as many on the brink of death claim to have seen), Rosemary replied there had not been lights or tunnels, but there had been fifteen Tony Bennetts in a semicircle, all holding Grammy Awards. Bennett had indeed won fifteen Grammy Awards, thirteen of them after 1993 in many of the identical album and vocalist categories for which Rosemary was nominated. Through 1998 Rosie had been the Susan Lucci of the Grammys, having not won a single award in her fifty-year career. (Rosemary Clooney was finally awarded a Lifetime Grammy in 2002.)

Miraculously, Team Clooney, led by Dante, Rosie's brother Nick, and his wife, Nina, nursed Rosie back to health in time for her to celebrate her seventieth birthday as planned after a month of shows at Rainbow & Stars. Due to a lease dispute with the landlord, Joe Baum had announced that he'd be closing Rainbow & Stars on December 19, 1998, making Rosie's seventieth birthday bash on May 23 a bittersweet finale in the room she adored and that had served as her home away from home for a full month each year. I was out of town working that night, but I hear that May 23 on the sixty-fifth floor was an especially joyous celebration of good friends and family, the highlight coming when Tony Bennett (just *one* Tony this time) took to the stage and sang the Gershwins' "They All Laughed." Then, for good measure and only 108 days late, Rosemary played the makeup date of the postponed Carnegie Hall concert on June 1, singing both with her Rainbow & Stars sextet and with the Count Basie Band. She closed the show with "In the Wee, Small Hours of the Morning" and dedicated it to Frank Sinatra, a lion of Carnegie Hall and in all of our lives, who had passed away two weeks earlier. She softly speaks a second "most" whenever she sings the final line of that song, as in "That's the time you miss him most—*most*—of all." When I didn't see it coming, it would take my breath away.

The next two years, 1999 and 2000, found me working extensively with Rosie, both in the recording studio and on the road. The first project would be an album Rosemary wanted to model after and dedicate to the spirit of the iconic bossa nova album made by Frank Sinatra and Antonio Carlos Jobim and arranged by Claus Ogerman in 1967 (*Francis Albert Sinatra & Antonio Carlos Jobim*). After getting calls from Allen and several from Rosie in the early months of 1999 to discuss arrangement and song ideas, we went into Village Recorders in Los Angeles (now simply called the Village), a former 1920s-era Masonic temple, now known for its state-of-the-art technology and vintage equipment, and as the place where historic sessions (Steely Dan's *Aja*, Fleetwood Mac's *Rumours*, the Rolling Stones' "Angie," Chick-Fil-A voice-overs) have taken place.

From my partisan point of view, there are too many high points on this record to adequately cover them here. Diana Krall and Rosemary, along with the brilliant Oscar Castro-Neves on guitar, collaborated on a "Boy from Ipanema" that will continue to be played for generations to come. The vocals approach the song from poles apart and yet settle into a compelling, unified piece, held on a bed of air by Oscar's beautiful playing and Diana's perfect piano lines. And yet despite the intentionally obvious contrasting forces at work vocally in this song, one can hear the Clooney influence in Diana's singing in general—in her phrasing, her directness, and her absolute respect for a song.

After our one-take effort on "Paper Moon" in 1992, Rosie and I took on five duets here, and I must say—I was much happier with the results this time around. (Of course, I'd had eight years to speculate on how I could have improved on our first effort.) "How Insensitive" felt particularly right, and I was gratified to hear Allen mention, on the way to dinner after the session, "That'll be one they'll be playing at night."

What I also recall from these days is that we adjourned to La Dolce Vita, a traditional Italian restaurant on Santa Monica Boulevard in Beverly Hills, on one of the evenings after the sessions. And there was a bottle of Dom Perignon involved. It was Rosie, Dante, John Oddo, and me (maybe a couple more people). But the night ended up being darker than one would have expected, following such a vibrant and upbeat recording experience. Then it came out that Rosie was in the process of finishing up her autobiography, *Girl Singer*, which was scheduled to be released later that same year. The remembering-and-writing process had dredged up a series of her most unhappy memories, such as her marriage to José Ferrer, her subsequent addictions, her friendship with and close proximity to Robert Kennedy when he was assassinated, and her violent reactions to his death. Clearly, the book had made it all raw and immediate again for her, and she was probably dealing with it constructively by talking through her emotions. But no one at dinner was whistling a happy tune. As we made our way out of the restaurant in a collectively somber mood, in the door walked—Betty White! Rosie turned on a dime, and it was no time before our entire group was laughing it up with Betty. So if you're out there, Betty, your timing was perfect, as always. Thank you for the lift, and thank you, as well, for guest-starring on the best episode of *The Odd Couple* out of the 114 of them that aired—"Password." (Oscar to Felix: "If Charlie Chan got these clues, he'd be running a laundry.")

Rosemary was devastated by the December 19, 1998, closing of Rainbow & Stars, the magnificent club she adored and considered to be her New York home. But a more practical consideration existed: although her annual Manhattan engagement was the hottest nightclub table in town, she needed a new base of operations. The prestigious Café Carlyle might have been a fit, but Bobby Short, Barbara Cook, and Eartha Kitt had already been booked to multiple-month engagements there. Fortunately, it was around this same time that Michael Feinstein and everyone's manager Allen Sviridoff had already begun discussions about the next phase of the singer/pianist's career—"I told him that I had always wanted a nightclub," recalls Michael. With Terrence Flannery, Michael and Allen came to form a business partnership with Loews Hotels (with the support of Sherrie Laveroni and Bob Tisch) to open Feinstein's at the Loews Regency Hotel on Sixty-first Street and Park Avenue. For performers and fans of the American songbook, Feinstein's has been a blessing and a godsend. Although the current location is closing on December 31, 2012, due to extensive hotel renovations, I suspect it won't be long before we see Manhattan's next first-class, five-star music room from Michael and his team.

Michael Feinstein and Rosie had been fast friends from the days when Ira Gershwin lived next door to Rosie at 1021 North Roxbury Drive in Beverly Hills, and Michael was his official archivist. Rosie lived for almost fifty years in the "Gershwin house," so named for the eleven-month period when George, Ira, and Ira's wife, Leonore, had rented it in 1936–37, when it became a hub of both social and creative activity. Coming off the mixed reviews of *Porgy and Bess*, George and Ira wrote *Shall We Dance*, *A Damsel in Distress*, and *The Goldwyn Follies* during those months, films that included some of their most celebrated songs.

On October 5, 1999, Rosemary introduced the world to Feinstein's in style, backed by her old (in the sense that she had played gigs with

At Feinstein's with everyone's adopted mother, Rosemary Clooney, and my son Johnny.

them previously) sextet from Rainbow & Stars, a triumphant kickoff for what has become an indispensable New York home for the variety of music I perform and go out of my way to experience in person.

The *Brazil* CD was released on June 6, 2000, in the middle of Rosie's gig at Feinstein's, to overwhelmingly positive reviews. More good news was that I had graduated from substitute guitar player to "Special Guest" in the print ads. We featured songs from *Brazil*, which meant that Rosie and I did three or four duets each night. After much discussion, we agreed we would skip the crowd favorite "Aguas de Marco" ("Waters of March"), an extended "list" song if ever there was one. Rosie had no doubt that she could memorize the song; her fear was that it would crowd out all the other songs on the evening's setlist, although we agreed that watching her cast about for lyrics did have some entertainment value. Also, she figured that if she did stumble, she'd randomly begin naming items that were on people's tables ("It is life, it is death, it's a trap, it's a gun"). So we skipped it—the no. 1 Brazilian song of all time in many polls—but I'll always treasure Rosie's sensible explanation of why she was taking a pass on it.

Rosemary and Allen agreed that it was best that she do two two-week engagements each year at Feinstein's, rather than the full month she'd had at Rainbow & Stars. In truth, the entire calendar at the new club would be built around Rosie's and Michael Feinstein's schedule preferences, and she was welcome to play there whenever she wanted. At least in the first year of Feinstein's she opened their season in early October, then played another two weeks of shows that ended in mid-June, just as New Yorkers migrate out of town for most weekends until Labor Day. The good news for me (and our trio) was that we had several dates scheduled with her that summer, as well as additional shows in the fall and right before the Christmas holidays, where we would appear as her opening act and I would accompany her on vocals and guitar as we sang some of the *Brazil* material.

A remarkable and memorable experience with Rosie took place at Grand Hotel on Mackinac (pronounced MACK-in-awe) Island, Michigan, that same summer. With no motorized vehicles of any kind allowed on the island (except on the golf course), countless horse-drawn carriages serving as transportation, and no access to the island except by boat or plane, Mackinac Island was the perfect setting for the 1980 time travel film *Somewhere in Time* (starring Christopher Reeve, Jane Seymour, and Christopher Plummer). And while there were only six hundred year-round residents on the island, there are over 130,000 visitors to Grand Hotel annually, many of whom make their plans around the musical guests and the Grand Hotel Mackinac Island Jazz Festival that is held over Labor Day weekend. (I played Grand Hotel for the fourth time over the weekend of July 13–15, 2012.)

It was evident early on during the show that this would not be a breezy and routine night at the office for Rosemary. She had suffered a serious asthma attack earlier in the day, and she was occupied with working the oxygen and her inhaler when we greeted her in her dressing room. And sure enough—one or two songs into her set John Oddo was already cutting songs and trying to bring the finish line closer, as Junior had done with Frank Sinatra five years earlier. "I don't think I can make it," she told the musicians early on in the show. I don't know a lot about medicine, but at that moment I wished I could have reached into my chest and handed her one of my lungs—her breathing was *that* painful to watch.

Then something happened. Rosie was hanging in there, not going for home runs but hitting a lot of singles and an occasional double. The crowd, perhaps sensing she needed their backing, became more vocal in support of her—and she fed off of that. The vintage concert hall is something like a barn out of the Victorian era, and Rosie looked around and remarked, "Hey, this is like the house in *White Christmas*." Then she sang "White Christmas"—on a Saturday night in early September. The crowd went absolutely crazy. When she reached the end of the show, she emotionally addressed the audience, thanking them for their enthusiasm and adding, "You are the best audience we've ever had." And she meant it. She never gave up that night and was rewarded with a long standing ovation.

What was more amazing was that she then had the strength to do a meet-and-greet after the concert, which at Grand Hotel meant about 150 people on line, each telling Rosemary Clooney what she meant to them and sharing their favorite Rosemary Clooney anecdotes. Rose sat in a wheelchair at the front of the receiving line, but she was beaming. I walked over to check on her progress—Jess and I were scheduled to have dinner with her after she'd met with the fans—and I had chosen my moment well. A mother had brought her young son to the show, and when they reached the wheelchair, the mother made it clear that Rosie was the singer of her son's favorite song, which she hadn't performed in that night's concert. So, with about half the original number of people continuing to wait patiently on the line, Rosemary proceeded to sing the full version of "Mambo Italiano" in a soft, deep voice just above a whisper, pointing at the kid whenever she'd hit the "Go, go, go." It was so sweet.

Rosemary somehow had energy for the dinner afterward, at which Jess and I and Maddie (she was then two and a half) joined Rosie, Allen Sviridoff and his wife, Linda, and Rosie's best friend, Jackie Rose, who had been her roommate in New York about fifty years earlier, after Betty Clooney went back home to Kentucky. Our group took things off-campus to the Polo Lounge, where Rosie sat down with a gin martini ("Scotch in winter, gin in summer"), and suddenly all subjects were in play—how Patsy's Restaurant (still on West Fifty-Sixth Street in NYC) floated them (Rose and Betty, and then Jackie) before Rosie hit it big . . . how there was no hanky-panky between either of them and Marlon Brando, whom they knew (Fun fact: Brando's NYC roommate—Wally Cox) . . . how Jackie had taught Rosie to cook . . . her audience with the pope, at which the pontiff let out a wild sneeze, Rosemary thought for a second, then said, "God bless you," to which the pope replied, "No, I bless you" . . . and if they are going to have so many Grammy categories, they ought to have one for "women over sixty who were born in the Ohio Valley." All the while two-year-old Maddie was multitasking—inhaling fries while carefully placing stickers on Rosie's face. Rosemary—the eternal and perfect grandmother—not only let her continue but encouraged her to do so, until her face was completely dotted in stickers by the end of the meal.

A few months later Rosemary asked our trio to open for her at the Foxwoods Resorts' holiday concert in December 2000. Her setlist lineup card took just about every Christmas song off the table, so for our closer we did our small group chart of "Sing, Sing, Sing" and killed the room. After we took our bow—okay, more than one bow, due to the finale—we walked off to more applause. A minute or so after the applause, the crowd was still buzzing, which most headliners cannot abide. Suddenly, Rosie walked up. "That's the *last* goddamn time I let you open for me," she scolded me, with a smile extending from ear to ear. She needn't have been worried—that night she did a version of Irving Berlin's "Count Your Blessings" that stopped clocks.

The following year Rosie came to see Jessica and me at Feinstein's, and we were beyond thrilled to see her there. When we asked for some feedback at the end of the show, her reply was one we try to live by—"Just keep telling the truth—because they always know when you're not."

In 1996 I was the recipient of one of her infamous holiday cassettes. I put it into the machine, and it was Rosie's voice singing "Easter Parade." She sang a chorus, and then spoke—to *me*. *"Hello, John. It's Rose. Thanks for helping us out on our gigs this year. And by the way, you do an amazing Billie Holiday impersonation!"* I couldn't believe that she had even thought of me at the holiday, but there it was. That was Rosie. I heard George Clooney telling an interviewer that Rosie explained on the family cassettes that she'd chosen "Easter Parade" that year because having done over thirty of these, she'd run out of Christmas songs.

When I heard Charlie Osgood report on a Sunday morning in late June 2002 that Rosie had passed away, my heart sank and I started to cry. The news came as I was about to depart a Dallas hotel room for a flight to LAX and a concert with James Taylor at the Hollywood Bowl, in Rosie's part of the world. Just three years earlier Rose had proudly walked me around the house on North Roxbury Drive she'd called home for almost fifty years, pointing out the home's rich history—where Harpo Marx, Oscar Levant, and Harold Arlen swam in the pool; where the crooner Russ Columbo accidentally killed himself with a dueling pistol; where the Gershwins wrote "They Can't Take That Away from Me."

My sadness came in two waves: for a woman who brought the warmth, honesty, and kindness that you hear in her singing to her friendship with her substitute guitar player. And for Rosemary Clooney, the performer with the unimaginable career—it was truly the end of an era for those of us of a certain age who are students of the American Songbook. To me, at least, Rosemary Clooney was the female Sinatra, our link to "the song that Crosby sings." I grieved for the wealth of information and the stories she took with her.

But when I listen to some of the best singers of the current generation—and Diana Krall certainly comes to mind—I am glad that Rosemary was around to influence them. And talking to singers after Rosemary passed away made me realize what a crucial role Rosie played in shaping how we approach a song and how generous it was of her to reach out to so many of us and embrace us as part of her life.

Margaret Whiting used to tell us that during the "4 Girls 4" days, she and Rosie would go for walks around cities while on tour, holding hands and singing. People would stop and stare, yet she said that she and Rosie couldn't care less. That's an image I am going to try to visualize whenever I need to smile.

Rosemary's brother Nick Clooney, a TV man and a journalist for all of his life, said it perfectly a couple of days after Rosie's death: "Rosemary's voice is now in heaven—where it came from."

Thanks for the memory, Rosie.

9

Come Fly with Me

MY TRAVELS WITH MR. SINATRA

What he is singing about has nothing to do with the Rat Pack, martinis, cigars and golf and everything to do with the essence of what it means to be human.
—Stephen Holden on Frank Sinatra, *New York Times*

Late one afternoon in June 1993 I was napping in Berlin, deep in the bowels of the Deutschlandhalle, the historic arena built for the 1936 Olympics. Bombed to the ground by the British in 1943, the arena had been rebuilt in the fifties and had become the setting for Ella Fitzgerald's Grammy-winning 1960 album *Ella in Berlin* (featuring her "Mack the Knife" with improvised lyrics).

A loud series of knocks on my dressing-room door roused me from what had been serious (jet-lag-assisted) sleep.

"It's time," said my visitor. "Let's go."

After negotiating about ten minutes of intricate underground corridors, we came upon signs marked "FAS" that were taped to the walls, all with arrows that showed us where to make the next set of turns. Finally, we reached a sign that simply read "FAS" with no arrows, taped to a door that was slightly ajar. After the requisite pat-down (only kidding), my accompanying adult supervision gave me a parental once-over, straightened my tie, took a deep breath, and then firmly rapped his knuckles against the door. Within seconds the door swung open, at which time my guide immediately launched into his introduction— "Frank, this is John Pizzarelli. He's our opening act. He's . . ."

At that point spoken words became muffled in my brain as though they were the plunger-muted trombone of Charlie Brown's teacher. My eyes no longer saw a person but, rather, a hundred flashing Las Vegas–style neon signs that read THIS IS FRANK SINATRA!

You've heard this before, now you'll hear it from me. The gods had blessed this gentleman with the bluest eyes I had ever seen, somewhere between the daytime sky of Rio de Janeiro and the color produced by the jets of my parents' gas stove. But after forcing Mr. Sinatra to endure about thirty seconds of the most lame patter produced outside the confines of a freshman mixer at Don Bosco, his famous eyes took on a certain blankness that unmistakably announced, "This conversation is *over*."

As his longtime production manager, a Sinatra insider for over twenty years, Hank Cattaneo had the pulse on Mr. S.'s moods and not-so-subtly began expediting my departure. After a handshake with Mr. Sinatra that I replay in my mind all these years later as having been about 54 percent too vigorous on my part, I caught up with Hank to reverse our course back to my dressing room. It was while walking away that we heard a voice—THE VOICE—calling out from behind me:

"Hey kid!"

It was Mr. Sinatra, perhaps realizing that he and I had more to discuss after all. I turned around. What did he so urgently need to communicate? Would it be career advice? A new recipe for red sauce? The security code to the main gate of his Palm Springs home? No. He took just a few seconds to impart the only explicit advice he would pass along to me over the course of our two months together on the road:

"Eat something—you look bad."

• • •

Rewind the tape (or its digital equivalent) by a week or so. My trio/ quartet (brother Martin on bass, Ray Kennedy on piano, plus Tony Corbiscello added to play drums) joined up with Frank Sinatra's World Tour on May 30, 1993, in Dortmund, Germany, where the itinerary called for an abbreviated late afternoon rehearsal to get us acclimated to playing with the twenty-six-piece band that Sinatra's organization had convened for the tour's European leg. When we arrived at the renowned Westfalenhalle, Frank Sinatra Jr.—his father's conductor and musical director since 1988—briefly shook our hands and then sat in the front row with Bill Miller, Sinatra's longtime pianist. Given the number of accomplished pianists with whom Sinatra had worked throughout his career, Miller's longevity with the boss he good-naturedly called The Old Man—about forty-five years, plus or minus seven years in the late seventies when he inexplicably found himself on

The trio—Ray Kennedy at the piano and Martin on bass (but minus Tony Corbiscello on drums)—that accompanied me on the Sinatra World Tour in 1993, here playing at Birdland.

the sidelines—should have qualified him for a Lifetime Achievement Grammy—or a Nobel Prize.

As we distributed the arrangements around the bandstand that day in Dortmund, I recall being greeted warmly and enthusiastically by the members of the orchestra. Some of them I already knew from New York—Tony Kadleck in the trumpet section, Dan Levine and Michael Davis on trombone, Jim Snidero, Walt Weiskopf, Charlie Pillow, Dave Brandom on saxes; others from Chicago and the West Coast I recognized by reputation—Mike Smith on alto sax, Herb Phillips, Buddy Childers and Walt Johnson on trumpet, Jim Huntsinger on trombone . . . and Sinatra's full-time rhythm section. Working with my charts for the first time and playing with my trio and drummer, the band ran through the songs as though they'd been playing them for months. For those keeping score at home, the day's schedule furnished by Sinatra's management called for us to rehearse for about twenty-five minutes (about the duration of our nightly sets), and we came in a little ahead of schedule. As we thanked the band, we heard Frank Jr. loudly share with no one in particular, "They're done already? This would have taken two and half hours with Shirley MacLaine . . . and she'd *still* want to go over two more songs."

We'd look back on the crowd of thirty-five hundred in Dortmund on May 31 as an intimate gathering in contrast to the sea of Sinatra fans we would see every night throughout the rest of the Germany trip. The aggressive schedule left no time to be nervous about playing in front of ten to twenty thousand people, although the sight of Mr. Sinatra eyeing us intently from outside his dressing room in Stuttgart caused me to almost stumble over a "baby" or two during our "Baby" medley ("Baby, Baby, All the Time" / "Gee, Baby, Ain't I Good to You"). The European shows were a blur—five shows in seven nights. I still get chills when I look back on singing and playing to eight thousand people outside the cathedral in Cologne's Roncalliplatz ("Roncalli Square"), then walking offstage and sitting down to one of the most incredible meals I have eaten in my life. When I later stumbled upon a telephone while taking in the show from the backstage area, I immediately called in my location to everyone's favorite Sinatraphile (and Sox fan and radio legend), Jonathan Schwartz, who asked me to hold up the receiver so he could hear Sinatra's singing over the international phone lines. The June 6 show in Cologne turned out to be Sinatra's final good-bye to Europe.

> I hope it won't be too many moons, before we come back and do some songs for you. In the interim, I wish you everything well, good health—God bless you, and take care!

Although it felt like a few hours had passed since we'd handed over our arrangements to the band for the first time, we soon found ourselves landing back in New York. But there was more to come . . .

Before we proceed further let's ask the obvious question—with all of the A-list talent available in the *world* in 1993, how did the John Pizzarelli Trio get the call to accompany Frank Sinatra on his World Tour? Believe me—more than a few Sinatra fans did not hesitate to raise this question with us out on the tour.

Fortunately for us (and bad for German-speaking comics), Sinatra's management had decided that the June and August concerts, particularly the ones booked at oversized venues in Germany, called for a musical act to open the show, as Frank had done over the years with Shirley MacLaine, Buddy Rich, George Shearing, and others. And while Germany is home today to any number of star-power comedians, we had heard that the promoters had not been successful in finding local comics or musical acts that passed muster with Sinatra's screeners in 1993. It also didn't hurt that my record label at the time was the Germany-based BMG (Bertelsmann Music Group), which put us in a position to be considered when the decision was made to open the show with a music act.

We believed our chances went far beyond simply being recommended by a German recording company. Right off the bat, there were my father's many collaborations with Sinatra—on recordings, on the road, at a White House performance during the Reagan years. Also, my last name begins with the word "pizza"—surely this had to grab the attention of Mr. Sinatra, who was actively promoting his own line of pasta sauces at this time.

After weeks of silence from BMG, unofficial word filtered down to us that Sinatra's people had decided to work the June and August dates without an opening act. The best-laid plans had not worked out for us—Dad's turns in the Sinatra guitar chair, "pizza" in my name, the "Coupla Guys from Jersey" Tour. Apparently, it hadn't been in the cards.

Then one glorious spring day at the Times Square headquarters of BMG, while doing a phone interview with an Australian newspaper, I heard frantic knocking on the conference room door. Without waiting for a response, a BMG executive burst in and uncharacteristically interrupted a press interview.

"You are going to open for Sinatra!"

A poster we saw hanging from a Berlin streetlight publicizing Frank Sinatra's 1993 World Tour.

I was completely stunned—speechless. I ended the interview, floated down thirty-six floors on the elevator, and, without touching the sidewalk, made it from the label's offices to the 21 Club, where our trio had been hired to play an early-evening private party. The first people I told were Martin and our pianist Ray Kennedy, who were jubilant when I told them the good news. ("I'm ready to take a bullet for the Old Man" became Martin's go-to line for months.) Our collective adrenaline rush produced a couple of sets at the famed West Fifty-Second Street restaurant that swung as hard as anything we had done in months. Ray channeled Art Tatum, and Martin was a freight train that night on bass.

I thought back on the incredible experience of seeing Frank Sinatra at the Brendan Byrne Arena (back when it was named after a human) in the Meadowlands in March 1986 and being jealous of the fantastic Red Buttons ("Saint Francis, whose own father called him 'Assisi'... never got a dinner!"), who opened the show that night. Now, just seven years later, *we* would be sharing the stage with our hero. I wanted to tell everyone we passed on the street in New York City that night—*we are touring with Frank Sinatra!*

So it was time for the U.S. leg of the tour. Our scouting report had told us to expect hot and humid weather in Atlanta. Summers in New Jersey do not begin to prepare those doomed to experience the "hot and humid" that comes with an authentic southern heat wave. It was as though the entire city was on the business end of a large but invisible blast furnace. As we arrived, local meteorologists were ducking thrown tomatoes from news anchors as they glumly reported that Atlanta had already suffered through eighteen consecutive days of ninety-degrees-or-warmer temperatures, accompanied by relentless humidity in the 70–100 percent range. And the forecasts offered no hope of relief during the time we would be there. Even the hometown *Atlanta Journal-Constitution*, a paper not known for whining about uncomfortable weather, took time to mop its brow and vent, describing the situation as "a sweltering funk."

The weather wouldn't have been such an issue had we the luxury of spending more of our Atlanta time indoors. But we'd been scheduled to play *outdoors*—the Chastain Park Amphitheatre, located adjacent to a tree-lined, upscale residential area of the city. It was also an area of the world fiercely determined not to give up a single cool breeze during our visit. Mr. Sinatra had not performed, indoors or outdoors, since his shows at the Desert Inn in Las Vegas about a month earlier, so a full rehearsal had been called for late afternoon on the day before the concert at Chastain Park. That rehearsal was also scheduled to take place at the amphitheater.

Thanks to our having already performed five shows in Germany with the band, we ran through our arrangements in about twenty minutes, wrapping up with an instrumental of "Sing, Sing, Sing" (with a Schvitz). Even the charts were sweating. With phone calls coming in that the elder Sinatra's plane was running late, Junior took his father's place out in front of the band to warm up the guys (and gals) and to help the sound techs get their levels. Stripped down to a white T-shirt, tuxedo pants, and a towel Junior had shaped into a turban—talk about a visual—he launched into a rousing rendition of "Lonesome Road," backed by the original Nelson Riddle arrangement. His speaking and singing voices took on a striking similarity to his father's on occasion, and this was certainly one of those occasions. I closed my eyes during "Lonesome Road," and it was like listening to *A Swingin' Affair* all over again. And that arrangement . . .

It was during Junior's third or fourth song while sporting the turban that we heard a commotion in the backstage area. By this time Ray, Martin, Tony Corbiscello (drums), and I had dried off, scooped up a pizza (still warm . . . no surprise), a case of Diet Coke, and a handful of towels, dried off again, and made our way to the fifth row center in anticipation of Ol' Blue Eyes running through his material. There had been speculation among band members that Sinatra would have some choice observations about the heat, which continued to hover around ninety-five degrees at six in the evening. When he appeared onstage in a black satin jacket with the words HURRY UP AND WAIT sewn onto the back, Mr. S. didn't let us down.

"What are we doing out here? Why aren't we rehearsing this in a *building*?"

"I *want* you to sweat," answered his son.

"What?"

"I wanted you to suffer."

Wow! That line came from so far out of left field that even Frank Sinatra was speechless!

After another brief exchange between father and son, the orchestra played Harold Arlen's "I've Got the World on a String," with Sinatra limiting his participation to snapping his fingers and humming his way through the tune.

"Okay," said Frank. "What time tomorrow?"

"C'mon. You have to sing the songs," snapped Junior. "You haven't sung in a month, and you need to *sing*."

What followed was a complicated series of hand gestures between singer and conductor, father and son. The signal from the son looked like a call to keep fighting; we interpreted the father's hand motions in reply to be either a dismissive Italian salute or the Dodgers' sign

This would be a good place for a photo from the U.S. leg of the Sinatra tour. But if you'd heard Mr. Sinatra's responses to backstage photo requests, you wouldn't have taken any photos either.

for the hit-and-run. Clearly affected by the heat, Sinatra removed the satin jacket, rolled up the sleeves of his cabernet-colored sport shirt, and began to chain-smoke Camels. After someone shouted, "Let's start from the top," all twenty-six pieces hit the intro, but the vocalist wasn't humming the lyrics this time. On an unbearably hot night in Atlanta and for three magical songs—"The House I Live In," "Come Rain or Come Shine," and "Luck Be a Lady"—the Old Man somehow recaptured his legendary swagger and his early-sixties pipes. Focusing on the five of us sitting just a few rows from the stage, he confidently smiled and played to us. It was the look of an aging pitcher, almost startled to realize during a random game in August that he still had his finest stuff. All too soon the singer polished off "Luck Be a Lady," leaving us in amazed silence for a few seconds before we began clapping wildly. I felt tears rolling down my cheeks. Sinatra winked at us. Whatever occurred between Frank and Frank Jr. had inspired twelve minutes of the best singing I had ever heard.

"*Now*," father growled at son, "*What time tomorrow?*"

The postscript was that *tomorrow's* performance was nothing like the stunning rehearsal. This is not to say that what Sinatra produced for the paying audience was anything less than stellar, particularly at an outdoor space that could have passed for the inside of an oven. Enthusiastic applause from the Atlanta audience greeted the singer's entrance, and it grew even louder after he landed his usual opener, "I've Got the World on a String."

"Thank you," responded Sinatra, as the cheers died down. "I'm melting."

As for my own set, the first of the U.S. leg, I will forever look back on it as the proverbial learning experience. The equivalent of the first twenty rows at Chastain Park were dining tables, filled with dinner guests who had brought stinky cheeses, baguettes, pesto chicken, red bliss potato salad, and red and white wines—mostly from California, all served on white linens. Believe me—I could see everything and smell most of it. And I could also see that no one with his or her back to me (a) considered turning toward the stage during my set or (b) gave thought to lowering the preshow decibel levels of their conversations. If anything, nearly all of those closest to the stage chose to shout *over* the music during my set. What flashed through my mind more than once was a 1970s bit by Albert Brooks about his disagreeable experience as the opening act for then-megastar folksinger Richie Havens.

"Are you Richie?" he was asked by the last security guard ("Last security guard before stage—Do Not Feed") before he stepped onto the stage, as chants of "Richie, Richie, Richie" rang through the hall.

"No."

"Then they're going to kill you."

But no one died at Chastain Park that night. In fact, the spectators politely clapped me off the stage, recognizing my departure to be part of a sequence of events that would result in a Frank Sinatra concert. As I dared not mention within 150 feet of a microphone at any point on this tour, it was now time for that "other" Italian singer from New Jersey to take the stage.

We knew Sinatra would be in a feisty mood on this evening. Unlike the Berlin setup, where our dressing room was closer to the Austrian border than to where Mr. Sinatra dressed, our Atlanta dressing rooms were practically adjacent—although I am guessing that Mr. S.'s came stocked with more than six Diet Cokes, four waters, and some Fig Newtons. And without talking out of school, I can vouch that on this evening the boss was agitated with:

> ➤ The weather ("Could you have found a place that was hotter?")
> ➤ The local promoters who wanted photos taken with him ("Jesus Christ—every time we come here!")
> ➤ The weather ("Somebody throw another log on the air conditioner.")
> ➤ No afternoon baseball on television ("Where are we? Turn on the game, and we'll know where we are. Find the Cubs.")
> ➤ The weather ("Are there any more shows at this place? Cancel them all!")

But following some gentle arm-twisting by Hank Cattaneo, we believed we heard the unmistakable sounds of guests arriving and photographs being snapped. Sinatra's initial reaction to the photo request, however, guaranteed that any requests for a photo of our group would need to come directly from Ol' Blue Eyes himself. As much as we (and our publisher!) wish we'd compiled albums of photos taken with Frank Sinatra documenting each stop on our musical expedition, the singer's (completely understandable) strong negative reaction in Atlanta scared us off. Things would have been different in today's age of hand-held devices, when *everything*—phones, eyeglass frames, blenders, golf clubs—contains a working camera. But in 1993 we knew we were the luckiest guys on earth to be playing that gig and didn't want to hand anyone a reason to send us home on a plane.

As I have indicated, the notorious Sinatra zingers still had some bite, and it was often Junior who found himself on the receiving end of them. Nearly every night came a version of "Say hello to Frank Jr.—my son. He's here because his mother said he needed a job." Harmless enough. But one night when Junior went one way, and Frank and the band went another, his father didn't hold back:

"Whaddaya mean you have the wrong song??? *The wrong song!!!*"

But 99.9 percent of the time Junior had the *right* song, and it was Junior who was most responsible for making sure that a concert featuring an aging and increasingly unsteady performer at its center remained securely on the tracks. Despite the Jumbotron-sized typeface on the teleprompter, Sinatra's eyes were beginning to fail him, making it necessary for Junior to more than occasionally feed him lyrics, song titles, and names of songwriters and arrangers. When he couldn't recall a name or read the words on the teleprompter, Mr. Sinatra often went with "Tom Mix," the silent film cowboy star of the singer's youth. These tasks were in addition to Junior's having to rehearse, manage, and conduct a twenty-six-piece band.

By the time we had met up with the Sinatra tour in 1993, Junior had paid his dues and jumped through enough hoops during the previous five years that it appeared to us that his musicians genuinely respected him on and off the bandstand. But while he was a well-trained musician when named musical director in 1988, Junior was still an inexperienced conductor, as well as the boss's son, which could have contributed to hard feelings among some of the band's holdovers. Included among those who didn't make it easy for Junior in the early days were his father's beloved concert drummer, Irv Cottler, and the man who assumed the chair for over a year upon Cottler's death in 1989, Sol Gubin. At least this was the story making the rounds when musicians would get together for distilled beverages at the end of the day. All agreed that it had become a happier environment in general with Gregg Field in the lineup. Field, a superb drummer and a faculty member at the University of Southern California from the time he was in his early twenties, could not only play the gig but won bonus points at the musicians' level for being welcome company, a wickedly funny man, and, oh yes, Henry Mancini's son-in-law.

Although the Trio took to Junior almost immediately, local and national press covering the tour, or writing about it afterward, was disposed to pointing out his more idiosyncratic qualities. First, one needed to get past his daily uniform, which, regardless of weather conditions, consisted of tuxedo pants, boots, and a white button-down shirt—all tied together by a green farmer's jacket. And his non sequiturs ("Have you seen the new Saturn? It's not a car—it's a machine.") froze us in our tracks a few times—until they oddly began to make sense. In fact, Junior made so much sense to us by the end of the tour that I knew I would one day come to appreciate the Basie-like arrangement of "Horse with No Name" he programmed into one of his first-rate New York concerts. That day arrived about three years ago.

Yet underneath it all, Frank Sinatra Jr. seemed like a guy who wanted nothing more than to blend in—even as he led the band and shared a name with the most exalted entertainer there has ever been. In the middle of the scorching heat of the Atlanta rehearsal, it was Junior who called ahead to the hotel to prepare three-course meals for almost fifty of us, then made the rounds to be sure we all knew that "Frank Sinatra bought us all dinner tonight." He went out of his way to welcome our group to the tour, including us in the afternoon exercise of choosing the movies to be shown on the band's extended bus rides. Before long we broke the code and realized it wasn't about getting our input but about Junior's wish to engage us on the subject of classic films. He could effortlessly quote complete passages from the forties film noir genre, then seamlessly slide into a director's cut–quality lecture on *Young Frankenstein*, replete with complimentary asides about Mel Brooks and Anne Bancroft, both of whom he knew well and obviously liked a lot.

With the passage of time, and after the experience of organizing my own big bands on the road, I have come to further appreciate Junior's role in the Sinatra organization. People who worked for the elder Sinatra privately compared an FAS show in 1993 to a performance by the Flying Wallendas—a high-wire act that had often chosen to perform without using a net. The responsibility defaulted to Junior each night to make sure everyone and everything stayed in the air—from a seventy-seven-year-old Frank Sinatra, dozens of musicians, and the sound production staff, to an opening act whose leader had never been part of anything like this in his life. And Junior had to do all of this in front of at least ten thousand fans, several of whom I witnessed suggesting to his face that his livelihood—leading Frank Sinatra's orchestra every night—was a piece of cake compared to any other occupation imaginable. In one instance near our hotel in Illinois I observed a fan chastising Junior for accepting a paycheck for conducting his father's band.

"The privilege should be enough," the fan barked.

And that knucklehead wasn't an isolated case. After almost every show we stood nearby and listened to fans compelled to inform Frank Jr. that *anyone* could conduct the band for his dad. The reality was far from what it seemed to the fans. In the summer of 1993, Junior was probably the *only* person who could have done that job.

Frank Jr. also had the nightly task of negotiating the minefields that defined one of the most public and complicated father-son relationships this side of Oedipus—whose father's name wasn't mentioned during my three semesters at the University of Tampa. Longtime tour veterans told us that Frank Sinatra continued to carry a roll of dimes in his pocket at all times, a holdover from when he needed to be able to use payphones during the two days Junior was missing after his Lake Tahoe kidnapping on December 8, 1963. Also noteworthy about the kidnapping were the astonishingly brief jail sentences served by the criminals, as well as the bungling kidnappers having to borrow eleven dollars (I wonder if they paid it back) from Junior in order to have enough gas to drive back to California.

Their well-known baggage and personal history made a Sinatra father-son moment in Mr. Sinatra's Atlanta dressing room all the more poignant. It was ten minutes of Frank Jr. attempting to reacquaint his father with "Imagination," a song Sinatra first recorded in 1940 with Tommy Dorsey, then rerecorded in 1961 in a slower tempo with a superb Sy Oliver arrangement (by Jimmy Van Heusen and Johnny Burke) on the Dorsey tribute, *I Remember Tommy*.

The exchange spoke to the father's fading powers of recollection and to a son who decided not to dwell on what had been forgotten but instead took the approach of trying to create a new memory.

> Junior: Let's try it—"Imagination . . ."
> FAS: "Imagination . . ."
> Junior: C'mon, you can do it.
> FAS: Why are we even doing this? Don't worry. I don't
>   like it when you worry.

I recall sitting in complete silence with Martin in our dressing room, trying to process what we were hearing next door. Our first reaction was a numb sadness, as we heard Sinatra unable to recall the lyrics to a song he had been singing so effortlessly for fifty years. But who better to be with him at that moment in his life than his son? Somehow, after all their shared history and for all the directions their relationship could have taken, here they were *together*, on the road, learning a song, the son teaching the father.

On most nights the production staff was on eggshells, waiting for Sinatra's voice to open up, which it usually did by about the second or third song of the set. But on a couple of dates in the United States, most notably on August 19, 1993, in Aurora, Illinois, nothing went right. Following applause for the preceding song, Sinatra dove into the spoken questions that begin Stephen Sondheim's "Send in the Clowns." The only problem was that the song being played by the orchestra and the one scrolling down the singer's teleprompter was "Guess I'll Hang My Tears Out to Dry." As his accompanist Bill Miller later told us, Sinatra hadn't sung "Send in the Clowns" at a concert in over twelve years.

When Frank Jr. walked up behind him and directed him to the words on the teleprompter, Sinatra appeared disoriented, shaking his head and saying, "I can't see. I can't hear. I can't do anything." But Junior quickly restored order—he stood nearby to steady his father through the next couple of songs, knocked a few numbers off the original setlist, and brought things home. While the talk among musicians afterward at the bar centered on how wobbly the performer had been, the night's real story should have been how Junior had quietly salvaged the show. Card players frequently point out that true skill in their world is demonstrated by playing bad hands well. Professional golfers often insist that they win tournaments not by making great shots on Sunday afternoons but also by minimizing the damage on the bad holes—getting away with a bogey when a possible triple bogey looms over the proceedings. Thanks to his son's behind-the-scenes work that night, Frank Sinatra made a bogey, the audience cheered the performance, and a few days later everyone flew to Jersey.

Another essential cog among Sinatra's core group of musicians on the 1993 tour was Bill Miller, who had been the singer's primary piano accompanist since 1951. Introduced by Sinatra during live shows as "Charlie Whiteface" or sometimes "Charlie Greenface," Bill's pallor was consistent with, let's say, a nocturnal lifestyle. As I said, Miller would refer to his boss simply as the Old Man, despite his being almost a year older than Frank Sinatra. As the story goes, he had been playing for six weeks as the lounge piano player at the Thunderbird in Las Vegas when Sinatra came to hear him at the suggestion of Jimmy Van Heusen and immediately whisked him away to work on his TV show and to accompany him at the Desert Inn for his first-ever live performances in Vegas. Except for a bump in their relationship that lasted several years beginning in 1978, Miller played piano and sometimes conducted for Sinatra from 1951 through the singer's final live appearances in 1995. When Bill passed away, it was while touring in Montreal with Junior in 2006. He was ninety-one.

We loved our time with Bill, who was young at heart, supportive of our music, and generous with his encouragement. The wobbly, high-wire concert in Aurora had such an effect on him, however, that he could be seen in the hotel lobby after the show drinking vodka directly from the bottle (and he wasn't the only one drinking from a bottle that night!). Wearing eighties-era eyeglasses that appeared to cover three-quarters of his face, he told anyone who would listen that when Sinatra stumbled into "Send in the Clowns," his pianist had been there for him.

"I had a nice little thing worked out if the Old Man kept going. Did you hear me start to fill?"

The most celebrated of Bill Miller's contributions to Sinatra's recorded and concert works was the solo piano coda that played under the spoken introduction and was woven as a theme throughout "One for My Baby (and One More for the Road)." "One for My Baby" was the "saloon song" on most nights, a seven-minute dramatic event whose props included a bottle of bourbon, a cigarette, a spotlight, a bartender named Joe played by the audience, and an extended spoken intro about a woman who had "flown the coop." The genius of Bill's accompaniment was laying down just enough structure, while allowing Sinatra free rein and the generous space needed to turn the song into theater. Great stuff. And I am not ashamed to admit that our group stole Miller's "One for My Baby" arrangement note for note to use in my trio's live shows. After having heard Bill Miller play this brilliant arrangement on the road for six weeks, I could not imagine the song played any other way.

The '93 World Tour wrapped up on the East Coast in late August, with one-nighters at the Garden State Arts Center in New Jersey and at SPAC in Saratoga, New York, followed by a week at the Sands in Atlantic City. I received so many ticket requests from my New Jersey friends for the August 23 Garden State Arts Center show that we probably could have packed a second show at the ten-thousand-seat amphitheater—just with my comps. The backstage area was packed before and after our show, not because it was teeming with people, but because *one* of the visitors took up such a considerable percentage of the available space—a member of the security detail for the former governor of New Jersey, Brendan Byrne, whom we mention by name in our international hit (played in the UK, Brazil, Canada, and the Café Carlyle), "I Like Jersey Best": "And our beautiful arena has 'Brendan Byrne' carved on the wall."

"I have a message for you from Brendan Byrne, and he wants you to know he's in the audience," reported the gentleman with the size 62 suit and no neck.

"Um, sure," said I. I knew what that meant.

But would it be "Jersey Best" for the governor, or leave it out because Sinatra's folks might plotz if the place went too crazy for the opening act? Again, I wasn't looking to make waves, particularly in Jersey, where it wouldn't even cost them plane tickets to send us home. Luckily, when I ran the yea-or-nay decision on the "Jersey" song past the person in charge of everything, Hank Cattaneo, he decided "Yea"—the song was *in*!

Spectators filled the eight thousand seats and another three or four thousand overflowed onto a hill ("lawn seating") in the distance. Yet it felt like a jam session on my parents' back porch. "I Like Jersey Best," played for the former governor, was a huge success, producing steady laughter, some of it arriving a few seconds afterward from the distant lawn seats.

It was a dream gig for me. We had brought in my dad as a special guest to play a solo number and a couple of instrumental duets with me during my set. The differences between the Sinatras and the Pizzarellis became even more apparent when I walked offstage after one of the guitar duets with my dad. Bucky and I laugh a lot during our instrumental performances, often communicating arrangement cues with our eyes and raised eyebrows.

On the other hand, Junior had gone from being a photo op on the day he was born to being the person most responsible for protecting the quality and integrity of Frank Sinatra's music during the final chapter of his father's performing life. I don't know anything about how they got along other than what I saw, and it looked complicated, as you'd expect many father-son relationships to be after fifty years. (I'd hate to see some of the transcripts of my dad's and my conversations after four hours in the car on the way home from a gig.)

"Wow!" Junior said to me, as Bucky and I came off the stage. "The last time my father looked at me like that was right after he told me to go fuck myself."

JOHN PIZZARELLI SETLIST—
GARDEN STATE ARTS CENTER, AUGUST 23, 1993

- ➤ Splendid Splinter
- ➤ If I Had You
- ➤ Three Little Words
- ➤ Baby Medley (Gee, Baby, Ain't I Good to You / Baby, Baby, All the Time)
- ➤ In a Mellow Tone (with Bucky Pizzarelli)
- ➤ I Like Jersey Best
- ➤ Sing, Sing, Sing

A week at the Sands in Atlantic City would be the final stop for the John Pizzarelli Trio (plus drummer Tony Corbiscello) on this tour. The availability of an up-and-coming comic named Don Rickles bounced us from the large arena shows that fall and from opening the Radio City Music Hall shows in early 1994. Martin and I found that our tour passes still worked at Radio City, so we paid a backstage visit to our old pals and made sure we didn't miss a chance at seeing the great Rickles, whose brilliant career afforded him the license to insult everyone. It got so that the regular targets of his insults were insulted *not* to be insulted. Included on Mr. Warmth's hit list were Frank Sinatra ("*When you enter a room, you have to kiss his ring. I don't mind, but he has it in his back pocket*") and Frank Junior ("*Do you know why the kidnappers let Junior go? Because they heard him humming in the trunk.*").

It was during the final shows of the tour at the Sands that we witnessed Mr. Sinatra's memorable method of vocalizing, after remaining in the pocket-sized backstage area to take in the singer's opening numbers. During the European dates we noticed Mr. Sinatra singing/yelling at the top of his lungs throughout our final number (a full-on, big-band arrangement of "Sing, Sing, Sing"). It turned out that in addition to a fairly comprehensive vocal preparation in his dressing room, he liked to scream backstage to warm up his voice to make sure he hit the ground running on the first downbeat.

"Go home!" Sinatra would holler repeatedly. *"The old man has nothing for you tonight!"* All the while, he would wear a mischievous grin, sometimes peeking out at the audience through a side curtain to see if they'd spotted him. Then he'd vocalize some more. *"Go home!"* One night he asked why there were bottles of Jack Daniel's on a backstage table stacked nearly up to the ceiling. *"What the hell is this for?"* When one of us told him it was probably in his contract, he laughed out loud. On another night, pointing at a too-large vat of ice near the bourbon table, he asked, "What am I—an ice skater?"

Although he'd miss a few shows during the Radio City engagement the following April, he missed just one show while we were with him, a Saturday night (August 28) in Atlantic City. The solution to the headliner's absence was simple enough—refunds were offered, and the audience members were invited to see a free show at which I opened for Frank Jr. and got to perform for thirty-five minutes. (About two-thirds of them stayed.) But the real story was Frank Jr.'s set, which absolutely soared. He hit Riddle's chart of "Lonesome Road" so far out of the park that the outfielders never turned around.

And it was in Atlantic City, of all places, that I began to get sentimental that I would one day miss all of this—a nightly master class of singing and living songs from Frank Sinatra . . . the free golf and being referred to as the Sinatra Foursome . . . not needing to check into hotels . . . marathons of seventies baseball trivia with the band . . . helping to choose the movies for the bus rides . . . and performing nightly while backed by the most skilled sound technicians and the most talented big band imaginable. But what I wound up missing most of all were the late-night hangs at the bar where musicians would gather to tell stories.

On one of our final nights in Atlantic City one of the older guys—trumpeter Buddy Childers—told a story about being out on the road in Texas with Stan Kenton's legendary big band during the early fifties. Kenton's lead trumpet player at the age of sixteen, Buddy explained that the band had stopped at a roadside restaurant and came upon Nat Cole, standing and eating dinner from a plate resting on the hood of his car. The restaurant, it seems, banned blacks from dining inside their establishment but explained that they'd decided to serve dinner to Cole and his musicians because twenty-four of the thirty songs on their jukebox were Nat Cole recordings. From the vantage point of 2012, I can't see how Nat Cole managed to control his rage when denied admission to that restaurant, or how he kept calm in 1956 when he was attacked on a concert stage in Birmingham (he never played the South again). Until my fellow musicians shared these first-hand stories, I had admired Nat Cole almost one-dimensionally for his musical contributions and virtuoso piano playing, his intelligent song selections, and for the trio format that I "borrowed." I was more than a little embarrassed for not having done my homework until then about Nat Cole's life and the challenges he faced in building a career on the road in the forties and fifties. Hearing Buddy's stories, as well as follow-ups by others among the elders of the band who had known him, helped me begin to see the lives and achievements of Nat and of other black musicians in the context of the aggressive racism they confronted on a daily basis.

My career experienced a definite uptick in the nineties, aided in no small way by my having joined the exclusive club of those who have opened shows for Frank Sinatra. My trio and quartet would soon be invited to play Carnegie Hall, the Hollywood Bowl, the Walt Disney Concert Hall, the Napa Valley Opera House, and the best clubs—Birdland, Dizzy's, and the Blue Note in Manhattan, Yoshi's in Oakland and San Francisco, Scullers in Boston, Shanghai Jazz in Jersey, Catalina Bar & Grill in Los Angeles, and Dimitriou's Jazz Alley in Seattle. And I was even invited to sing the national anthem at Fenway Park in 2009 (Red Sox 14, Yankees 1). I often reflect on Mr. Sinatra and my time with him on the road, with the memories all returning in

2006 when I decided to craft an all-Sinatra album, introducing fresh arrangements and alternative approaches to songs identified with my one-time employer and my all-time hero. And performing songs from this album in concert at the Kennedy Center on New Year's Eve of 2009, carried live nationally by NPR, allowed me to thank Mr. Sinatra from the stage for paving the way for all of us who follow him, a microphone in our hand and a song in our hearts. His lifetime body of work is nothing short of stunning.

As I look back on our days with Mr. Sinatra, it is with a combination of admiration and deep affection. He was a little over three months from his seventy-eighth birthday, and suffered the unfortunate fate of being unfavorably compared with his younger self. And his fans had the records and CDs to prove it. But man, he put a lot of employees on his back (me included), he had ten thousand people leaving their homes and counting on him every night, and he did his job.

I will always be grateful to Sinatra, to Frank Jr., to Hank Cattaneo, to Tony O., to the ladies and gentlemen of the band, and to the entire Sinatra staff for giving me the opportunity and for treating us so well. Sinatra's people, nothing but generous with their encouragement, often suggested that if I could open a musical show in front of ten thousand people, all of whom wanted me to dissolve before their eyes onstage, then I could play *anywhere* and keep up with *anyone*.

As I drove home from Atlantic City after the final show of the tour, I decided that it was time to put into action what people were telling me about myself. I made a quick detour for a jam session at my parents' house, to make absolutely sure that I could still keep up with my father.

10

Team *Dream*

You're going out there a youngster, but you've got to come back a star.

—Producer Julian Marsh to understudy Peggy Sawyer in
42nd Street

I went out there a thirty-six-year-old and came back with mediocre reviews and a lovely wife. Please don't reverse those two adjectives.

—John Pizzarelli

Things were looking up in early 1996. Not only had the trio's bookings been on the rise during that time, but we had also begun receiving offers and inquiries from larger halls and performance spaces. And while we hadn't attained "no blue or brown M&Ms" status in our concert riders, we began to see fewer week-old crudité platters and more recognizable brand names of soft drinks (Coke, Pepsi, Snapple, Mr. Pibb) and bottled water (e.g., Poland Spring, Fiji, Evian, San Pellegrino) in the backstage area. I like to advise the youngsters coming up through the music ranks that it's never a good thing when the brand of bottled water in the dressing room happens to share its name with the condemned pond behind the theater where you are performing.

So when I received a call from my manager at the time, Buddy Morra, about the possibility of costarring in a Broadway show, I was intrigued. Honestly, I was at a point where I was reluctant to stop the momentum of our group but eager to try something out of my comfort zone. The project he had in mind was *Dream*, a musical that would feature loosely associated scenes set over four decades, combined with music—vocal and instrumental—set to highly choreographed dance sequences. The unifying theme would be that all of the forty or so songs would feature lyrics written by Johnny Mercer. Did I mention there would be a lot of dancing? Buddy's pitch was typically low-key: "If it's a hit, you might win a Tony. If it's not a hit . . . hey, you've done a Broadway show, you'll make good bread, and you won't have to travel."

Buddy had more good news. I wouldn't have to make my Broadway debut as King Lear or Willy Loman. Or as Ben Franklin in *1776*. No, I would be called upon to stretch my acting chops by playing a crooner who leads a guitar/piano/bass trio through the evening's various song-and-dance-driven vignettes. Martin (on bass) and Ray Kennedy (piano) would play a jazz bassist and a jazz piano player, respectively. And there would be no dancing required of our trio, which just about sealed the deal.

Before I had hung up with Buddy, I knew that we were going to accept the offer to be part of the cast of *Dream*. After a couple of days of discussions with Buddy, and then with the guys, we made it official. More good news was that the always dicey audition process had been waived for us—it turned out that the producers and casting people for *Dream* had seen us around New York City, most often at our annual monthlong runs at the Algonquin Hotel's Oak Room. (Typing "Algonquin Hotel" instantly produces in my mouth the taste of a Bombay martini, straight up.) Our trio's two hundred nights away from home each year playing jazz had apparently demonstrated to them that we had the necessary acting chops to portray . . . a jazz trio.

My first stop on the way to what I believed would be a sure Tony nomination was not for method-acting lessons at the Strasberg Institute but to a backers' reading at the apartment of producer Louise Westergaard. My mission at this gathering was to (a) smile at all times and (b) keep the cast on my right hand out of sight and out of the conversations. I even thought of following Bob Dole's example and holding a pen (or a Wusthoff classic eight-inch chef's knife) in my hand to give pause to hand-shakers. In a fit of frustration, I had sustained a "boxer's fracture," an actual medical term for the consequences to one's knuckles of "punching a skull, or a hard, immovable object, such as a wall." In my case, it was a stack of books that *felt* like a wall. The injury caused discomfort for sure, but it didn't prevent me from strumming the guitar. A left-handed punch, on the other hand, and I would not have been able to perform at all.

Louise was joined at this event by three other producers—Mark Schwartz, Jack Wrangler, and Margaret Whiting. Jack and Margaret were a married couple who frequently caught the attention of *People* magazine, Page Six of the *New York Post*, *US Weekly*, and countless print publications that loved to chronicle their colorful May–December romance. It didn't hurt that the Wranglers represented a slice of the boy-meets-girl love story that could come true only in the United States—and certain parts of Amsterdam. Fiftyish actor noted for his work in the field of gay porn in the seventies and eighties decides to

Martin, Ray, and I in the company of two of our favorites— Margaret Whiting and George Shearing.

settle down with one of Capitol Records' star singers from the forties, a woman twenty-two years his senior.

Margaret had always been great to me, one of my strongest and earliest supporters, and a frequent audience member at jazz and cabaret rooms in New York City. Her rich association with Johnny Mercer went back to when she sang for him at her family's Beverly Hills home at the age of six when Mercer was there to collaborate on songs with Margaret's father, the noted composer Richard Whiting ("Hooray for Hollywood," "Ain't We Got Fun," "Beyond the Blue Horizon," "Sleepy Time Gal," "Too Marvelous for Words," all with Mercer's lyrics). When Richard Whiting died suddenly of a heart attack at the age of forty-six, Mercer was there as a surrogate father to thirteen-year-old Margaret. As legend has it, his advice to her at the time was, "I have two words for you: *grow up.*'" And when she followed his wisdom and turned eighteen, Mercer was also there with professional support, offering Margaret a recording contract almost immediately after cofounding Capitol Records in 1942. In short order she made Mercer look like a genius, recording the hits "Moonlight in Vermont" and "It Might As Well Be Spring."

Jack's given last name was Stillman; he took the moniker "Wrangler" from the company name on the labels of the jeans and shirts he wore in his films. One of the architects of the Great American Songbook, Jimmy Van Heusen—composer of such standards as "Darn That Dream," "Here's That Rainy Day," and "Love and Marriage," and stalwarts of the Sinatra song-book like "Come Fly with Me," "My Kind of Town," and "Ring-A-Ding-Ding"—had also lifted his professional name from the label on his shirts.

By the time we met up with him, Stillman/Wrangler had moved from acting to producing, with a focus on off-Broadway and regional plays, as well as cabaret. Over many years Jack would invariably stop me backstage after concerts or at parties to insist there was a perfect song for me hiding on the soundtrack to one of his old films. And languish in obscurity is what that soundtrack will do until I work up the substantial nerve I'll need to drop by Colony Records and casually announce that I am working on a project that requires the sheet music for *The Devil in Miss Jones* 2.

Fast-forward a few months from the backers' evening at Louise's apartment, and the cast of *Dream* is gathered in a big empty rehearsal hall, appropriately named Raw Space, on West, West, West Forty-Second Street. Any mistakes in choreography during rehearsals and a dancer could find himself or herself swimming in the Hudson River.

New to the boards and not clued in on dress-code protocol, I wore the same tan poplin suit and a tie to rehearsals for about ten days, leading several of my cast mates to mistake me for a producer, with others assuming I owned an extremely limited wardrobe. My first observation as a newcomer was that this Jessica Molaskey (more on her later) really had the goods vocally. She had arrived a few days late from doing *Time and Again* in San Diego, and the first song I heard her sing was "Skylark" to an arrangement that sounded like Mike Oldfield's "Tubular Bells," which was also known as the theme from *The Exorcist*. In fact, *every* arrangement we heard for the first few weeks had the same DNA as "Tubular Bells," almost as though we were rehearsing Linda Blair's nightclub act. (Linda's role in *The Exorcist* was that of the possessed little girl with the spinning head, an asset to any stage act.) Despite the considerable vocal talents of Ms. Molaskey and the rest of the cast, I could barely decipher the melodies of standard songs I'd been hearing for most of my life. I was no David Merrick or Manny Azenberg when it came to knowing what works in the theater, but I did know arrangements. And these weren't cutting it.

And it wasn't just the arrangements. The entire premise for *Dream*, dance-heavy vignettes based on the *lyrics* of Johnny Mercer, might have been a flawed concept. The title of the iconic Sly Stone song wasn't "Dance to the *Lyrics*"! Take, for instance, "Jamboree Jones," the musical story of the swinging clarinet player who singlehandedly engineers a Rose Bowl comeback. There was so much dancing stuffed between verses of the song that you forgot there was a football game being played. Or that the score was "seventeen to nothing."

The cast talked about the structure of the show occasionally, but not too loudly or too often. As Dave Frishberg once said in the studio after a session with an off-key female singer: "I wanted to say something, but we were getting paid, man." And the same was true with *Dream*—a lot of people were getting paid, and it didn't pay to rock the boat.

It would be fair to say that when we left for Nashville for the out-of-town previews of *Dream*, we didn't have much of a show in place yet. There was no shortage of clutter, with rewrites and suggestions pouring in every day from the director, the producers, and the music supervisors. Some good news—the "Tubular Bells" instrumental arrangements behind the singers were slowly but surely being exorcised (sorry, I couldn't resist) from the lineup in favor of new, swinging charts by the brilliant Torrie Zito. Still, I couldn't imagine how, in a matter of weeks, a theater would be presenting our show to paying audiences, particularly in a state in which such a large percentage of the population are gun owners.

Dream also had no shortage of drama. And I'm not referring to the "Goody Goody" S&M vignette and the ten minutes of tap dancing that accompanied it. No, our drama centered around our star, our leading lady, Oscar and Emmy nominee, Queen of the Miniseries, Cinderella herself (the 1965 version)—Lesley Ann Warren. The fun and games began as we learned that unlike the rest of the cast, Lesley Ann would be rehearsing in private. The short plays-within-the-play structure allowed us to rehearse the non–Lesley Ann scenes normally, that is, with a full complement of actors, assistants, producers, and other staff on hand. For Ms. Warren's scenes, however, the room needed to be cleared, which on one magical day meant having my dad bounced from the rehearsal. I soon learned we had seen merely the tip of the Lesley Ann Warren iceberg.

Somehow the Nashville stop on the road to Broadway did not turn into the horror show I expected it to be. With tickets sold, actors and crew hired (and housed a good half hour out of town), and the sets in place, those in charge made the decision to open the doors to paying audiences. And while our show might not have been *A Chorus Line* or *My Fair Lady*, it certainly didn't approach the depths of *Frankenstein—the Musical*, *Urban Cowboy*, *Carrie*, or the legendary *Moose Murders*, productions whose posters were doomed to hang in theater district bars and restaurants like Joe Allen that celebrated colossal flops. Perhaps it was a question of availability at that time of the fall, but the audiences did not throw a single piece of fruit, ripe or otherwise, during the entire run. No thrown fruit combined with (a) not-horrible accommodations and (b) checks that cleared had me reclassifying *Dream* in the "decent gig . . . so far" category.

A few weeks into the Nashville performances, it was clear on most nights that the actors and actresses whose names appeared in smaller type on the *Dream* poster were becoming the audience favorites by the end of the evening (and three matinees). Jonathan Dokuchitz, Darcie Roberts, Kevyn Morrow, that Molaskey chick, Susan Misner, and the rest of the cast were getting huge applause throughout the show and at the final curtain.

Brooks Ashmanskas was given one of Sinatra's (and everyone else's) favorites, "Come Rain or Come Shine." The highest compliment I can pay Brooksie is that after hearing him sing it each night and witnessing audiences' reactions, I am beyond surprised that one of the stars in larger type—myself included—didn't swipe it out from under him. I also love the reaction of straight men when Brooks (who can behave flamboyantly on and offstage) finds an excuse to put on display his far-reaching knowledge of the 1977 NBA Champion Portland Trailblazers.

This was not a big deal to me, a member of a working trio who was used to being overshadowed on many nights by *everyone*—Ray, Martin, a horn section, a special guest star (especially a hometown guest), the local NPR jazz guy who introduced me, or a bird getting loose in the theater. But when our star sensed the spotlight drifting to other members of the company in the Nashville production of *Dream*, what happened next could have been lifted from the pages of Lesley Ann's old show, *Mission: Impossible*.

One of the highlights of Act 2 was a three-woman song-and-dance performance of the Harold Arlen–Johnny Mercer war song "I'm Doin' It for Defense." Unlike about 60 percent of the show's numbers at that point, "Defense" was clicking (no pun) on all cylinders and was a reliable crowd-pleaser. Then one day Jessica Molaskey and Darcie Roberts arrived in their dressing rooms and noticed that the heels of their dancing shoes for "I'm Doin' It for Defense" had been cut down by the wardrobe department, the first time this service had been provided to either of them in their careers without their having requested it. Amazingly, the ad hoc shoemaking continued on an almost daily basis—Jess and Darcie arriving for the show and seeing their dance shoes slowly evolving into flats. Not close to being a short woman, Lesley Ann appeared to be experiencing a relative growth spurt with each performance as her dance partners were gradually shrinking. I recall a postshow session backstage one night when we figured the next step for Darcie and Jess would be channeling Tim Conway's Dorf character and dancing on their knees.

As *Dream* settled into its Nashville run, I began to feel as though we would be okay. One reason for this was that we knew we had our closer in the bullpen, Jessica Molaskey, ready to come in every night at ten thirty (and four thirty at matinees) to sing the Mancini/Mercer classic from *Breakfast at Tiffany's*—"Moon River." We didn't have time to put it into the show during rehearsals in New York, but we needed the song in there ASAP. "Moon River" was specifically listed in the ads in Nashville, and the audiences began to complain when it wasn't being sung.

Whether it was the memory of seeing Audrey Hepburn singing it on her balcony in the film or from so many years of hearing Andy Williams croon it, it was clear that most of the audience members felt a deep emotional connection with this song. This can be a mixed blessing for a singer, because how do you measure up to people's personal recollections of something so overpowering? It might explain why audience members have taken me to task both for singing songs in the style of Sinatra *and* for deliberately going in a different direction than Frank did. It clashed with the memory of the song in their heads and hearts. As I have learned along the way, this is a serious business for audiences and has a significant impact on the show.

What I can definitively say about Molaskey's version of "Moon River" is that in the face of the obstacles I described, she began nailing it regularly in rehearsals. Tom Petty knows that the only place to go after "American Girl" is out of the building. Springsteen once played "Rosalita" at the Wollman Rink in Central Park, after which Anne Murray came onstage as the headliner (look it up!). Didn't work. Similarly, there was nowhere to go after Jess's "Moon River." But the producers had sprung for a large train set to be built, it allowed everyone to wave good-bye, and that's the stuff finales are made of.

Jessica says she felt the vibe one night after rehearsal that she might be asked to walk away from "Moon River." I do not pretend to know the specifics on how it all came about. However it happened, the result was director Wayne Cilento calling together the entire company at morning notes and announcing: "Jess, you're not going to sing 'Moon River' anymore. Lesley Ann will be doing it from now on."

What? I was speechless. I didn't know whether I was reacting to the startling news—or how it was delivered. I was hardly a Broadway veteran—the show hadn't even made it out of Nashville—but we seemed to have taken a left turn in Albuquerque. When the color came back to Jess's face a short time after the announcement, Jess explained to me in no uncertain terms that in our little show, Lesley Ann Warren had all the leverage, and that was that.

I'm no theater critic, and as I write this today, I most assuredly have a pro-Molaskey bias, given that we have since shared marriage vows in front of God, our families, twenty-five musicians, five cases of wine, and Tony Bennett. Thus, I am in no position to review the quality of Lesley Ann's roughly 150 performances of "Moon River" (remaining Nashville shows, plus the Broadway run). I can objectively state that after the role change, there was no longer audible weeping coming from the Nashville audiences during the song. As for the reaction on Broadway, the esteemed critic Douglas Watt of the *Daily News* noted that it was the first time he had ever heard the song sung and had not cried.

Very late in the Nashville run we gathered together to receive happy news from our producer. For all its wackiness on and off the stage, *Dream* was all set to move to Broadway. Tech rehearsals would start in February 1997, a month of previews would begin in March, and an opening night was penciled in for early April. Hello, Sardi's, Joe Allen, Barrymore's, and McHale's (actors had a hockey bar back then)—we'd been called up to the Big Leagues.

11

On Broadway

I saw the play under the worst possible conditions: the curtain was up.

—George S. Kaufman

After we'd escaped Antioch, Tennessee, and had gotten our sea legs back under us in Manhattan, Jess had the idea to wander over to the Royale Theatre (now the Schoenfeld) on West Forty-Fifth Street to watch the load-in and maybe check out our names on the Broadway marquee.

I must admit—I've played a lot of places ("seen pictures of the rest . . ."), but there is nothing that prepared me for the thrill of seeing my name in lights on the marquee of a Broadway theater. Since about 1970 our family had packed all six of us into the car for the annual holiday trip to see a show. Usually, it meant a trip to Broadway—*Brigadoon* in 1980; Frank Langella (Mom's favorite) in *Dracula*; Jim Dale in *Barnum*; Doug Henning in *The Magic Show*. In the early eighties we made the trip to see *Peg*, Peggy Lee's one-woman show, which featured my father as both the guitarist and as a speaking character who played guitarist Dave Barbour, one of Ms. Lee's husbands.

Bucky's reading of "I love you, Peg" served to mess with my head. Though Bucky's scripted words had the stiffer-than-stiff cadence of Jackie Gleason's "Oh, it can core a apple" on *The Honeymooners*, it was mind-blowing, even on a stage, to hear Bucky throwing around the "L" word to a woman who wasn't my mom.

Standing under the neon lights of the Royale brought back all the memories of those holiday pilgrimages and the four Pizzarelli kids riding in the back of the Cadillac, where it never seemed crowded. The theater doors were open for the crew, so Jess suggested that we take a look inside at what would soon be our new home. The empty theater was magnificent—and it freaked me out. *This is real*, I thought. *What have I gotten myself into?* The odd thing was that I had played Carnegie Hall, the Hollywood Bowl, the Garden State Arts Center, SPAC in Saratoga, New York, the Ridgewood Bandshell (just seeing if you were paying attention), and any number of ten- and twenty-thousand-seat arenas in Europe when we opened for Sinatra. Yet I had never before had the feeling of excitement and panic I experienced at the Royale that day. When I told Jess that I needed to go home to collect myself,

Posing with Jessica during the run of *Dream* on Broadway in 1997.

she seemed to understand. It would be a feeling I'd experience only one other time—when I walked into an empty Radio City Music Hall in 2003 before I opened there in *Sinatra: His Voice, His World, His Way*.

It took about a full day of hyperventilating, several dead-of-winter walks past the marquee, and at least six visits to my analyst's couch before I completely made peace with my initial reaction to our historic new home. When I walked back into the Royale when we reassembled in February, the feelings of panic/intimidation/sense of upholding theater traditions/fear of disappointing audiences were nearly all gone, replaced by the familiar set of butterflies that preceded having to do something that fell outside my usual comfort zone. Tech rehearsals began soon thereafter to get everyone's heads back into the show and to tweak some of the scene-blocking to fit the constraints of the Royale's stage and backstage areas. I recall enjoying this time a lot— the time spent with my cast members on and off the stage, as well as the sense of calm professionalism that had come over the entire company. Things were even quiet on the Lesley Ann front. Ensconced in the St. Regis in a suite whose square footage was reported by our spies to be somewhere between a New York City two-bedroom apartment and Madison Square Garden, Ms. Warren still wasn't interacting with the cast, but at least she had chosen to rehearse with us. It was the calm before the storm.

The clouds gathered slowly when someone got ahold of an early release of the upcoming Sunday's Arts & Leisure section of the *New York Times*, which contained the full-page color ad for *Dream*. What I noticed in real-time order was: (a) a blurry photo of a dancing Suzy Misner, (b) the font used for Lesley Ann's name was larger than mine, in violation of the contract my manager had negotiated, and (c) this ad must be extremely confusing for people who know nothing about our show. No concerns here on Font-Gate; smaller-than-agreed-upon font size in a full-page *Times* ad for a Broadway show is a high-class problem for a jazz musician. The truffle pig in me says that when our names are mentioned as part of a *Times* full-page ad in *any* font, it means there must be a paying gig lurking nearby—and that is more than good enough for a jazz musician.

Lesley Ann's reaction to the *Times* ad, however, was the stuff that legends are made of. She immediately sought out the producer, Mark Schwartz. And fortunately, being assigned to the dressing room directly below the producer's office in an antiquated (and not exactly sound-proofed) Broadway theater placed me in the perfect spot to listen in on one of the most colorful, take-no-prisoners, Tony Award–worthy performances one could imagine. From the early volleys I gathered that Lesley Ann had expected a photo of herself to be the centerpiece of both the *Times* ad and all of *Dream*'s advertising. Instead, there was an out-of-focus dancer, names of cast members (Lesley's name *was* on top in the largest type), and an impressive song list. "How dare you put her bleeping picture in the bleeping bleeping ad" was her opening salvo, and it escalated from there.

"Call your effing manager."

"I'm going to call my effing manager right now."

Schwartz reminded me of a valiant goalie on an overmatched hockey team. He made some early saves ("No, fuck *you!*"), but eventually couldn't keep up with the irrational arguments, novel combinations of obscenities, smashing of furniture, and sheer hysterics that Lesley Ann carried in her toolkit at that time. But Mark must have stopped more shots than I thought; the blurry ad with the dancer continued to run, although alternative print ads also began to appear.

Previews for *Dream* began in early March, and I must say that I loved the entire Broadway routine. After a couple of years of spending over two hundred days on the road, I felt almost like Ward Cleaver when I got to make my daily trip to the office. I loved getting to watch how Broadway people prepare for their performances. Molaskey wanted no sign of me during "half hour"—the call by the stage manager that it's half an hour until curtain time. Martin's "special" time usually included confirming the hand signals he'd be getting from the stagehands and crew to communicate hockey scores to him while the show was in progress. All was going well, although we could feel the tension ratchet up as we approached the final week of March. Soon, the critics' previews would play, followed by April 3, 1997—*Opening Night!*

Having stepped back and critically watched our play in the weeks leading up to the big night, I did not have high expectations of our becoming the next *My Fair Lady*. As much as I had hoped to walk beneath the marquee of the Royale one day and read: "*Dream*—In Its Fifth Record-Breaking Year" and "Pizzarelli Still Getting It Done," the realist in me hoped against hope we'd make it to our fifth record-breaking *week*. The high-concept ad of the out-of-focus dancer didn't create the rush on the box office our producers were hoping for. We began to hear through the reliable theater grapevine that advance ticket sales were not what one would call robust. But there was still hope—*the opening night reviews*.

From what I could gather from the grizzled Broadway veterans in our cast, the review we would receive from the *New York Times* would determine our theatrical fate more than all of the other reviews (the *Daily News*, the *New York Post*, Jeffrey Lyons, NY1, the *Wall Street Journal*, *Variety*) combined. Word also filtered through the same highly reliable grapevine that the *Times* had sent Peter Marks and not its no. 1 critic at the time, Ben Brantley. Always a presence in theatrical criticism over many years, the *Times* had accumulated unprecedented power in the theater world during the thirteen-year (1980–93) period in which Frank Rich served as chief theater critic for the paper. I was glad that Frank, nicknamed the Butcher of Broadway, had moved on to the Op-Ed section by this time and would not be writing about our show.

For a couple of days I tried to convince myself that Opening Night was essentially a victory lap, to take place in front of the home crowd— our friends, family, and . . . investors (uh-oh!). The critics had already paid their visits during the previous week, and their reviews were likely already written as we took to the stage that night. There was nothing to it but to do it—relax and share my first opening night on Broadway with Martin, Ray, and all the new friends I had made in the cast.

There was one story for the ages that I take away from that night's performance. Act 2 began with my playing and singing a low-key version of "I Thought about You" on stage right, which also happened to put me directly in front of my parents' second-row seats. I was positioned in front of a closed curtain for my song, whose primary purpose in the show's structure was to get the laggards back from intermission and back into their chairs before the curtain-up, full-blown "And the Angels Sing," which immediately followed.

Anyway, we're talking about one of the wildest moments of my life and my career. Move over, Frank Langella, Jim Dale, Bernadette Peters, Doug Henning, Madeline Kahn, Len Cariou, Angela Lansbury, Rex Harrison, and the other stars we had braved the holiday traffic from Jersey to see in person over the years. Here I was *on* Broadway, it was opening night, and I was singing directly to my mother, who was seated less than ten feet from where I stood at the edge of the stage. The house lights were brighter than usual to make it easier for people to find their seats. I could clearly see my mother's face.

And she was reading the Playbill!

Nothing on earth could have been more distracting. My mind went nearly blank (referred to by theater people as "going up") on the lyrics to a song I had sung at least two hundred times over the previous six months. As I racked my brain to get the correct lyrics in the queue, my inner voice kept asking what my mom could possibly be reading in the *Playbill* at that particular moment that trumped watching her second-favorite son on the stage of the Royale. My bio? ("This is John's Broadway debut.") Someone else's bio? ("Suzie dedicates this performance to her loving and supportive *mother*.") It even crossed my mind that she could be reading one of those perfect written-by-the-restaurant's-publicist restaurant reviews. ("Patti LuPone says the prime rib is the 'John Raitt of entrees.' Strong, tasteful, and dependable.") It didn't hit me until about three-quarters of the way through "I Thought about You" that my mother's head buried in the *Playbill* as I sang to her from a Broadway stage on opening night was, in the end, one of those stories I would be telling for the rest of my life—both from the stage and to interviewers, as well as to a wide array of disbelieving mental health professionals.

Once you've made it to the closing curtain on opening night (check), taken the bows (check), gotten directions to the opening night party (check), and ensured that one's parents are settled safely inside the bash, there is nothing to do but wait for the reviews. These days it's all about the Internet, that crazy World Wide Web, and something the kids call social media. But in 1997 the world still had one foot on the boat and the other on the dock, with the dock representing a hard copy of the *New York Times*. And in this instance, the "dock" reference was literal, in that someone affiliated with our play ran over to the *Times* Building's loading dock, dialed a secret number, gave the password "swordfish," and was soon in possession of a stack of the next day's newspapers.

I almost expected someone to stand on a chair, bring the assembled group in close, and read the review through a megaphone. Fortunately, cooler heads prevailed, leaving us each to grab a paper and show off our Evelyn Wood speed-reading skills. The first words of Marks's review were "Steve and Eydie." *Where was this going?* Then "For nostalgia buffs . . . *Dream* may be a godsend." *Hey, that's not bad . . . there's a nugget for the marquee.* Then—"But for virtually everyone else, the revue may seem pretty lame." *Hmm . . . "Lame" . . . not a good word for the marquee.*

Okay, this was going to be a mixed review—at best. Time to make sure that Marks didn't throw out the Pizzarelli baby with the bath water. I skipped over a few words about the play itself ("dreadful," "cheesy") that told me things weren't getting better, and looked for references that were specific to me and my performance. And I spotted one: "The evening's stars, however, have lesser degrees of success." *I'm not what you'd call a star . . . maybe they don't mean me.* "Pizzarelli . . . never establishes a rapport with the other performers, who seem at times to be passing the baton back and forth at a celebrity telethon." But this was nothing compared with what I heard from the brothers at Don Bosco when I "forgot" my homework. Or read in a Chicago newspaper a few months ago about my most recent album. Or the review of this play written by Clive Barnes of the *New York Post* that referred to my style as that of "an amiable fire hydrant." Ouch.

Actually, several members of the cast received favorable notice. Peter Marks opined that Lesley Ann's talents were wasted in our show and suggested she be considered to replace Julie Andrews in *Victor/Victoria*. Brooks, Angelo Framboni, Susan Misner, and Kevyn Morrow all received "played-well-in-a-losing-effort" mentions. But Marks also cut to the fundamental flaw inherent in dancing to the lyrics—"The revue never considers what they might mean." In the end, when someone writes the words "You may begin to fear that a big luau number is coming next," only the most cockeyed of optimists would come away thinking he or she had read a rave review.

The next day brought what I would learn is another ritual in the world of the Broadway stage—the meeting in which the producers tell the cast and crew that despite a shaky review from the *New York Times*, the investors were committed to keeping the show alive and running. Someone forgot to tell our top-of-the-poster star, Lesley Ann, however, who phoned in that she would not be making the trip down from her suite at the St. Regis for the second regularly scheduled performance. Fired up from our pep rally and the reading aloud of several positive reviews for the show, I then actually phoned Lesley Ann and told her that the cast was counting on her, that her behavior was unacceptable, and that goddamn it, she owed it to the Theater (capital T). Her reply to me was essentially "Yeah, yeah, yeah . . . I'm still not coming." The best I could muster as a reply was "You're unprofessional" and "You're not a trouper" (not my best work), and I hung up. Lesley Ann's understudy, Jane Summerhays, was called in, reportedly from a restaurant in the middle of dinner. Jane had figured when six o'clock had come and gone without a phone call from the theater, she was free for the evening. It was an assumption she would never make again during the run of *Dream*.

Yes, for a Johnny Mercer musical there seemed to be a lot of melodrama in the air. But I must confess that once the pressure of opening night and the reviews had passed, I came to enjoy the daily routines of being a stage actor. As a musician who is usually on the road, I definitely miss the ten-block commute I had from my apartment to the Royale Theatre during the run of the show. And I so liked hearing the half-hour call announcement that I tried to time my arrival time to be about five minutes ahead of it. ("Ladies and Gentlemen, this is your half-hour call. Half-hour, please. Thank you.") And before the cast members would go out after performances, we'd sign autographs for fans outside the stage door and pray that they weren't rogue investors with guns. And because we needed to keep our jazz chops in order, our trio would take our instruments to Puleo's, an Italian restaurant across the street from the Royale, where we had talked the owner into allowing us to play (unpaid) whenever the spirit moved us, which turned into three or four nights a week.

Meanwhile, I had the distinct feeling that my night-after-opening-night call to the St. Regis had succeeded in making things frosty between Lesley Ann and me. Truth be told, Lesley Ann had reeled in the backstage antics as we got a few weeks into the regular run. Oh, there was the occasional "What the fuck?" and a high-octane tirade punctuated by an act of destruction heaped upon a piece of furniture. But hey, it was backstage, and she wasn't the only one dropping F-bombs back there.

When it came to raising profanity to an art form, Buddy Rich,these days an Internet sensation with the famous bus tapes, was the only person I knew of who was in Lesley Ann's league—although I never had the opportunity to hear the legendary Packers' coach Vince Lombardi do his thing at halftime. If a revival of the play *Lombardi* is ever done, the producers should bring in David Mamet to punch up the coach's salty language, then bring in Lesley Ann to play Lombardi's wife. Smells like a hit to me.

Speaking of hits, it was becoming clear as it got closer to Memorial Day that *Dream* was not going to be one. Our show had been available at the TKTS half-price ticket booth since shortly after we opened, with increasingly more audience members dressed as empty seats. To recycle a joke Martin and I would make in the early trio days about sparsely attended gigs—the balcony at the Royale Theatre was starting to resemble a map of Montana. Or as the old baseball announcer said of his team's fans, "If they're coming to the games, they're doing it dressed as empty seats." A friend called the box office and asked for the curtain time of a Tuesday evening show; he swears the receptionist's reply was, "What time can you get here?"

Then real trouble began. Two of Molaskey's weekly paychecks bounced, after which she prevailed upon the producers to pay her in cash. This resulted in a German woman appearing on the scene each week with a cloth sack of money, counting out in heavily accented English a pile of ten- and twenty-dollar bills, and handing them over to Jessica. Then one of *my* checks bounced. Then the dancers' checks began bouncing. Our savior was a guy named Bruce at the bank who cashed the checks we presented to him within seconds of receiving them. His services also included a courtesy phone call and a few days' grace period for all involved when the checks inevitably bounced. We joked that there could be an ad in the paper once a week that read "Come meet the cast of *Dream*—at Chase Manhattan Bank."

At some point during *Dream*'s financial nightmare, I got it into my head to have some fun with the situation in the form of a lighthearted practical joke that would no doubt amuse my brother and pick up the spirits of my fellow cast members. And as with nearly all of the ill-conceived, half-baked schemes I had plotted over the years with a Wile E. Coyote–like sense of purpose, I wished I could have had this one back about three seconds after I put it into action.

The first song of the Rainbow Room scene in Act 1 was "You Were Never Lovelier," a Jerome Kern melody from the 1942 film of the same name, sung by Fred Astaire to Rita Hayworth. But after about five minutes of channeling Sammy Cahn, the Patron Saint of Special Material, I came up with a new title: "Checks Were Never Bouncier." I figured my cast mates would get a kick out of my new and improved (and up-to-date) lyrics—"Checks were never bouncier / In their bounciest days."

During the planning stages I figured my stunt was following in the tradition of Pete Seeger and Bob Dylan, raising my fist to management on behalf of labor. In the execution of it, though, I felt more like Weird Al Yankovic. And the looks of horror on the faces of the other cast members when I saw them backstage let me know that I had pole-vaulted beyond the parameters of acceptable Broadway behavior.

The response was immediate. About six seconds after closing bows, stage manager Diane DeVita burst into my dressing room. Diane cut straight to the point: "You realize that you can never do that *ever* again." Harkening back to a strategy that served me well after I had cut Mr. Pfanner's gym class at Don Bosco, I went into full-agreement mode. "You are correct" and "Never again" were my replies to about six questions seeking assurances that I would not even think of changing a

Johnny Mercer lyric again as long as I was in this show, even as the idea for singing "Seats Were Never Emptier" began percolating in my brain.

As our run on Broadway came to a close, so did the Broadway Show League softball season. And consistent with the reviews of its stage performance, Team *Dream* struggled in those late-morning games on the softball fields of Central Park, despite the menacing presence of the thirty-seven-year-old spitballing rookie, steroid abuser, and Knights Day Camp alum, John Pizzarelli, on the mound. There is an esoteric baseball stat called BABIP—the batting average for batted balls in play—and our opponents' average was about .990. If they hit it, they got on base. To put it in theater terms, it looked like the dance scenes from *West Side Story* anytime there was a fly ball hit to the outfield. And the infielders wore baseball gloves primarily for ornamental purposes; they probably would have stopped more grounders by stabbing at them with forks. I just kept smiling and

I got to take my Saddle River spitball to the mound in the Broadway Show League. Team *Dream* managed one win, versus *Defending the Caveman*—a one-man show.

shouting out "Tough hop." But win or lose, a figure of speech for our group (we did beat *Defending the Caveman*—all right, so it was a one-man show), the enthusiasm for the games was always sky-high, and the attendance was practically the same 100 percent we'd get at Chase Manhattan Bank on payday.

It was this grit and desire that Team *Dream* brought to its final game of the 1997 season, a grudge match against the best team in the Broadway Show League, *Victor/Victoria*. You hated to play against the long-running shows because the word on the street was that those teams tended to accumulate the best softball players the longer they stayed open, and *Victor/Victoria* had opened back in 1995. According to the scuttle, they'd happily settle for spotlights on wrong actors, slow curtains, and missed cues in the third year of their run, as long as crew members hit for power and fielded their positions. The goal of everyone on Team *Dream* was to have our show run long enough to allow us to field a Broadway Show League team of ten softball ringers, as *Victor/Victoria* did. For now, we had to go with the players we had, half of whom had initially put their baseball gloves on the wrong hand, and all of whom were wearing makeup of some kind. Striking a contrast, *Victor/Victoria* had guys who wore actual baseball pants (as opposed to cut-off denim shorts for our squad) and carried their own customized Worth aluminum bats in special bags.

As if the talent differential wasn't enough to do us in, *Victor/Victoria* turned to a secret weapon in the second inning—the arrival of Julie Andrews. Having just departed from the show earlier in the year in favor of Raquel Welch (sadly, a no-show on this day—I was ready to pitch to her), Ms. Andrews sat in the bleachers behind the *V/V* bench and immediately checked in with a loud and unmistakable "Go, team!" I do a pretty good Julie Andrews (available on the audiobook), but imagine Mary Poppins herself cheering on her former colleagues and offering them refreshments, which she brought along in bulk. "Would anyone like a *dayooooonut?*"

It was too much to handle for Team *Dream*, the vast majority of whom considered Julie Andrews to be royalty, up there with Judy Garland, Liza Minnelli, Shirley Bassey, and Barbara Cook. Our infielders called timeouts continuously, much to the consternation of the notoriously grumpy Broadway League umpires. "She's gorgeous," was the subject of one huddle on the pitcher's mound. "I wonder if I can get her to sign my mitt," was the conversation at the next mound session. "Do you think we can get her to sing?" was another conference. Meanwhile, her voice proved to be a happy distraction, particularly when she'd say, "Have another *dayoooonut!*" She'd brought along a lot of doughnuts. Ms. Andrews stayed for the entire game, which the "mercy rule" brought to a halt a few innings early with *Victor/Victoria* ahead by about twenty runs. The game went down as a moral victory for Team *Dream*, as our cast immediately surrounded the ever-gracious Julie Andrews and hit her up for doughnuts, coffee, and Christopher Plummer anecdotes.

Our hopes of staying open long enough to someday challenge the *Victor/Victoria* softball team to a rematch were dwindling with every half-filled house. There is always hope that Tony nominations and awards will build buzz and momentum for a sinking ship, but when Wayne Cilento's well-deserved nod for Best Choreography was our only nomination, we were clearly running out of options. Enter the marketing department, with an ad campaign that still has me scratching my head all these years later. (When you see me scratching my head for no apparent reason, assume I am still baffled by the "Hail Mary" ad campaign for *Dream*.) The message on the bottom third of the ad was—*Pas besoin de connaître l'anglais pour apprécier ce spectacle sensationnel!* No disrespect meant for Don Bosco Prep, but I was stumped. Maybe it was an invitation to French people. Then, *Para disfrutar esta fantastica obra, no se necesita saber inglés.* Hmmm—"Don't go to a Beckett play starring Marty Ingels"? There were about four more languages, including Chinese. So I brought a copy of the ad over to the people at Chiam, a Chinese restaurant (RIP) on East Forty-Eighth Street, and they translated it for me—"You don't have to speak English to love this fantastic spectacle." *What?* We were trying to sell tickets to a work based on the *lyrics* to Johnny Mercer's songs, yet our ads were telling people that the words don't matter. Uh-oh.

But I was having a ball doing the play. I loved singing those great Mercer lyrics, taking bows every night, and getting unexpected backstage visits from my heroes, including my old neighbor Pat Summerall and the late film director and husband to the Broadway softball league doughnut lady Blake Edwards. I was not missing the Friday night gigs in Bismarck, North Dakota, the four o'clock wake-up calls, followed by the Saturday night in Jupiter, Florida. Ten blocks was my idea of an ideal commute.

But as Yogi Berra might have said about theater audiences, "If they don't want to come, you can't stop them." So after a month or so of rampant rumors of our demise, the producers gathered the cast and crew and told us that July 6 would be our final performance. Shaky review from the *Times*, no Tony awards, no buzz about the play in general, only one win for the softball team, uncertainty about how to market a dance-centric play that is based on lyrics—and they put a fork in us.

The show didn't completely close for Jessica Molaskey and me. From the first moment she arrived directly from a show in California, I loved her voice. Soon afterward, I began to fall for everything about her, starting with a lunch at which both Jessica and Brooksie each believed I had a crush on them. (Actual conversation, I'm told, one day when I left to use the men's room—Brooks: He likes me. Jess: Um, I think he likes *me*.) Despite complications up to the sky in our respective personal lives, Jess and I grew close during the Nashville leg of the tour and became even closer when we got back to New York. There was no finger-snapping or wishing for a life together that made it so; there was a lot of pain for both of us in ending long relationships. But on August 1, 1997, Jess and I were married. The stage at the bar at our wedding was filled all day with our musician friends, sometimes fifteen instrumentalists at a time.

The wine flowed, too, with a special vintage (Beringer Private Reserve—1991) assigned to the table of Tony Bennett, who had just flown home that day to be with us. He'd been working in Italy for three weeks, which, combined with a long day on the plane, produced a voice that he could barely push above a whisper. He apologized for not being able to sing "with that swingin' band up there," but his friendship and support by just being there meant more to us than a song. And

Tony Bennett flew home early from Italy to be at our wedding.

he'd already given us *so many* songs. What I didn't share with him that day, however, was that a friend of mine who does one of the better Tony Bennett impersonations around had been calling my answering machine that week as a raspy Tony, apologizing for a voice that was rapidly going south as the week progressed.

Now that you know the story behind *Dream*, you can understand why I scratch my head upon hearing some of the introductions I am given in advance of my concert performances across the country. "You saw him on the Broadway stage . . ." That's what they said at the Napa Valley Opera House. Not sure they "saw" me. Had people in California (not to mention Colorado and Utah) gotten onto planes to see me in *Dream*, the damn thing would still be running. And if it were still running, we'd have put together a powerhouse softball team by now!

Dream was also an unforgettable experience because I got to hang out five days a week with the classiest woman I'll ever meet, the sensational Margaret Whiting. There might have been more than our share of wacky behavior associated with the show, but Margaret's presence added balance and calm. She also was our link to Johnny

Out on the town with (right to left) Tony Bennett, his wife, Susan Crow, and one of my favorite singers, Ann Hampton Callaway.

Mercer, the man who gave her a start and to whose music and lyrics she then devoted her life. It was an honor for Bucky and me to play for Margaret in her final years, both at the Shanghai Jazz Club in Madison, New Jersey, and at the Lillian Booth Actors Home in Englewood.

Not everyone gets to be on stage in a Broadway show, and I am more thankful than I let on for being given that opportunity to be part of the cast of *Dream* back in 1997. Sometimes it was an amazing sideshow to behold at a distance; at other times it wasted our time and energy. In the theater world, there is a great tradition of actors who are just a little off, and Ms. Warren follows and leads this tradition. But there is a reason why she was living in a suite the size of Radio City Music Hall while I was playing free gigs at the Italian restaurant across from the theater— she is a *star*. People came to our show to see Cinderella and the woman they have grown up watching on their TVs for most of their lives.

Finally, I shall always remember *Dream* because it is where I met my wife. And although we haven't assembled the softball team you'd expect us to have, we're still running after fifteen years.

12

On the Road (Again)

If you get far enough away, you'll be on your way back home.
—Tom Waits

In the previous chapter about our experiences on the road (the one that covered our trio's travels and travails from early 1990 until 1994), I mentioned that our first piano player, the excellent Ken Levinsky, had grown tired of the travel schedule and departed the group in early 1993. "What a wimp!" was the implication. But then after writing about Ken's departure I happened upon our 1992 travel itinerary in the process of doing some research for the book's chronology. You know—Ken might have had a point. In a two-week period in June 1992 we flew from New York . . . to the Robert Mondavi Jazz Festival in Napa Valley . . . back to New York on the red eye. Then that night we flew to the Umbria Jazz Festival in Perugia, Italy. There was also a trip to Denver, followed by the drive to Boulder Creek, then home the next day—all on the day following our two-week run in Montreal. I think there might have been the classic Omaha-Croatia-Tulsa trip since Ken's departure, but I had forgotten what we'd put him through in 1992.

So with Kenny's departure, we were left without a piano player in the early months of 1993, employing instead a series of guest stars (thank you to John Bunch, Tony Monte, and Dave McKenna) to fulfill the scheduled home dates, but we needed a full-time player for our ambitious 1993 schedule to support *Naturally*. In the early months of that year my father and bassist Jerry Bruno told me there was a St. Louis native I needed to hear. Halfway through the first song of Ray Kennedy's audition at my parents' house, Martin was tapping his foot loudly to the music (while also playing bass, a balancing act) and nodding his head "yes" in an exaggerated fashion. As the audition continued, it turned out that Ray had already taught himself several of our arrangements of trio songs, which was a nice touch. I hired him on the spot, things moved quickly, and Ray found himself in the piano chair and playing in front of twenty thousand people just three months later when we opened for Frank Sinatra in Germany.

Truth be told, Ray should have been holding auditions to replace the trio leader/guitarist/singer and the bass player, who were soon trying their damnedest to keep up with his inspired playing. The model of our trio had always been the Nat Cole Trio, but Ray, an Oscar Peterson disciple, couldn't help but push our trio in the direction of the soulful and rhythmic sound of Oscar's piano, Ray Brown's bass, and Herb Ellis on guitar. Leonard Feather took some shots at us for mentioning Oscar's Trio as our idols and model and then not measuring up, but I saw no shame in that, as long as we were working each day to play *our* best music—and to narrow the (considerable) gap. And regardless of the self-inflicted comparisons with Oscar—Ray had written a tribute with Oscar's nickname in the title, and we invoked Oscar's name often at our shows—both Martin and I believed that Ray's work on piano was often nothing short of stunning.

Martin and I were thrilled when Ray's playing began to attract attention on its own, but the week in late 1993 at London's Pizza on the Park (RIP, 2010) went over the top. The club manager/announcer gravitated to Ray's playing from the first set of the first night, so his introductions went along the lines of—"And on piano, we're hoping someday he'll bring his own group here to Pizza on the Park, the great Ray Kennedy."

On the Letterman show, with Ray Kennedy on piano and Martin on bass.

And to the wild clapping at the end of the set, the announcement would go—"And with Martin Pizzarelli on bass and John Pizzarelli on vocals and guitar, the great Ray Kennedy. Ray Kennedy! Ray, please bring your own group back here anytime you'd like." Two announcements per set, and there were ten sets that week—twenty times we got to hear Ray invited to bring back his own trio, with the strong inference that it should be a different crew than the one he brought to this particular gig.

The flip side of Ray's devotion to music, orchestrations, composition, and his idol Oscar was that he was occasionally oblivious to cultural icons. I'll give him credit—he recognized Frank Sinatra and would sneak peeks at Ol' Blue Eyes' shows along with the rest of us. But Oscar Peterson had done an album of Sinatra songs, Sinatra is Sinatra, and St. Louis is so hip that they probably teach *Songs for Swinging Lovers* in kindergarten. But when our trio was called to open a few shows in Las Vegas for Jerry Seinfeld, at the height of *Seinfeld*'s first run of popularity on NBC back in the nineties, and Jerry graciously stopped by during our sound check to ask how we were doing, Ray was lost. Not having any idea that the guy in jeans and white sneakers was the most popular television star on the planet, Ray immediately began ordering him around, even asking if Jerry could find him a telephone book for the piano bench. Seinfeld's response to our trio's first set with him (made as an aside to us) has stayed with me over the years as well—"What a sophisticated little group."

Just as Ray filled the vacated piano seat for us, we had an almost identical amount of good fortune in filling the manager's spot. The events of 1990–93 made me realize that things were getting busy in a hurry, and that a manager might not be a bad idea if we were both pulling in roughly the same direction. I put out an APB for someone who specialized in reducing disorder, putting out fires, and helping acts at our level move the ball up the field professionally. Buddy Morra's name came up often, and I am glad that we decided to work with him. He immediately (and calmly) righted the ship, he made sensible decisions, and he seemed to command the undivided attention of record company executives. One of the magazines in L.A. had written that Buddy was the last guy left in that town who could keep a secret. Most important, he was 180 degrees from where I had been, and that saved me.

In the course of doing my due diligence on Buddy and his firm (MBST), I recall reading a quote from him about how the older comedians and comediennes (Benny, Burns, Hope, Berle, Lucille Ball) had worked for so long on their craft that by the time they were given TV series, they were ready. He said the difference between the new breed and our elders was that today's "talent" waits for the opportunity rather than preparing for it. It was an observation that thoroughly resonated with me.

As I pointed out in the previous chapter about the road experience, moving over to Buddy provided some quick fixes. I was now allowed to work again with my father—who had acquired such a lineup of collaborators, colleagues, and costars by that time that he wasn't even taking my calls. Unless there was golf involved. Seriously, Bucky did some great duo work back then with Howard Alden and Jerry Bruno, conducted master classes at high schools and colleges all over the Northeast, accompanied pianist Russ Kassoff, and continued New York Swing with

Jay Leonhart and John Bunch until John passed away in 2010 at the age of eighty-eight. And while interested in my live performing, Buddy didn't stand over me and grade me ("ninety-eight puh-cent tonight") as was the case with the previous administration. He also allowed me to go back to holding the guitar over my shoulder with a strap during the entire set—standing in front of a mic without the instrument, I felt naked—and thought I looked as awkward as a camel.

Buddy's connections (did I mention he also represented Billy Crystal and Robin Williams?) also did wonders in getting me booked on *The Tonight Show with Jay Leno*, *The Late Show with David Letterman*, and *Late Night with Conan O'Brien*. Conan has been particularly supportive of our group, having us on his twelve thirty NBC show eleven times and on his TBS talk show *Conan* once so far. It's another one of those situations where you don't believe anyone is watching—until you get about ten people stopping you in the airport on the day immediately after the appearance. By the second day after a late-night guest spot, I return to being the same anonymous guy in a Sox hat I was on the concessions line at Fenway Park about twelve minutes after singing the national anthem up there.

The travel became more rational right away when I hired MBST, and it has even improved further with Ted Kurland & Associates, the firm that books our group (and my wife and me) today. And credit also goes to Bennett Morgan and his firm, as well as Kenny DiCamillo at William Morris, who both worked extremely hard for us for a long time. It's not easy to match the needs of venues with open dates on performers' schedules, and then go the extra yard and make the schedule feel as though there is some logic to it. Our itinerary back in Ken Levinsky's day looked as though it had been assembled with a dartboard, and we are happy to be beyond that approach. We couldn't have afforded the cost and downtime involved replacing travel-weary piano players the way that Spinal Tap needed to replace its unlucky drummers.

Among the benefits of staying in the game as long as we have are the annual return trips to many of the same destinations and venues. Besides the month at the Carlyle (which doesn't qualify as "the road," even though it now requires a crosstown cab) and our weeks at Birdland (no. 1 train), we can count on annual trips to Tokyo, Los Angeles, San Francisco, St. Louis, Sarasota, São Paulo, Rio de Janeiro, all over North Carolina, Napa Valley, Minneapolis, Boston, Seattle, and plenty of other stops. And there was a 2012 trip to Paris, which I am hoping to make into a regular engagement, although I didn't follow Eddie Izzard's lead and attempt to do our entire act in French.

One of the highlights of nearly every summer since 1992 has been our groups' appearances at the Festival International de Jazz de Montreal. And it's been "groups" plural because we have gone up there with a trio, a quartet, the Swing Seven, and in 2004, a whole lot of Brazilian people to perform the *Bossa Nova* CD in a live setting. In 2009 the festival conferred upon me the honor of being the eleventh winner of the prestigious Ella Fitzgerald Award, whose previous winners and lofty award description I am reluctant to include here lest the festival's cofounder and artistic director, André Ménard, read the qualifications closely, reexamine my high school grades, and request that I bring the hardware back with me on my next trip.

I had no choice but to publicly comment on the award because it was presented to me at my concert at the Theatre Maisonneuve at La Place des Arts. In acknowledging the honor, I said to the audience, "Most of you must be asking 'Why?'" Jessica and Maddie had come up to watch me accept the award, but even their first question at the conclusion of my show was, "Do you think they'll let us see Jackson Browne?" (He was finishing up his show at the building next door to ours at the same time.)

No one should tell André, but I didn't need a special award—twenty years of trips to Montreal have been an honor on their own. And it's been a lot of fun—from the night I went down the hockey road and was gloating about the 1994 Rangers and wound up calling the audience "habitants," which actually means "farmers." (The H on the Canadiens' jerseys—*La Sainte-Flanelle*—stands for "hockey.") Or when Brian Setzer bought me a beer and asked me if I was the same John Pizzarelli who used to beat him up in high school on Long Island? (No, sorry.) Or when Wynton Marsalis, fresh from his sold-out concert down the street, sat in with a late-night trio at a bar, called easily a dozen songs ("You *must* know 'I Can't Get Started'"), and had it turn into the jazz version of the Monty Python "Cheese Shop" skit—the pianist was not familiar with a single one. Or when I asked for a check at Le Latini on the night I received the Ella Award, only to be told that one of the restaurant's patrons had already covered it. "Thanks for all the great concerts," the gentleman told me. Wow.

The Festival International de Jazz de Montreal audiences were also extremely supportive of two of my records that didn't get much label encouragement upon release—the first being *John Pizzarelli Meets the Beatles* (RCA, 1998) and the other being *Bossa Nova* (Telarc, 2004). Fully aware that today's record listener is more likely to either purchase a single or stream specific cuts of a record, I still choose to tell time by the albums—they are how I look back on my career, how I recall a recording process, and how I build tours soon after releases.

The Beatles record is an incredible animal. Standing ovations in Montreal, pandemonium in São Paulo, a pat on the back from Paul McCartney ("It's very good, you know")—and stunned silence in the RCA conference room. I recall a publicist breaking the silence by saying she heard her phone ringing on the other side of the building as she quickly left the room. And RCA and BMG Music's president and CEO Bob Jamieson listening to "You Can't Do That" at the Nola Studio, taking a shot of tequila, and declaring, *"That one's gotta go!"*

Then we played "I Feel Fine." Bob's response: *"I hate it."* And he wasn't feeling fine.

I'd worked with Don Sebesky to come up with arrangements that approximated charts we'd heard on older records—for example, "Things We Said Today" was patterned on Van Morrison's "Moondance," "Can't Buy Me Love" was constructed like Woody Herman's "Woodchopper's Ball," "Get Back" channeled Wes Montgomery, "Oh Darling" had a Basie groove. But nothing seemed to matter. RCA released it with just a red cover, with no photo of me—or of anything else, for that matter. I later went to them with my own photos and asked that some Beatles-like photos of me be added for a U.S. rerelease (which they did in February 1999). The decision was made to drop the record from the main RCA label, past Novus, and down to one they used for obscure soundtracks. No publicity machine behind this one—not even an intern.

The *Bossa Nova* album on Telarc at least ends on a happier note. The project took flight after a late-night dinner with Russ Titelman (three Grammy Awards, James Taylor's producer, also producer for George Harrison, Eric Clapton, Steve Winwood, Randy Newman, and others). Russ had just seen João Gilberto at Carnegie Hall, and didn't break stride on the way to Gino to inform me he wanted me to make a bossa nova record. I didn't need to be convinced, having been 94 percent of the way to the same conclusion prior to our conversation.

The album, with Titelman producing and featuring the Brazilian superstar Cesar Camargo Mariano on piano, Daniel Jobim (grandson of Tom) on vocals, Harry Allen on tenor sax, Jim Saporito on percussion, and Paulinho Braga on drums (along with Ray and Martin), was the most enjoyable time I have ever had in the studio. And besides the Brazilian greatest hits ("Ipanema, "Estate," "One-Note Samba," "Aguas de Marco") we added James Taylor's "Smiling Face," Stephen Sondheim's "I Remember," and several others.

Paulinho Braga listened to the playback and memorably said the music "flowed like a river." (The name of the album was almost changed at that point to *Like a River.*) And I sent it out to Jonathan Schwartz, a critic who does not mince words at the early stages of my projects—and he also loved it. So why was I not surprised when the head of Telarc at the time, Bob Woods, who was chilly back when Titelman and I were pitching the idea, *hated* the album? Fortunately, there were significant pockets of support for *Bossa Nova* within Telarc. I felt vindicated when *Swing Journal*, the Japanese jazz bible from 1947 to 2010, named *Bossa Nova* its Record of the Year in 2004. For all the grumbles of "inauthentic," both from reviewers and online commenters, the crowds in Brazil went nuts over the live show in support of the record. It went on to have the highest sales of any album I have ever released.

Bossa Nova was also an important release for us because it marked the point at which our trio became a quartet. While Daniel Jobim and Cesar Camargo Mariano joined us at various locations throughout 2004 and 2005 to reprise the roles they played on the album, we needed a full-time drummer to play this style of music every night on this tour. We also needed a bigger sound to fill the fifteen-hundred- to two-thousand-seat halls where we were beginning to be booked into and also to keep time for us on symphony and big band dates. All roads pointed to a guy I have known around the music scene for over thirty years, the talented Tony Tedesco, the drummer with the wildest résumé you'll ever see—even Tiny Tim is on it. Tony's approach to the drums is summarized by the way he tells students we teach at master classes how to work behind singers. "You have to know what not to play," Tony often says.

What I didn't fully get until he became a member of our group was Tony's attention to detail in everything he does. When I pass around a set list or stage direction ideas, I can see his wheels turning, with the result being helpful suggestions that both complement and respectfully challenge mine. In his playing, he listens attentively and drives the music forward—taking in background riffs, then following them, coloring them, and starting new ones. His focus on the little things extends to his use of brushes and sticks and sometimes his hands to achieve the sound he knows will work for us. Our performances also can occasionally veer onto theatrical turf between tunes (and sometimes midsong), and his solid sensibilities about

Drummer Tony Tedesco brought much-needed organizational skills and a stylish mustache to our traveling quartet.

where it's all going—the man played drums for Donald O'Connor, Mickey Rooney, and Uncle Miltie after all—are always on the money.

Toward the end of 2005 Ray Kennedy began expressing a desire to get off the road and spend more time with his family. For someone who actively disliked flying, Ray hung in there with us for almost thirteen years, made all the trips, raised the collective level of musicianship in our trio (later quartet), and succeeded in leading us to a better place musically than where we were when we met him.

Through my pal the West Coast drummer Jeff Hamilton, we were able to find the wonderful Larry Fuller, who was Ray Brown's piano player at the time of the famed bass player's death in 2002. Larry played a gig with us in Brazil in early 2006, during which Martin again began stomping his foot and nodding his head "yes." Jeff's scouting report—that Larry was the nicest guy in jazz—was also welcome to hear, given that our quartet travels so extensively and spends such a large number of our waking hours together. And fortunately for Jeff, it was a completely accurate scouting report—Larry is a first-class guy, and there is no question that he can play the gig.

The quartet at work in Westchester, New York, in May 2012.

What I have also realized as I put in more years on the road with a touring band is the importance of the gentlemen in the group being 100 percent invested in the music. With Larry this has turned out to be a nonissue—*this* music is his life. He has an appreciation for all the things that I throw at him, but it is the jazz sensibility at the center of his playing that pushes our current quartet. Make no mistake, he had a tough act to follow in Ray Kennedy. But while there are things that Ray did that no one else can do, there are also elements in Larry's playing that set him apart from other piano players, particularly the way he drives our mid-tempo numbers. At the heart of it is what I continually hear from his fellow musicians about Larry's playing: "Man, he swings hard." My wife says that when he's playing the piano, he looks as though he is about to murder someone. I'm assuming she meant that as an analogy and didn't catch him glaring one night as I was driving the quartet into an onstage ditch.

What is also unusual about Larry is that for someone whose playing is always on the attack, he is an absolutely first-rate accompanist and soloist on ballads—instrumental and vocal—that make up a significant portion of our book. After almost seven years together I have come to admire how his fundamental love for the melody informs his chord structure and his overall approach to a song—and that he happens to have the driest and slyest sense of humor on the planet.

Meanwhile, I have found another manager. Buddy had retired from MBST, and Andy Tennenbaum served us well in his stead. But while leading the band for Billy Crystal's Mark Twain Award at the Kennedy Center, I was asked by the director repeatedly if I knew anyone who could perform a number on the televised portion of the show. I said I would do it (many times), and he said no thanks (many times), until finally he said, "Well, you know, like a name. You know—like Madeleine Peyroux." It was at that moment that I decided I needed to be with a management company that gets me, where something like the Kennedy Center conversation wouldn't happen.

Joel Hoffner, my current manager, has done a great job in taking all the aspects of what I do and boiling it all down to a sane operation. And while he likes our music, he allows me to handle that part, which

With Andy Fusco at the fall 2011 recording session at the Jacob Burns Film Center in Pleasantville, New York.

is so important to me. He has been a savior for my career and my sanity (not in that order). And as I have long believed, it's not the business you're doing but how you do your business.

You don't get to be a leader with the captain's C sewn onto your Brioni suit without accepting a couple of other jobs on the road—sound and check—and I don't mean sound check; I am talking about two separate functions. We essentially have taken Oscar Peterson's old sound rider—mic on bass, one on piano, and two overhead on the drums—and we've gone with that. I want the piano player hearing the bass in his left ear, and I need the drummer to hear the vocal monitor. It's important at every sound check to remind the outside sound people that we want to sound more like Oscar Peterson and less like Lynyrd Skynyrd. We need the bass to sound like "Do, Do, Do," not "Bong, Bong, Bong." Setting up can always turn into an adventure, but, for the most part, we've gotten our sound checks down to about forty minutes, and we'll take that.

Finally, it falls to me to pick up the check for our gigs, or at least the percentage of the fee that remains after a down payment to the booking agent. There are stories from the trenches, and if I am hearing them or telling them, it means that someone didn't get paid or didn't get paid in full. The worst situation we've experienced with checks? Okay, here goes.

An entity that no longer exists and that will remain nameless (in my next book, I name names and blow the lid off the upholstery business) hired our group to accompany their orchestra for a December holiday show. Two days before the show they called and asked if I would entertain at a mall to promote the show. Sure, I said, even if it meant beginning the day with an unpleasant wake-up call at four thirty in the morning because I needed to fly two hours to get back to New York City. But I made it to the mall by twelve thirty, and played there (for free) from one to two in the afternoon. From three to five we had to rehearse the entire show with the local orchestra, with whom I would play in both halves of the show. There then followed three hours of time-killing during which I could not eat, because it is not conducive to singing. The eight o'clock show ended at ten fifteen, after which I was asked to come to an off-site restaurant to help the organization woo potential donors. I did this until eleven thirty, after which I needed to depart—or collapse.

I was already home when I realized—*the check*! I had neglected to ask for it. When I called on the following Monday, I was informed there would be no check. The reason cited—*"You didn't use our orchestra enough."*

"Um, but we agreed ahead of time what would be played and who would play it. And I sat at the mall—and I wooed donors. And . . ."

Sorry to take you behind the scenes to reveal the unsavory side of what we have to deal with on the road, but I must admit—I love traveling, and I love being in front of an audience. As it happens, the promoters and the producer wind up paying us nearly all of the time, or else I might have to find another line of work. And while technology moves forward in breathtaking advances, there hasn't been enough progress to do away with the need for musicians to get on planes and buses and play venues that are close to the homes of the audience members. Springsteen, Roger Waters, Madonna, and performers at that level have access to the best information and technology, and they don't appear to have found a better way to put themselves in front of people. And once in front of them, it comes down to making certain that the people sitting in the seats each night return to their homes overjoyed at having decided to leave their homes and hear live music.

That's our job.

13

Let Me off Uptown (but with a Stop at 76th and Madison)

We are all a little weird, and life's a little weird, and when we find someone whose weirdness is compatible with ours, we join up with them and fall in mutual weirdness and call it love.

—Dr. Seuss

From 1979 until 1996, Mel Tormé turned his annual New York City engagements at Marty's, later named Michael's Pub, into master classes in pitch-perfect singing, impeccable phrasing, and accomplished musicianship. Mel wrote many of his own arrangements and often took over at the piano and behind the drums. But as Peter Watrous once observed in the *New York Times*, Mel had an "entertainer's urge," one of which was to pay homage to reviewers during his otherwise impeccable rendition of Billy Joel's "New York State of Mind." He'd perform the vocal flawlessly and without embellishment until—without warning—he embellished. "And now I need a little give-and-take," he'd sing, while softly making a fist that showed his thanks. "The *New York Times*—thank you, John Wilson / The *Daily News*—thank you, Rex Reed."

While I can't imagine ever reaching sufficient career stature that would allow me to sing my thanks to reviewers in the middle of a set, these days I can identify with Mel's sense of gratitude. In my case the thanks would be directed toward the audiences and the press who have embraced the five years of engagements Jessica and I have enjoyed at the celebrated Café Carlyle in Manhattan. Most helpful were the prominent accounts of our work in the first year or two, particularly (but not limited to) those of Stephen Holden in the *New York Times*, Rex Reed in the New York *Observer*, and Jonathan Schwartz on WNYC in New York and Sirius/XM Radio. More than being generous with their appraisals, they also took the column space and air time to explain our act (even to *us*). It had the effect of making audiences aware of what we were up to—and prepared them for the varied and unconventional (at least for the Café Carlyle) song combinations—from the moment we walked onto the stage.

Every so often I find myself sneaking peeks at articles and comments about our Carlyle shows from newspapers, websites, blogs, podcasts, and tweets. I read them simply because they allow me to appreciate how far things had come in the twelve years since my wife Jessica and I lifted our ban on performing onstage together.

It was 2000, we'd survived the Y2K scare, and our trio's main Manhattan cabaret room was Feinstein's at the Regency. A joint effort on the part of Michael Feinstein, Terrence Flannery, manager/promoter/booker Allen Sviridoff, and Loews Hotels' Bob Tisch, the club came together quickly and efficiently. And a triumphant curtain-raising (well, there was not exactly a curtain) engagement in October 1999 helped Rosemary Clooney to immediately feel at home in her new Park Avenue digs. It also didn't hurt that Rosie and Michael headlined the schedule, which gave Feinstein's a string of early sold-out shows and provided the room with instant exposure and credibility.

Since our trio was also a regular act at Rainbow & Stars, we found ourselves needing a new room when it closed. When Feinstein's came calling, it was with the understanding that our trio needed a girl singer to give our lineup of three men (and sometimes four when Bucky was the guest star) a measure of vocal and visual balance. Jazz historians (and I) have conveniently forgotten the names of those who were pushing the idea of a female vocalist, but I am happy to report that it was *not* the late George M. Steinbrenner, the famed Yankees owner and a resident of the Regency Hotel when he came up from Tampa to see his team. It was always a pleasure to hear Mr. Steinbrenner's friendly words when we'd see him in the Library Bar (where hotel staff would set up a television so he could watch the end of games) or when he'd sneak into a back booth a few nights a week to catch our show, often wearing his trademark navy blue windbreaker adorned with his team's interlocking "NY."

During the first two years of our marriage Jess had been fond of joking that she wanted no part of the existing Pizzarelli family act because she didn't want to be seen as (a) Jackie Kennedy disrupting the Kennedy brothers' touch football games, or (b) Lucy (as in *I Love Lucy*) wandering onto the stage and ruining the gig at the Tropicana for the Ricky Ricardo Orchestra. (She had observed during an interview I was having with writer Jacques Steinberg that Christmas with my family was like being with "the Von Trapps on martinis.") So you can imagine that I almost fell over when Ray Kennedy, Martin, and I were asked about the idea of working with Lucille Ball's real-life daughter, Lucie Arnaz. And she's great. And so was Cybill Shepherd, who had performed with Jack Shelton and some big bands in L.A., as well as headlining at Reno Sweeney on West Thirteenth Street (before it became Zinno). But I didn't feel the chemistry, nor did I believe we needed a female vocalist. I mean, we were performing almost two hundred nights a year, and I can assure you—*the act wasn't broken*.

After considering a few more vocalists and "name" TV stars who also sang (Bea Arthur might have been mentioned, as well as two of the actresses from either *Alice* or *Dallas*—we had a bad phone connection), we essentially gave up and hoped the audition process was over, especially after we finally agreed to bring on Jessica for three or four songs every night. But a weird dynamic began to take place in the room—from the moment she and I (stiffly) shook hands and said

"Hello" to one another, people started laughing. And we had no idea why. Then we began riffing on the subject of her being onstage with the Pizzarelli boys. And they laughed some more. It was like the Bugs Bunny's aha! moment when he and Elmer Fudd realized the seltzer bottle bit had improved their vaudeville act. And around this time three fortuitous events transpired: (1) Allen Sviridoff and Michael came to us and strongly recommended that Jess and I create a full set for our shows at Feinstein's; (2) after seeing us at Feinstein's, Don McCollough, a radio producer who creates and syndicates shows, wanted to take our conversations, bottle them, and put them on the air; and (3) Jerry Kravat, who booked the Café Carlyle, began angling to get us on the schedule at that Upper East Side jewel of a music room.

Our first radio show, named *Radio Deluxe* by our producer Don, went out over the airwaves on December 3, 2005. So before there was a Café Carlyle (not until May 2007), we had a radio show. When the television variety show we were pitching hit the proverbial wall, the idea of taking our chatting onto the radio with Don sounded appealing. Concocting a made-up backstory for ourselves, we became a composite of socialites—equal parts Irene and Roger from Woody Allen's *Radio Days* and the couple they were loosely based upon, the Barcelona-born model/actress "Jinx" Falkenburg and her publicist husband, Tex McCrary, who created the radio show, *Hi, Jinx*. In addition to discussing the goings-on at their home, general gossip, and theater openings, the real Jinx and Tex tackled some of the more controversial issues of the day—the atomic bomb, the creation of the UN, and U.S. relations with Russia. Our show, on the other hand, avoids controversy in all of its forms; whether or not to play the Puppini Sisters' cover of "I Will Survive" is about as contentious as things get.

Staying in character as a faux society aristocrat, I introduced that first show with the words "From high atop Lexington Avenue in the Deluxe apartment . . ." It seemed to work, and we were off and running. Originally, the plan was for *Radio Deluxe* to be structured primarily around live music performance—our quartet and my dad played a ton of live music on the early shows—but this became a scheduling nightmare on our end and overwhelmed the production people on the

West Coast. Almost by necessity we needed to go for a more simple and basic format. Once the syndicators volunteered to insert the non-live music later in postproduction, a two-hour show now took just forty-five minutes to record, which also made it easier for us to talk guests into doing the show.

Exceptional guests began to visit us, and it didn't take them long to have fun with the format and our assumed characters. The elegant and delightful Margaret Whiting complimented us on how well we had decorated the Deluxe apartment, with the curtains coming in for particularly high praise. Columnist Frank Rich made a point of saying how much he loved the shag carpet and the bean bag chairs. (We taped both shows in a small booth in a recording studio.) Our thing was to make it feel like home by saying the first "Hello" to guests on the air, with a "Put your coat over there. Isn't it cold outside today? Can we get you some cheese?"

This was our approach with singer Kurt Elling when he came by for the first time. Within a few minutes he had concluded that Jess and I were crazy. He observed, "You guys are like a cartoon show," which I interpreted to be high praise. But as the caffeine wore off, and Jess began asking him about Fred Hersh's *Leaves of Grass* song cycle (with Elling and Kate McGarry on vocals), he spoke seriously and passionately about how he puts poetry to jazz solos, his love for Dexter Gordon, and the not-to-be-missed music sessions on Wednesday nights at the Green Mill in Chicago.

While discussing *Tuesdays with Morrie* with author Mitch Albom (whose appearance resulted in the most comments we've ever had for a show), it came up in conversation that Mitch had cowritten a hockey song with Warren Zevon called "Hit Somebody! (The Hockey Song)." Zevon had recorded it with Paul Shaffer on the Hammond B-3; David Letterman jumped in with a cameo vocal ("Hit somebody" was his line). The song centers on a Canadian player named Buddy who must fight to earn a living and who scores his first goal in his final game, just as he receives a fatal stick to the head. The NHL, however, refuses to allow the song to be played in their arenas due to the subject matter, limiting the scope of what many call the best hockey song ever written or recorded.

Of course, the same league that iced Mitch's song has not banned *actual* fighting, a clumsy, irrelevant sideshow doctors have blamed for over 10 percent of the concussions sustained by NHL players.

Another extraordinary day on *Radio Deluxe* featured a guest we'd wanted for the show within ten seconds of knowing we'd be radio hosts—the late Kenny Rankin. On the day Kenny was to join us, Jessica was delayed across town on an errand, so not knowing how long she would be, Kenny and I plugged in and forged ahead. I began with the usual intro ("From high atop . . ."), after which Kenny launched into a logical opener, "Haven't We Met?" When she entered the lobby and heard the music, Jess heard a voice and guitars she later told me sounded so pristine that she thought it was a CD. When she walked back to the studio and saw us playing and Kenny singing, she nearly lost it. Here we were with one of our beloved artists on *our* show, and he was playing a song that had been a treasured record for both of us since we were kids in the seventies. "Haven't We Met" was the beginning of two hours of nonstop live music with Kenny that embodied everything we wanted our show to be.

Regis Philbin came on during Christmas season one year, then immediately afterward called his pal, the singer/pianist/Carlyle regular Steve Tyrell, and told him (according to Steve), "You're going to love doing this show." (And Steve did.) Our time on the air spent separately with Barbara Cook and Liza Minnelli, both of whom were lively and colorful guests, reminded us why we love our format (very loose) and why Jess and I have always loved radio. We got so caught up in Liza's career—and later with her alternately claiming she couldn't sing, then breaking into song—that we forgot to mention her famous mother until the end of the show's second (and final) hour.

> *Note from Jessica:* The thing about *Radio Deluxe* was that it came
> about when I first worked with John and his band at Feinstein's
> (which I thought was a horrible idea). Every time we opened
> our mouths, people began laughing. It was really odd. I would
> say, "Hello, John," and they would laugh. I think it has a lot to
> do with people's ideas of a couple working together and knowing

going in how different John and I are—he being the vaudevillian clown, and me being the dry straight man. The weird thing is that we didn't know this going in. It just happened organically, and we never plan out our speaking ahead of time—we develop it in front of an audience. Several people in radio suggested that we take whatever was happening onstage and put that energy into a radio show. It just feels like the two of us sitting around the house having coffee and talking about our day. To me, I often think, "Who cares?" But I guess people enjoy either the company or the stories about the music. Early on, we were on the verge of quitting the show several times because it was like the question of the tree that falls in the forest—was anyone hearing it? Then we started to get the most beautiful letters about such personal experiences from the people who were allowing us to come into their lives each week. It was moving and reminded us what we got into this for—the personal connection that radio has with people. We feel it now through the letters and from people around the country, who greet us as though we are family.

As for onstage performing Jessica had a highly successful 2005 solo debut at the now-departed Oak Room of the Algonquin, the room that launched the careers of Michael Feinstein, Harry Connick, Maude Maggart, Peter Cincotti, and Diana Krall, as well as defining the careers of Julie Wilson and Andrea Marcovicci (as well as Sylvia Syms, who passed away at the feet of composer Cy Coleman as she was leaving the stage on May 10, 1992). By popular demand Jessica was invited back the following year with a group that included Larry Goldings. And with singer/songwriter/pianist Dave Frishberg, she made a final visit to the landmark Oak Room in March 2011. "Quality Time," "My Attorney Bernie," "Slappin' the Cakes," "Blizzard of Lies," "Do You Miss New York?"—that last Algonquin show featured Dave's hits, which Jess had rehearsed with him in Portland during our West Coast swing a few weeks earlier.

But it was Jess's infamous two-week gig with Dave at Feinstein's in October 2006 that has become literally unforgettable in the Pizzarelli/

Molaskey household—and it has resulted in flowers being delivered to our home on the same October date every year. By all accounts the first week of shows had passed without a lot of drama. Sure, there had also been plenty of music stars in the audience, with Bette Midler, Donald Fagen, and Diana Krall among those who dropped by to honor one of Dave's infrequent visits from Portland. But that was all the excitement for the week—until Dave developed a kidney stone. He tried to play through the discomfort, prompting Jessica to point out to anyone who would listen that "Morphine and patter songs make for a dangerous combination." Unable to endure the pain any longer, Dave found himself in a cab one night, bound for the emergency room of Lenox Hill Hospital in the company of his singing partner. Things worked themselves out (easy for me to say), and Dave soon found himself well enough to be able to fly home to the Pacific Northwest.

A year to the day following Dave and Jess's mad dash to Lenox Hill, flowers appeared at our door, commending "Kidney Stone Day." And flowers have arrived from Dave on that October day every year since the blessed event. We are convinced that Dave has made provisions to continue the tradition after he is gone and possibly after we all are gone.

Then came the blessed day in late 2006 when we received a call from the longtime booking agent for the Café Carlyle, Jerry Kravat, with the news that Jessica and I would be performing a nearly monthlong engagement (May 1–May 26, 2007) in the world's most prestigious music room. When she'd begun sitting in with us at Feinstein's, Jessica used to joke (though it's not *really* a joke) that as a Broadway and theater actress, she had never appeared in front of audiences without a wig and a script, and not until her performance had undergone weeks of rehearsals. But after our performances together at Feinstein's, two stints of thinking on her feet (and inside the ER) alongside Frishberg, and two solo engagements at the Algonquin, she and I believed we were ready for this. But it was still the Carlyle, and there were butterflies all around, to be sure.

For those of us who have ever aspired to play the world's great singers' rooms, the Café Carlyle—located on Madison Avenue and East Seventy-Sixth Street in Manhattan—is the ultimate goal and everybody's endgame. Shaped by the banquettes and decorated with the Marcel Vertes restored murals (which were rumored to have been finished by the Carlyle's president when Vertes fell ill and couldn't complete the job), the Café's idiosyncrasies are what push it so close to perfection—think Fenway Park. With Bemelmans Bar (with Ludwig Bemelmans's murals) about twenty feet across the hall—and Loston Harris and Chris Gillespie filling the room every night—and the quiet of Central Park a block away, the entire Carlyle experience harkens back to a fedora-wearing, better-mannered, stay-up-later New York City. The room transported you, if everyone cooperated, back to the days before Foo Fighters' ringtones and the unmistakable bright lights of midsong texting were capable of interrupting an evening's performance or distracting the performer.

At least as compelling as the room's design was the rich history of the Café's first two primary musical performers. In 1955 the hotel hired forty-seven-year-old George Feyer to open the room, even hiring a Hungarian decorator to make the Budapest-born pianist/singer feel at home. Feyer's informal but sophisticated act, sprinkled with popular and classical music, lyrics in foreign languages, highbrow humor, and medleys that wove it all together, was successful in drawing a crowd of well-heeled regulars who made tables hard to come by. Nat Hentoff's liner notes to Feyer's 1960 live album from the Café stated that there probably had not been five unoccupied tables (usually with a complete turnover of tables every night) during the first five years of his Carlyle run.

Having held forth at the intimate Café for thirteen years, by the summer of 1968, George Feyer did what he always did in August—he booked a two-week vacation in Nantucket. Meanwhile, the management of the hotel and the Café began asking around for the name of an entertainer in the same style to fill in the two-week slot. Peter Sharp, who ran the place back then, had the wisdom to seek the advice of his close friends Ahmet and Nesui Ertegun, who, along with Jerry Wexler (who coined the term "rhythm and blues"), were running label giant Atlantic Records. Atlantic had recorded a live record from Town Hall three months earlier with singer Mabel Mercer and a pianist and singer named Bobby Short, leading the brothers' strong recommendation to hotel management that Short fill in for Feyer. A known pianist-for-hire among Manhattan socialites and a veteran of the Blue Angel and five shows a day at the Apollo in his younger days, Short made the most of his opportunity, packing the Café each night with his fans and friends (including the Erteguns).

Upon his return from the little island off Cape Cod, George Feyer found himself with a first-rate tan—but no job—after being told his contract at the Carlyle would not be renewed. For the fans of Manhattan supper clubs who are also rooted in baseball history (all nine of them), George has always been "The Wally Pipp of Cabaret," named after the Yankees' first baseman of the twenties who took a day off and found himself replaced by the Bobby Short of Baseball, Lou Gehrig—who didn't miss a game for the next fifteen years. He immediately landed at the Stanhope, where he would soon afterward make medley/"mash-up" history by combining Beethoven's Ninth Symphony and Jimmy Webb's "By the Time I Get to Phoenix." He was also a longtime volunteer at Memorial Sloan-Kettering Cancer Center (simply Memorial Hospital when he started out), playing once or twice a week for patients from the early sixties until shortly before his death in the early nineties.

The Carlyle was able to allow Feyer to depart because they immediately offered a long-term contract to Bobby Short to play at the Café for eight months a year. (He'd eventually cut back to six.) Rather than performing as a cocktail pianist and competing with the audience's conversations, Bobby's sets became cozy concerts at which the audience's silence was expected. And it all worked—by the time the nineties rolled around, and thanks to the countless sets of Cole Porter, Gershwin, Rodgers, and the thousands of songs that resided in the performer's head, Bobby and the Café Carlyle had been awarded "living legend" and "landmark" status, respectively. All this time he continued to record—his perpetually hoarse baritone combined with soaring talent, solid sidemen, and impeccable song selection to win him three Grammy Awards. To say that the Café Carlyle became Bobby's room for the next thirty-six years, until his final performances in 2004, would not be accurate. The Café remains Bobby Short's room, and a fortunate group of us gets called in to sub for him.

To old souls in our town who continue to fight the good fight to preserve essential rituals to be shared among generations, Bobby Short at the Carlyle always represented timeless style, culture, and class. Whenever Woody Allen, our city's definitive filmmaker, wished to shout *"Incompatibility!"* in shorthand to his audience, all he needed to do was place a couple inside the Café Carlyle and show that one of the parties was bored and distracted while Bobby was at the piano (as he did with the Dianne Wiest character in *Hannah and Her Sisters*).

Those were the shoes we had to fill, both onstage and emotionally, as we looked forward to our month at the Café Carlyle with equal parts anticipation and anxiety. We've explained the mystique of the Carlyle, but our nerves were also the result of having exactly one song combination in place in early 2007 (with the help of Eric Stern, a superb music conductor and arranger who had worked with Jessica on *Parade*)—a "money" medley—"Plenty of Money and You" (Jess) along with "We're in the Money" (which I'd sing). We soon came up with two more pairings—"I Didn't Know What Time It Was" and "Just in Time," as well as "If I Were a Bell" (from *Guys and Dolls*) and "Ring-a-Ding-Ding" (from Sinatra's phone call to Van Heusen and Cahn), which succeeded in tripling our repertoire.

> *Note from Jessica:* We wanted to do a real set of Jazz at the Carlyle, but we knew that the sum of the parts needed to have more of a theatrical arc than what we might do at a jazz club. So we began to think of musical give and take. How to have a musical conversation in song. We didn't want to do medleys. We wanted to have a dialogue where the juxtaposition of one song next to another would make the audience feel something different. Sometimes it is the music, and other times it is the lyrics—but many times it is both. I think the term "mash-up" became famous after we'd been doing this for a while. Often the ideas come to us in dreams or from a very visceral place—as in "The Waters of March" wrapped around "Circle Game"—or "My Guitar Gently Weeps" and "Killing Me Softly," which are two different perspectives on the same moment.

The making of Jessica's *Sitting in Limbo* (my favorite of her CDs) also helped immensely in the process of figuring out song combinations. Since we needed to be in the studio during the winter months

At the Carlyle in November 2011. Below, sitting in with Loston Harris on piano and Chris Berger at Bemelmans Bar.

Channeling Johnny Cash at the Café Carlyle.

leading up to the May 2007 Carlyle show, we experimented with changing the center of songs from major to minor, often creating that Meryl Streep moment from *Ironweed* where a song can turn on a dime from happy fantasy to a fear of broken dreams (as with "Small World" from *Gypsy*). And by swimmingly pooling our resources, we even managed to come up with a new pairing while taking a dip at the hotel before a gig in Hawaii (the electric guitar drew some concerned looks). Our idea was to combine two Victor Youmans and Irving Caesar compositions—"Songs about co-dependency before the term had been invented"—"I Want to Be Happy" (from my old favorite, *No, No Nanette*) with "Sometimes I'm Happy" (1927).

A dream, specifically one of mine, is what brought us the conversation between Joni Mitchell's "Circle Game" and Antonio Carlos Jobim's "Waters of March." With song combinations on the brain 24/7, both for Jessica's record and for the month at the Carlyle, I literally woke up in the middle of the night with these two songs interwoven in my thoughts and immediately wrote it all down—and we have been singing that song combination for five years. I know, I know—had I dreamed of lottery numbers instead of the merging of two songs, we could have finally built the place in Branson, Missouri, and we'd be performing in one place year-round. But you take what your dreams give you.

As with so many New Yorkers, we (and especially Jessica) have a particular fondness for the songs of Stephen Sondheim, and I am excited that we have been able to create a number of song conversations around some of his best material. One grouping began with a two-song combination that Jess had assembled with Jason Robert Brown (piecing together the pages of sheet music like a puzzle on the floor) and which we recorded in 2007—Lambert, Hendricks, and Ross's "Cloudburst" and Sondheim's "Getting Married Today" from *Company*. Both are rapid-fire songs that audiences love because there is a good chance the speed of the song will defeat the singer. (People oddly like this.) For the first Carlyle show we expanded it into a "marriage trilogy" by slowing things down for Sondheim's "Sorry-Grateful" (also from *Company*), then added a fourth song, finishing with Jess's perfect reading of Paul Simon's "Hearts and Bones." For our 2011 shows we tied together a bossa nova version of Billy Joel's "Rosalinda's Eyes" with "In Buddy's Eyes" from Sondheim's *Follies*—two songs about seeing ourselves as we believe another person does. That the excellent revival of *Follies* was running on Broadway at the time had us even more aware than usual of that show's impressive songs as we prepared for our 2011 set.

One day we were joking about a George Feyer–like combination—then actually came up with one. We felt we needed to set limits on songs we would ever consider putting together, so we did—the joke was that we would never do "Lush Life" and "God Bless America." But with Irving Berlin's name in play, we came up with one of Rosemary Clooney's favorites of his—"Count Your Blessings," and Jess put it with an improbable partner song, "Seasons of Love," Jonathan Larson's song from *Rent,* with both songs linked by the word "Counting" in Berlin's song and the "Five Hundred Twenty-Five Thousand Six Hundred Minutes" of Larson's. And it somehow evolved into a song conversation that seems to work everywhere, including Carnegie Hall and at the Disney Concert Hall in December 2011.

Besides being in a place where we have been pushed to grow artistically, we are thrilled at the enthusiastic audiences who come to see us. Given the rich tradition of the hotel and the Café, the music room has been filled with boldfaced names—Paul Newman and Joanne Woodward, Tom Brokaw, Jimmy Fallon, Katie Couric, Trevor Nunn, Bill Bradley, Elaine Stritch ("You kids knocked it out of the park!"), Stephen Sondheim, James Lapine, Hal Prince, and Frank Rich. (Who could imagine the one-time Butcher of Broadway wiping away tears?) And (no pressure) Eartha Kitt, Elaine Paige, and Barbara Cook. And Brooks Ashmanskas.

Note to readers—get yourself hired to sing for a month at the Café Carlyle, and they'll throw you a suite at the Carlyle for the extent of your run—*with cable television*. Besides providing a couple of nights of housing for out-of-town friends and family members, having the suite presented us with an everlasting and indelible vision burned onto our retinas—the sight of legendary actress, New York treasure, and full-time Carlyle resident Elaine Stritch knocking on our door for a visit, wearing only a towel. More than being snapped by the paparazzi with the rapid-fire flash camera, it was another one of those moments—like listening to Bucky shouting at *The Price Is Right* from his bed—when no one needed to tell me that I was now officially in show business.

There's an old axiom about marriage along the lines of "I signed up for 'sickness and health'—not for lunch." But it's been at lunch—as well as in the car, hanging out at the cabin, swimming in the lake, talking over coffee—that Jessica and I have come up with most of our ideas for the Carlyle shows. We are occasionally baffled at the amount of usable (and borderline compelling) material we've been able to create (or sometimes dream up) and with the larger "When Worlds Collide"–type approach we've devised for the Carlyle shows. And as with *Radio Deluxe*, where it hit another gear for us when we began hearing from listeners, we are overjoyed that people appreciate what we are trying to do. Bobby Short and George Feyer invested almost fifty years creating the expectation that a night at the Café Carlyle would always be a once-in-a-lifetime experience—even when it's your second visit to the room in a week.

I am thankful and honored that Jessica and I are handed the keys for a month each year and asked to uphold Bobby's tradition—and maybe try to create new ones.

This Old Guitar

Sattinger's Law:
It works better if you plug it in.

I have played a number of different guitars in my thirty years of playing professionally. It has, however, taken me a while to land on what feels and sounds right for me and what I am trying to accomplish each night.

My first seven-string was my dad's Gretsch. In typical Bucky style, he suggested backstage before a 1980 gig at the Morristown (New Jersey) Library, "Play the seven-string today. That way, when I solo, you accompany me and vice versa." No rehearsal, no warning—just "Swim!" I had been accompanying him until then on a six-string Aria 175 Copy (a Gibson knockoff, very reliable guitar). I then "stole" one of my dad's seven-string Benedetto guitars. It was the first one Bob had made for him, and I loved how it looked and played.

When I was about to go out on the road in 1991, I looked at purchasing a little Oscar Moore Epiphone six-string or a Charlie Christian Gibson ES150 Archtop. But Bucky insisted that Bob Benedetto had a seven-string laminated archtop that would be good for me. We drove to Stroudsburg, Pennsylvania, where

Bob had a house and a workshop. He put a little strap-holder on the guitar for me, and I was off to the races for the next eight years. Laminated guitars always worked great for me on the road because they aren't affected by the extreme outdoor weather conditions of either summer and winter shows. As my old buddy Rick Haydon from Southern Illinois University likes to say, an archtop guitar sometimes thinks it's still a tree.

There was a morning show in Minnesota where they asked me to play outside at seven o'clock, with a game-time temperature of ten below zero. Nothing was going to prevent that (or any) guitar from going up a tone and a half in pitch in those conditions.

It was around 1999 that I met Bill Moll who, with his wife Denise, makes guitars in Springfield, Missouri, at Moll Custom Instruments. I had loved the Benedetto guitar that had been so great for me for so long, but I thought it was the right time to forge my own relationship with a guitar maker. Bob had always been Bucky's guy, and I wanted it to stay that way. Bill impressed me immediately as one of the best luthiers I have ever met, and we have spent thirteen years developing the Workingman's Hero and the John Pizzarelli models from the ground floor.

Although Bill was originally averse to working with anything but solid wood, I have nudged him (successfully) to come up with a laminated guitar that would be more affordable for students. He built me a terrific carved-top seven-string that I played acoustically on Jessica's *Pentimento* (her first CD), a travel classical, and a gorgeous classical seven-string that I played on my 2012 CD, *Double Exposure*. The 16-inch John Pizzarelli Model 7-String is my go-to guitar now. It has a bronze tailpiece on it and, although laminated, has an acoustic sound that is about as good as it gets.

All of this from a guitar maker who had previously shied away from laminated (plywood) guitars.

14

The Long and Winding Country Road

JAMES TAYLOR AND PAUL McCARTNEY

The secret of life is enjoying the passage of time.
—James Taylor

When I sat down at Capitol Records Studio A a little after one in the afternoon on April 8, 2011, and played rhythm guitar for the man in the booth singing Irving Berlin's "Cheek to Cheek," I had officially hit the exacta. Working on the sessions for Paul McCartney's *Kisses on the Bottom* meant that I had now provided musical accompaniment on studio albums for two of the voices of my generation—Sir Paul McCartney and James Taylor.

For those of you who haven't played professionally with James and Paul, I can assure you that it is career-changing. For instance, most folk music coffee houses that require auditions have backed off the requirement that I provide two references from previous gigs. When I let it slip that I have recorded and played live shows with two of the most essential writers and voices in the history of music, all but two places have waived the second reference.

The good news for fans of theirs is that there cannot be two nicer people on earth than Paul McCartney and James Taylor. Really. For those of you who love their music—and what is not to love—I urge you to embrace it even more because I'm guessing James and Paul must have good karma playing and singing backup on every note they play.

But just because I love and admire them both doesn't mean I can't take you behind the scenes for recording sessions and live performances—first with James, then with Paul.

James Taylor Recording Session—*October Road*
Clinton Studios, New York City
A Sunday Afternoon in August 2001

The phone call from Russ Titelman to make this record is up there with the one from BMG that we'd be opening for Sinatra and the one from Tommy LiPuma that I would be accompanying Paul McCartney. Russ often tells the story well of how we met, but let's just say it took place on a boat and leave the rest of the telling to Mr. Titelman, should you ever run into him. A few months before this session I had worked for the first time with Russ, laying down a handful of new guitar parts on a male singer's album of standards (don't want to offend the credited guitar player)—and things seemed to go well. As an avid James Taylor fan over many years, I had been following Russ's work as Warner Brothers' in-house producer on some of the best work in James's catalogue (*Gorilla* and *In the Pocket*).

The only track scheduled for this session was a JT original called "Mean Old Man," which Russ believed felt like a standard more than a pop song and could benefit from a rhythm guitar behind the vocal. In five takes we had finished, and the next thing I knew the other players, Larry Goldings—piano, Jimmy Johnson—bass, and Steve Gadd—drums, had descended on my sound booth. "Man, that was just like the old days," said Gadd, who knows about the old days—having been a recorded drummer in five different decades on a stack of the most iconic albums of the past forty years.

Adrenaline pumping, heart beating out of my chest, I couldn't help myself. "Hey, James," I asked. "Any more originals?"

Titelman shot me a look that sliced me to ribbons, but James answered my question with one of his own.

"Want to try the other one?" he asked the group.

The "other one" was the holiday chestnut "Have Yourself a Merry Little Christmas."

James wanted me to play behind him on the song's seldom-used verse and showed me the sheet music. It read *A—two-three-four . . . E—two-three-four* in the melody. I started to play what was written above the staff until I heard the portable Bucky who travels in my head saying, "Look at the bass notes, ya' (fill in term of endearment here)!" It was A, but with C# in the bass. E, but with B in the bass, and down the line.

With my great friend, Grammy-winning producer Russ Titelman.

A beautiful little work of art and, more importantly, a nick-of-time solution that I was able to locate by looking below the staff in the basement
(or bassment). The verse was the only slight bump in the road, we got
back on the rails—and James's singing took it home from there. I went
home from the session impressed by how cordial and considerate James
Taylor had been to the new guy (me) throughout the entire day.

My next call from James came in December 2001, but so much
had changed in our city and inside all of us since our August session, which had taken place a few weeks before 9/11. He wanted me
to accompany him on the *Today* show, for which there would be a
rehearsal the night before at Sir Studios. We ran through the two songs
we'd be playing—"Have Yourself a Merry Little Christmas" (with the
verse) and "The Secret of Life"—for three and a half hours. You watch
James effortlessly perform and speculate that he must be able to get
out of bed and sing "Fire and Rain" better than the recording in our
heads. But as I sensed about three hours into the rehearsal, he was
taking this television appearance seriously.

In Capitol Studios in February 2012 with James Taylor, who came by to rehearse
Beatles songs while we worked on the McCartney material for the Apple and
Grammy performances.

At five o'clock in the morning we all arrived at the streetside aquarium of a studio that had been built for the *Today* show on West Forty-Ninth Street, just south of 30 Rock, the world-famous Christmas tree, and the glorious skating rink (onto which John Belushi and Dan Aykroyd would flip pizzas after freezing them on a window sill, according to a friend whose east-facing office they used as their base of operations). After we played the sound check—a loose, playful version of "My Blue Heaven," which was not on the setlist—it seemed that everyone in the building wanted to meet James. But James wanted to meet Madeleine Albright, who was scheduled to be a guest that day to discuss world security issues during that troubled time.

Soon we got the word that we'd be "up after Mister Rogers," who immediately had our group speaking in hushed tones as he and his cardigan walked past us in the hallway. Fred Rogers was one of the rare people in the world capable of eliciting such deference and borderline reverence from a collection of musicians who had been asked to rise before three thirty in the morning, following a late rehearsal.

My next visit with James was in 2002, for the Fourth of July concert at the Hollywood Bowl that featured James and John Williams. As I was about to leave my Dallas hotel room for L.A., Charles Osgood delivered the sad news about Rosemary Clooney's death. And while I was on the West Coast, we would learn of the death of Ray Brown, who passed away in his Indianapolis hotel room after his usual round of afternoon golf. Joe Cosgriff and I, along with bassist Jay Leonhart, had played golf with Ray at Metedeconk National in New Jersey about seven weeks earlier. Ray had been immensely proud of his space-age driver, an overgrown monstrosity that weighed less than a swizzle stick, a gift from friends in Japan. "This is what you'll be using when you're my age," he told us, as we each took a whack with it on the eighteenth tee. As I mourned my two friends, I found no small amount of comfort in working with and being around James.

It was John Williams and James again that summer at Tanglewood a couple of weeks later for the same show, this time in front of twenty-five thousand spectators, including Maria Traversa and my son Johnny. But after the orchestra packed up and called it a night, James summoned together the band (Larry Goldings, Jimmy Johnson, Gregg Bissonette on drums) and suggested, due to the traffic that had caused people to miss the early part of the show, perhaps we could perform "a little extra."

"Do you guys know any of my songs?" Only since I was twelve years old, I resisted the urge to shout out. "Sure" was my answer, as it was everyone's. I recall thinking *I am actually on a stage performing "Steam-roller" with James Taylor!* I think we also did "You've Got a Friend," "The Secret of Life," and the local favorite, "Sweet Baby James." Maria and Johnny made their way close to the stage for the impromptu encore and came backstage all smiles. And Johnny summed it up well for everyone who had been there—"That was *so* cool!"

Paul McCartney Recording Sessions—*Kisses on the Bottom*
Capitol Studios, Los Angeles
Friday, April 8, 2011

The McCartney project fell out of the sky. We'd finished a family dinner, and Martin had come back to stay at my place because we were leaving early in the morning to fly to a gig. On my voice mail were three calls in a row from star producer Tommy LiPuma. When I called Tommy back, he let me know he wanted me for a recording session with Paul McCartney.

The plan was to record a series of thirties- and forties-sounding songs with Diana Krall's small group, with Johnny Mandel writing string arrangements for certain others. They wanted me in Los Angeles on April 8 and 9, which presented scheduling issues. I was off after a Thursday concert in Savannah, and while I could get out there for the Friday, I had to be back in Nashville for a show on Saturday night, April 9. But I told them if they could get me there, I'd play all day on Friday. About a week later they called me and asked about Bucky for Saturday, the ninth. ("Does your father still play?") My dad had a gig with Ken Peplowski that he was able to finesse, thanks to Pep being the ultimate Beatles fan.

As I was leaving the hotel in Savannah at four in the morning, my brother was waiting for me in the lobby. He said it was important for him to see me off and mentioned all the Beatles' tunes we had performed at the hundreds of gigs we played at Nobody's Inn and dozens of other rock clubs and bars in the early years. It was sweet of the knucklehead.

The flights were Savannah-to-Atlanta and Atlanta-to-L.A., which put me at the hotel at ten forty-five in the morning Pacific Time. Of course, the room wasn't ready. So, seventy-five minutes early, I strolled into the front lobby of Capitol, where next to the reception desk stood a life-size cutout of the four Beatles. My playful nature undimmed after an eventful morning, I confidently walked up to the receptionist and announced "I am working with *that* one," pointing to Paul. She wasn't at all charmed by the attempt at humor, but found my name and waved me through—past the gate and the fine-trimmed lawn.

Engineer supreme Al Schmitt and I were the first to arrive that afternoon. Eventually, everyone wandered in. Paul arrived at about twelve thirty, after which there were introductions all around. When he reached me, LiPuma said, "Paul, this is John Pizzarelli." I shook Sir Paul's hand and said, "Nice to meet you." His first words were, "You made a Beatles CD." My eyebrows must've been raised cartoonlike above my brow. I stammered out, "Yes, I did." Paul allowed for a fat and dramatic pause, and then added, "It's very good."

As the great TV sportscaster Warner Wolf would announce over a film clip of the play that had sealed a team's victory, "You could have turned off your sets right there."

The interesting part of the process, which Paul has addressed in subsequent interviews, was that we were all figuring it out on the fly, which was also the way he characterized the Beatles' way of doing things in the studio. He told us that it almost always fell to him and John, as the primary songwriters, to teach the new songs to George, Ringo, and even to George Martin. The next step was coming up with an arrangement and then, finally, recording the song. They did two in each session, as I recall him saying. He said it wasn't until after they'd made a few records that they felt they had the stature to request an acetate to take home and evaluate their day's work.

In all the excitement, Bucky walked through the door at about one thirty, twenty-two hours early for his assignment the next day.

His idea wasn't just to be characteristically early for the gig; he also wanted to listen to what was going on. But as it turned out, as soon as Bucky settled in, LiPuma wanted us to re-create the feel of an old Ukulele Ike arrangement on "Paper Moon." So the Pizzarellis marched in together to play. Later on that day, Paul would say how cool it was that we were both there, to which I responded, "When McCartney calls, *all* the Pizzarellis show up." Bucky loved Paul's energy level and told him so. "You could go all night doing this; you're fresh as a daisy!"

The real turning point in the session came when we recorded Frank Loesser's "More I Cannot Wish You" from *Guys and Dolls*. Paul sang it beautifully, the guys carried him along, and Diana capped it off with a tender piano ending. I added a few little harmonic things that I do, and he seemed to like them, too. There was a little vocal thing he did after he sang the line about "Wisdom, when your hair has turned to gray . . . mmmm." The "mmmm" was so perfect that I had to tell him so. His instincts were unfailingly spot-on and musical.

Paul McCartney Recording Sessions
Avatar Studios, New York City
June 20–21, 2011

I had managed to sneak Jessica and my daughter, Maddie, a *huge* Paul McCartney fan, just inside the reception area, but outside the studio. Paul asked for his jacket at the end of the session, and I grabbed it and put it on him and asked if he would mind saying hello to my daughter. He said, "Certainly." As he walked out of the studio directly toward Maddie (with a giant brace on her knee from a scorekeeping mishap—don't ask), I saw her mouth the words "Oh my god!"

I started off the introductions: "Paul McCartney, Madeleine Pizzarelli, Madeleine Pizz—" but couldn't get all the words out. I was starting to cry, so I backed away as I heard my hero say to her, "Come on, give us a hug."

I assure you it was as perfect as a moment can get.

Paul McCartney Rehearsals

Capitol Studios A, Los Angeles
Monday, February 6–Saturday, February 11, 2012

iTunes Concert
February 9, 2012

On Monday morning I put on my jacket and tie and again headed back across the street to Capitol Studios. When I entered the studio, I noticed they had put in a big lighting rig and laid down a black floor. With my JazzKat amp in one hand and the travel guitar in the other, I asked Al Schmitt, who was engineering and mixing the session, where I should go. He showed me to where I would be stationed, commenting that I was again an hour and a half early. Paul wouldn't be coming around on this day, but Diana, Anthony Wilson (Diana's guitar player), bassist John Clayton, and drummer Karriem Riggins all made their way in for a one o'clock faceoff. We ran down all the charts without much fanfare. The main thing Diana wanted to accomplish was having the tempos straight and the road maps worked out. We were pretty much done by six o'clock.

Tuesday was album release day as we awaited Sir Paul. He was, as he always is, in an upbeat mood, but on this day he had more reasons than usual—the majority of the reviews for *Kisses* had been favorable. It was customary for him after that first handshake to now greet each of us with a big hug as he said hello. Unlike a lot of boldfaced musicians I can mention, Paul's arrival and presence among us seemed to relax the room.

We ran down the songs in record order with the rhythm, planning to add the strings the next day. There didn't seem to be any questions, as Paul indicated that everything was going well. He liked the tempos. I was asked by Diana what I had done on the record for "My Valentine," and I responded that I played a complementary part to Paul's guitar. Paul swung around and looked at me and said, "That's absolutely right . . . and I liked what you did there." Whew! I was in the clear.

Wednesday was the busiest and most harried day. First stop that morning was Nordstrom's by ten thirty to pick up a black suit I needed to buy (what happened to tuxes?). It would be all that I would wear for each of the week's big three events. The strings would be in that day, as would be Joe ("My Maserati Does 185") Walsh, who would play Eric Clapton's parts from the record. We were then all mic'd up and interviewed about the experience of making the record and what it is like to be there and what the music means to us. I mentioned in my interview how much I liked Paul's song selection. And how authentic I thought the project was, given Paul's love of these songs.

Paul liked to mention to us how the Beatles had worked out "And I Love Her" (almost forty-eight years earlier, to the day), with George playing the memorable critical four notes after the count-off that defines the song. He said that George just played them without any prompting or advance discussion. "Can you imagine that song without those four notes?" Paul asked more than once. As Martin and I did as kids when my dad's pals stopped by to tell stories, I reminded myself constantly to make sure I was listening and absorbing *everything*.

Joe Walsh was a terrific teammate. He introduced himself and sat between Anthony Wilson and me. At one point he remarked (since he was assigned to only two tunes) that we were schooling him with our playing. I leaned over and told him it was payback for all those nights in high school spent trying to learn his solos when I should have been sleeping. Of course, I ended up playing my "Fast Lane" lick for him, and he told me the song had begun as nothing more than a little warm-up riff he was doing. Glenn Frey and Don Henley heard it and built an entire song around it. *I gotta get me a lick like that*, I thought.

So now we've reached Wednesday, and it's the final day of rehearsals. As we hit around two o'clock in the afternoon, Paul seems to like the idea of starting with "I'm Gonna Sit Right Down and Write Myself a Letter." Nice and swinging. The strings were adding the touch that was missing the day before, and the elements were falling into place. As time marched on, we began cramming a lot into the final minutes of the rehearsal day. With the day running long, it was no time for me to be stumbling over an easy solo on "Always." I began getting annoyed with myself. LiPuma finally halted the proceedings. Tomorrow Paul would be getting a star on the Walk of Fame in front of Capitol, then doing a live streaming concert (a first ever for anyone) of the new record from Capitol Studios A and B. And in the face of it all he was cool as a cucumber.

I, on the other hand, was more than a little under the weather and couldn't wait to head across the street to get some rest. But just then I looked up and saw James Taylor and Paul hugging it out and exchanging pleasantries. I remarked to Anthony Wilson that my entire foundation of music during my formative years was standing twenty feet away—"Fire and Rain," "Day Tripper," "The Secret of Life," and "The Long and Winding Road." Those songs alone nearly made up a set at Nobody's Inn—time to pass the hat.

Having worked with James about eight years earlier in this same room, I thought I would wave hello as he passed. I did, and he said, with genuine warmth, "Hey, John—how you doing? You bring your seven-string here?"

I must say—his friendliness put a jump back in my step. He moved over to Diana, with whom he was going to rehearse his version of "Yesterday" for the Friday night MusiCares event.

My playing at the end of the day left me a little upset. I was run-down and could use the rest. I talked to Jess for a bit. My son was going through some bumps at college, and we were talking about dealing with that. It was already ten thirty on the East Coast—they didn't waste time back there. My cell phone's second line rang in the midst of this—it was Diana.

"Where are you? James is looking for you."

"I am across the street in the hotel."

"Well, come back."

I got back to the other line to talk a little more about Johnny, and then the hotel phone rang. It was Shari Sutcliffe, Tommy LiPuma's coordinator. "James Taylor would like to see you come back!" Me: "Jeez, okay. I will be right there."

"Uh, Jess, James Taylor needs to see me right away. Gotta go." I said it eight more times to her. We laughed, and I ran back. I sat in the studio, unseen, as Diana, James, and John Clayton rehearsed "Yesterday" with James on vocals, then ran through "For No One" with

Diana singing. After about forty minutes, Diana announced, "Well, John Pizzarelli is here." No sooner did she say that than James put down his guitar and said, "Hey, John! How is it going? Listen, I got a question for you. How do you do that *Radio Deluxe* program?" Man, I thought. Just when you think you have no listeners, here's James Taylor explaining to anyone who will listen that it's his favorite radio program. Listens all the time on WAMC, it seems. We talked for about fifteen minutes, after which he asked to be a guest on the program. At that point you pretty much have to declare victory and get out of there. Which I did—picking myself off the floor and heading back to the hotel.

Thursday started off with our needing to enter Capitol from the back entrance. Paul was getting his star, and the place was mobbed. We were in a little eating area almost overlooking where the event would take place. This was the day we would get a glimpse of what it is like to be Paul McCartney, the Beatle. People brought their Beatles basses, "Let It Be" T-shirts, and signs that read, "All You Need Is Love." But for Paul, this wasn't close to Shea Stadium 1964. He could've handled this one in his sleep. Neil Young introduced him at the ceremony, and I was struck by the spectators' arms in the air. Think of a thousand people waving hello with their right arms, all holding camera phones. I heard Paul thank the "other three," saying that nothing would have been possible without them.

Just ten minutes later, Paul was in the studio for a full dress rundown. He wore a great black blazer that I asked him about. "Stella designed it." He showed me the one button that is unbuttoned on each jacket sleeve. He was very proud of his daughter's work and would continue wearing the clothing she'd made for him throughout the weekend, including a beautiful white dinner jacket at the Grammy Awards. We ran down the show. I finally hit my stride during "Always." We finished at six. At seven we were live to the world on iTunes. In the parking lot was a buffet—vegetarian, of course.

Joe Walsh saw me and asked if I had five minutes. To paraphrase Chico Marx, *I got a plenty a' minutes*! He led me up some stairs to his makeshift dressing room, opened a guitar case, and pulled out a

Stratocaster tuned to an open E chord. Then he got out a clear glass guitar slide, put it on his middle finger and started to play, all the while explaining what he was doing. "Don't press down . . . just place the slide over the frets. . . . This is how Duane Allman did it. . . . Got it?"

Duane Allman . . . "Yes."

A huge smile came to my face when he said that. I was gonna give him the slide back, until he said, "No, that's for you. Now go fishin'!"

"That," I told him, "had been the best guitar lesson I'd ever had!"

Ten minutes later we were all gathered for the live show. Capitol A and B studio combined. The strings would be conducted by Alan Broadbent, who played piano for Irene Krall, whose records I had heard so many times on Jonathan's program. I had pretty damned good company: Diana Krall at the piano, John Clayton (who had arranged my *Dear Mr. Sinatra* CD with his big band) on bass, Anthony Wilson (whose father wrote the "Perdido" arrangement to which Jess had put lyrics for our Ellington CD) and Joe Walsh (my new guitar teacher and a pretty fair little player himself—he tore up "Get Yourself Another Fool") on guitar, and Karriem Riggins (who played with Larry Fuller on the final tour with Ray Brown) on drums. An audience of thirty-five to forty-five people were scattered around the room and the booth. Eric Idle in the house. Herbie Hancock and Don Was in the booth. Paul sang "Sit Right Down" and "Home" to start. As Paul performed the third number, Frank Loesser's "More I Cannot Wish You," I could not help but think of my son on the other side of the country, struggling to figure out college and life. As I searched for insights I could pass along to Johnny, here stood Paul singing "More I Cannot Wish You," a wise uncle's song about hope for the future and finding your way when you're young. There could not have been a more perfect song for that moment—and it was a brilliant choice for Paul's record. It was quite touching. I was tearing up and hoping my son was listening. Hoping as many people as possible were hearing this. As the concert ended, I got my hug and headed across the street. I called Jess and said, "You know what hit me tonight. It's all the things I have been writing about in the book. You just saw me on the computer, like my mother saw my father on TV in the fifties. I was thinking about Maddie and Johnny and you

With Paul McCartney for the Apple iTunes Worldwide Live Streaming Concert in February 2012.

watching me. Thinking about all the life decisions that brought me to a place where I was sitting behind Paul McCartney. I cut out cardboard guitars when I was five to be a Beatle. Now that Beatle hugs me when he sees me."

When I go to Southern Illinois University at Edwardsville to give clinics to Rick Haydon's guitar students, I tell them to make sure they know how to play an intro, how to accompany a singer, and how to play an eight-bar solo. I tell them to be prepared for those things as much as they should be ready to cut up some guy on "Cherokee." And here I was on a large stage getting to practice what I preached to them every time I went there.

It wasn't about impressing Paul McCartney as much as it was about being ready to do my job when the bell rang. I thought also about Bucky and all his hard work and what that tremendous work ethic has instilled in me. I still have a long way to go, both as a musician and as a person, but I was also going to take a few hours and enjoy this sense of accomplishment. I was called because I was John Pizzarelli, and that was a pretty great feeling.

Finale

The Best Is Yet to Come

What they don't tell you when you sign up to become an author is how many times you will end up reading your own book. I have already gone cover-to-cover on *World on a String* more times than my lifetime totals on *Green Eggs and Ham*, the indispensable *Looney Tunes and Merrie Melodies* by Jerry Beck and Will Friedwald, and *The Essential Groucho*. I can also tell you that I have been around the block so many times with this manuscript that I'm beginning to have issues with this vaguely familiar John Pizzarelli character who seems to get a lot of airtime in this book.

As I write this, I find myself encouraged by a series of positive developments in my career that are carrying over to many components of my life away from the stage. It was an honor and a really big deal for me to work with Paul McCartney, Tommy LiPuma, Diana Krall, and team on all aspects of *Kisses on the Bottom*. Part of me (okay, nearly 82 percent of me) looked around in awe with my head on a swivel. Part of me—okay, nearly 82 percent of me—looked around in awe with my head on a swivel. But an increasingly larger part of me every day is arriving at the conclusion that I was precisely the right person to have

An essential for life on the road is to make sure it passes through Boston during baseball season. Here we all are—Jess, Maddie, and me—high above the field at Fenway Park with the man whose voice magically comes out of our radios and computers all summer, Dave O'Brien.

been in the rhythm guitar chair for this project, with Bucky pitching some relief. I have been working at this for over thirty years. I have learned technique and work ethic from the best, and now, more than at any time in my life, I am confident in my abilities and in what I bring to the table. What I came away believing, and this has probably cost me tens of thousands in therapy bills to get here, is that I *belonged* in the company of the musicians who surrounded me at Capitol's studios that week—particularly given the styles of music needed on the sessions.

I realize that to jazz fans and musicians of a certain age I will always be my father's son ("Nice playin', kid—you still can't hold a candle to your old man"); to jazz purists, I'll be the guitar player who sings (and who should stick to the standards). One day a newspaper will call our performance "jazz-infused cabaret," then the next day it's "cabaret-infused jazz." And I'm cool with all that. But what I can also say definitively,

It's always a treat to come off the road and head into the studio. Lately we've taken to trying out new material and arrangements at New York City clubs prior to our recording sessions.

however, is that everything feels as though it's moving to a better place, particularly when it comes to our concert performances.

Speaking of concerts, this book is part of a dedicated effort to get closer to those of you who currently attend or have wanted to attend our live performances. We already have conversations with our loyal fans on Facebook, on my website, and when we don't have a four o'clock wake-up call for an airport run, after our shows. But by sharing stories in the book about my family, our musician friends, and our years on the road, we hope to bring the songs to life and have them resonate with our audiences for the same reasons they have special meaning for us. Perhaps when we break into "Jamboree Jones," instead of keeping score of the game (and wondering how a clarinet player personally erases a 17–0 deficit in the final minute), you'll picture (as I do) the great Bobby Troup, sitting on the edge of his legless couch in Encino, silently listening to his own vocal recording of the song. Or you'll stream/download/buy Bobby's album of Johnny Mercer songs. Or be the hit at a fancy dinner party or at your table at

Birdland or Yoshi's as you regale your guests about the "Jamboree Jones" composer and lyricist Johnny Mercer, who once said after attending a trendy play in London's East End—"I could eat alphabet soup and shit better lyrics."

In *The House That George Built* Wilfrid Sheed writes that the magnificent composer George Gershwin so believed that the rising tide of songwriting would float all the boats of his peers that he would anonymously purchase pianos and have them delivered to their residences in order to allow them to work at home. Similarly, I can't wait to see what the next artistic step will be for the singers in my space who float the boats—Tony Bennett, Kurt Elling, Diana Krall, Cyrille Aimee, Judy Collins, Michael Feinstein, Tierney Sutton, John Proulx, Jane Monheit, Kate McGarry, Harry Connick, Michael Bublé, Jessica Molaskey, the Callaway sisters. And Paul McCartney. And James Taylor.

At its heart, jazz should be about compelling and pleasing interpretations of some of the most gorgeous songs ever written, and we need to do a better job of holding this simple message above the fray. Too often, jazz is held up as an intellectual exercise that can be understood only by the chosen few who can whip out their Village Vanguard matchbooks from the night in 1962 when Eric Dolphy cut loose while playing alongside Coltrane.

The exclusionary approach of many of its enthusiasts has almost turned "jazz" into a dirty word. A story that makes the rounds among musicians is that when George Benson had his monster commercial hit with "Breezin'", the word "jazz" was ordered removed from his publicity material—as if realizing they were listening to—gasp—jazz would stop people from buying his records and attending his concerts.

The goal with *Double Exposure*, as it has been with all my CDs (but even more so in this case), was to get the nonjazz listener to the party. We *have* had some great successes with *Bossa Nova* and with the Sinatra CD, and I truly hope that we can continue to provide the nonjazz listener a place where he or she can always be making new discoveries. In a perfect future world, I would love to be involved in projects with Michael McDonald, Joni Mitchell, Billy Joel, James Taylor—be they concerts or releases on CD or DVD, or in creating new material. It would also be satisfying professionally to continue to challenge the artificial distinctions between categories and to have our music worlds blend together by simply recording and performing exceptional songs.

You can only hope that imagination will win out—that musicality will win out—and that people will listen to what our group has to offer, do their homework, and find their way to Tony Bennett, Tormé, and Krall.

I make a point of driving my dad to master classes when I am home because watching him play "Honeysuckle Rose" for young people is truly inspirational and reminds me why I do what I do. They are floored by an eighty-six-year-old man playing insane chord solos; I marvel at a song that has sat on our family's stove for over seventy years like a pot of soup—and we have all added our seasonings over the years to arrive at the way we're playing it today. It also floored me last year when kids at two different college shows mentioned seeing me play on *Late Night with Conan O'Brien* back in the day and letting me know they decided on the spot that they wanted to do *that*—what I was doing. It's important to remember every night that someone is always watching—always watching.

As you can imagine, the changing landscape of music has resulted in more than my share of navel-gazing and lake-staring about where it's all heading and how I should proceed. We schedule fifteen or so concerts a month, catch planes, rent cars, set up the sound, and somehow you find us. That is a small miracle. As I've mentioned many times in this book, I recognize that we have to do a better job of communicating—both our schedule and what we are up to in general. And keep sending in comments and questions—maybe you'll give us some ideas for the next book, which hinges on our good behavior at the book signings and parties for this one.

This is the point where, if this were a concert, I would probably introduce the quartet one last time.

From the University of Ray Brown, on piano—Mr. Larry Fuller.
On drums, the final drummer to give a rimshot to Uncle Miltie—and
    there must be a better way to phrase that—and someone I'd already
    known for twenty-five years ten years ago—Tony Tedesco.
And last but not least, a man with whom I slept many times until I
    took my Farrah Fawcett poster and moved to the attic—always my
    mother's favorite—Martin Pizzarelli.

I cannot emphasize enough how much I enjoy being in front of an audience and making music. And I have never had more confidence in a group's abilities and where the music will take us than I do with the current squad of Martin, Larry, and Tony. Whether this ride takes us to television shows, back to Broadway, or even if the plan one day involves us setting up a stage on a vineyard in Napa Valley for a year and inviting audiences to travel to see us, I am blessed with three guys who will always be reminding me that it begins and ends with the music. Everything else is just noise, smoke, and mirrors unless we swing every night.

My small regret is that given our wild touring and travel schedules, the singers I have mentioned throughout this book (and many others who deserved a shout-out) don't have opportunities to meet, team up, and stage blowout gigs together in major concert halls to celebrate the Great American Songbook. But whether it's together or separately, it's important that we're all out there, constantly striving to move our music forward.

Thank you for making it all the way to the end of the book. We hope to see you at a live show soon—maybe for meatballs and lasagna if you can make it to Birdland in New York City. My usual closing line (right after "Carnegie Hall does not validate parking") is "Music is good." I'll always remember the brilliant Brazilian drummer Paolo Braga shouting back to me onstage one night at the Montreal Jazz Festival as we took our final bows, "Yes, John, I like that. Music *is* good!"

My Favorite Things

He has Van Gogh's ear for music.

—Billy Wilder

Since 1942 the BBC has been airing a radio program called *Desert Island Discs*, on which celebrities are invited to imagine themselves as castaways on an island, to which they are allowed to bring along eight pieces of music, a book, and a luxury item. The guests and the interviewer then use these items as a basis to discuss guests' lives and the reasons for the choices.

A lot of people over the years have selected Dante's *Inferno* and a good chair.

Since I would find it impossible to limit my selections to eight pieces of music, let's assume that if there's electricity to play the eight pieces of music, then there is a place to plug in a vintage Seeburg jukebox with fifty selections of my favorite music. I'll keep this list on my website, and swap out songs from time to time to keep the music fresh. So here are the fifty songs I would make sure were installed on my improbable island jukebox (in no particular order):

FIFTY SONGS ON PIZZARELLI'S ALL-TIME JUKEBOX

Toninho Horta, "Aquelas Coisas Todas" (All of These Things), *Toninho in Vienna*

Zoot Sims, "Lady Be Good," *Zoot Sims & the Gershwin Brothers*

Zoot Sims, "It's Alright With Me," *If I'm Lucky: Zoot Sims Meets Jimmy Rowles*
Zoot Sims, "Somebody Loves Me," *Somebody Loves Me* (originally *Nirvana*)
Oscar Peterson Trio, "Brotherhood of Man," *Oscar Peterson Trio Plus One*
    (Clark Terry)
Oscar Peterson Trio, "Mumbles," *Oscar Peterson Trio Plus One* (Clark Terry)
Oscar Peterson Trio, "How About You?" *Oscar Peterson Trio at the Stratford*
    Shakespearean Festival
Miles Davis, "Freddie Freeloader," *Kind of Blue*
Bill Evans, "You Must Believe in Spring," *You Must Believe in Spring*
Bill Evans, "Theme from M*A*S*H," *You Must Believe in Spring*
Tony Bennett and Bill Evans, "You Must Believe in Spring," *Together Again*
Tony Bennett and Bill Evans, "Some Other Time," *The Tony Bennett and*
    Bill Evans Album
Tony Bennett, "Moments Like This," *The Art of Excellence*
Tony Bennett, "Emily," *The Movie Song Album*
Mel Tormé, "Lulu's Back in Town," *Lulu's Back in Town* (with Marty Paich
    and the Dek-Tette)
Mel Tormé, "Pick Yourself Up," *Live at Marty's*
Mel Tormé, "Clear out of This World," Mel Tormé and George Shearing,
    A Vintage Year
Wes Montgomery and George Shearing, "Love Walked In," *George*
    Shearing and the Montgomery Brothers
George Shearing, "Mack the Knife," *Grand Piano*
George Shearing, "It Never Entered My Mind," *Grand Piano*
Dave McKenna, "C Jam Blues," *Solo Piano*
Dave McKenna, "Time Medley," *An Intimate Evening with Dave McKenna*
Joe Venuti (with Dave McKenna), "At the Jazz Band Ball," *Joe Venuti—*
    Alone at the Palace
Joe Venuti (and Zoot Sims, Bucky Pizzarelli), "String the Blues," *Joe & Zoot*
    & More
Joe Venuti (and Zoot Sims, Bucky Pizzarelli), "Dinah," *Joe & Zoot & More*
Joni Mitchell, "Circle Game," *Ladies of the Canyon*
The Beatles, "The Long and Winding Road," *Let It Be*
The Beatles, "One After 909," *Let It Be*
The Allman Brothers, "Jessica," *Brothers and Sisters*
Peter Frampton, "Shine On," *Frampton Comes Alive*
Billy Joel, "Laura," *Nylon Curtain*
Billy Joel, "She's Right on Time," *Nylon Curtain*
Bruce Springsteen, "Thunder Road," *Born to Run*
Chaka Khan, "Through the Fire," *I Feel for You*
George Benson, "Affirmation," *Breezin'*

Jonathan Schwartz, "Haunted Heart," *Anyone Would Love You*

Nat King Cole Trio, "Body and Soul," *Nat King Cole Trio: Instrumental Classics*

Nat King Cole Trio, "Paper Moon," *The King Cole Trio* (1944)

Nat King Cole, "Portrait of Jenny," *Cool Cole* (Boxed Set)

Dinah Washington, "Blue Gardenia," *The Bridges of Madison County Soundtrack*

Frank Sinatra, "River Stay Away from My Door," *Come Swing With Me*

Frank Sinatra, "Come Rain or Come Shine," *Sinatra & Strings*

Margaret Whiting, "All in Fun," *Margaret Whiting Sings the Jerome Kern Songbook*

Les Paul and Mary Ford, "Tiger Rag," *Best of Capitol by Les Paul and Mary Ford*

Les Paul and Mary Ford, "How High the Moon," *Best of Capitol by Les Paul and Mary Ford*

Cesar Camargo Mariano and Romero Lubambo, "Joy Spring," *Duo*

João Gilberto, "Estate," *Amoroso*

George Barnes and Bucky Pizzarelli, "Rose Room," *The Town Hall Concert, 1971*

Ella Fitzgerald and Louis Armstrong, "Under a Blanket of Blue," *Complete Ella and Louis on Verve*

Ella Fitzgerald, "But Not for Me" (and every other track), *Twelve Nights in Hollywood*

RANDOM FAVORITES AND BESTS

Best Jazz Club Food—The Dakota in Minneapolis

Best Post-Gig Hang—Mistura Fina in Rio (now closed)

Best Post-Gig Food—Palace Kitchen in Seattle after Jazz Alley shows

Best Karaoke—The Again Club in Tokyo (almost all Sinatra songs)

Best New York City Bartender (decided by a shootout in overtime)—Doug Quinn, late of PJ Clarke's, wherever he takes his bow tie and sets up shop.

Best Lamb Chops—Gene and Georgetti, Chicago

Best *Match Game* Panelists—Bret Somers and Charles Nelson Reilly (they can't be without each other)

Best Batman Phrase—*"Careful, Robin. It's quite a drop."*

Best Batman Exchange—

> Robin: Where'd you get a live fish, Batman?
> Batman: The true crime fighter always carries everything he needs in his utility belt, Robin.

Best Play Attended—*Beyond Reasonable Doubt* in the West End of London, Summer 1988

Best Football Game Ever (TV)—the 15–13 Giants/49ers NFC Championship Game at Don Gardner's house with Martin Pizzarelli and Rick Marchesi

Best Hockey Game Ever Attended—Game 6, NHL Eastern Finals, the Messier "Guarantee" Game, May 25, 1994

Favorite Spot in Nashville—Priest Lake

Worst Thing about New York City—It is starting to close earlier and earlier.

Silver Lining—PJ Clarke's on Fifty-Fifth and Third Avenue is not closing earlier.

Best Thing about New York City—The people are tremendously nice.

Favorite High School Albums—*Frampton Comes Alive!*; Robin Trower, *Bridge of Sighs*; Jackson Browne, *Late For the Sky*; Eagles, *Hotel California*

Favorite High School TV Viewing—Saturday Night on CBS, 1977

Best Martini—The first one Danny pours at Smith & Wollensky

Best Gin—Bombay (not Sapphire)

Zoot Sims's Favorite Gin—Gordon's

Bucky Pizzarelli's Favorite Gin—Steinhager in the clay bottle after it sits in the freezer. A shot of that with an ice-cold Rheingold, and you have Saturday afternoon in front of the fire watching Chris Schenkel call college football on our black and white TV after a long week of studio work, circa 1972.

Best Thing about the First Billy Joel Concert I Attended, St. Petersburg, Florida, 1978—When Billy closed with the words, "Good night, St. Pete. Don't take any shit from anybody!"

Best Springsteen Concert—On September 30, 1978, I listened for four hours in my Tampa dorm room to Bruce and the E-Street Band performing live from the Fox Theatre in Atlanta. I didn't move. Stumbled upon broadcast by accident.

Best Frozen Pizza—Tree Tavern

Best Restaurant Pizza—Kinchley's in Ramsey, New Jersey

Favorite Mario Batali Pasta—Mint Love Letters

Favorite Mario Batali Advice—"Don't overdress the pasta."

Favorite Observation from Batali—A major difference between home cooking and restaurant cooking is the time restaurants spend searing and browning the meat.

Best Knife Skills—Jacques Pepin. Watch his hands. Runner-up—Emeril Lagasse

Best Food-Related Paul Lynde Answer on *Hollywood Squares*—

> Peter Marshall: Sophia Loren has written a cookbook which will be published this spring entitled *Cooking with* . . . "Cooking with" what?
> Paul Lynde: Cooking with a Three-Foot-Long Spoon.

Best New York City Italian Meals—Chicken Parm at Gino (RIP), Veal
   Milanese at Ballato's, Risotto at Luca/Cavatappo, Pasta tasting at Babbo,
   Meatballs at Spiga
Favorite Italian Food Outside New York City—The salumi at Salumi in
   Seattle; the pasta with the egg yolk in it at Mozza in L.A.; La Taverna in
   Perugia, Italy
Best Chinese Dinner—Any meal at Cathay in Waldwick, New Jersey, from
   1985 to 1992
Best Meal Outside New York City—Napa Valley, with five or six winemak-
   ers in the middle of Crocker & Starr Vineyard. The only buffet(t) I've
   ever enjoyed other than Jimmy from Key West.
Second Best Food-Related Paul Lynde Answer on Hollywood Squares—

> Peter Marshall: According to the French Chef, Julia Child, how
>   much is a pinch?
> Paul Lynde: Just enough to turn her on . . .

Best New York City Theater Experience—Opening night of the Round-
   about's *Sunday in the Park with George*

FAVORITE COMEDY ALBUMS

Comedy Minus One, Albert Brooks
Why Is There Air?, Bill Cosby
AM/FM, George Carlin

FAVORITE ORIGINAL SONGS OF MINE THAT NO ONE KNOWS OR
WILL EVER HEAR

"Captain of My Heart"
"Make Every Moment Count"
"Reinvented"
"Journey On"
"Arizona Boy"

FAVORITE ORIGINALS FROM MY CDS WRITTEN WITH JESSICA
MOLASKEY

"I Wouldn't Trade You"
"The Girl with His Smile and My Eyes"
"All I Saw Was You"
"Da Vinci's Eyes"
Favorite Molaskey CD—*Sitting in Limbo*

FAVORITE RADIO

The first hour of Jonathan Schwartz's Sunday show on WNEW-AM from
   1978 until it went off the air on December 11, 1992. (Now—*any*
   Jonathan Schwartz Sunday show)

Car Talk, NPR, while driving with the quartet to or from anywhere in the
    United States
Wait Wait, Don't Tell Me, NPR
Mike and the Mad Dog (and now, just Mike), WFAN in New York City
Vin Scelsa, "Idiot's Delight," WFUV.org
The late Pete Fornatale, "Mixed Bag," WFUV.org
Dan Ingram *("Big Dan here, laughin' and scratchin'")*
Casey Kasem's Top 100 from anytime in the seventies. They rerun them
    now on Sirius on the weekend
Arthur George Rust Jr. (RIP)

MEMORABLE JAZZ MOMENTS

Maynard Ferguson Big Band at some nutty restaurant in Belleville, New
    Jersey, circa 1975–76. Went with Bucky, very exciting. It was like a rock
    concert.
Al Cohn playing over the phone to an ill Zoot Sims at the Dick Gibson
    Jazz Party, 1984
Playing rhythm guitar for Marshal Royal, Buddy Tate, and Lockjaw Davis
    while playing "Shiny Stockings" at the Dick Gibson Jazz Party, Labor
    Day, Denver, 1985
Al Klink playing "September Song," Waterloo Village, in 1992
Pat Metheny at the Beacon Theatre, New York City, in 1988
Toninho Horta at Dizzy's Club Coca-Cola in New York City in May 2011
Kurt Elling anywhere
Freddie Cole in any setting—on land or sea

FAQ

*Outside of a dog, a book is man's best friend. Inside of a dog,
it's too dark to read.*

—Groucho Marx

Welcome to the back section of the book. Special thanks to those
readers who have gotten here by reading from the beginning. My hope
is that you've read about people and subject areas you expected to be
covered, as well as two or three you might not have seen coming. For
my dozens of loyal followers, I trust I have filled in some gaps about our
family's musical history, given the wildly inconsistent chronologies I have
apparently been providing to reporters and interviewers over the years.
Clearly, I was not a history major; in fact, my college transcript (available for $2.73 on eBay) will reveal that I didn't spend enough time at the
University of Tampa to even declare a major. But I defy any of you faced
with a ringing phone in Eugene, Oregon, at nine o'clock in the morning
(six Eastern) to string together coherent answers when a reporter starts
asking about Sandy's Hollywood Bar in Paterson, New Jersey, back in
the forties. Or about playing on the Wes Montgomery records back in
the mid-sixties (um, that was the other John Pizzarelli—my dad). Or
whether I believe my playing has improved since my dad passed away . . .
six years before he blew out the candles on his eighty-sixth birthday.

Still, there may be questions that I have not answered adequately
to this point. As a performer who goes out of his way to communicate

with audiences both at concerts and through electronic media (website, Facebook, ham radio, telegraph), I get hit with more questions than you'd think. Backstage at concerts; on the telephone with interviewers for newspapers, magazines, and blogs; shouts from the audience; e-mails to the website; comments on Facebook—the stream of interrogation is constant. And because I like to talk about *everything* from the stage and all across the World Wide Web, people seem to believe that most (I typed this twice as "moist") subjects are in play—homemade pasta, Vin Scully, high-end neckwear, my father's whereabouts, wine pairings, best airports, West Coast hockey, *Frampton Comes Alive*, and, of course, all aspects of jazz music.

But there are specific questions that come up often, both from reporters and from people who follow our music. This section of the book features actual questions I have received over the years, both in writing and in person. They are divided into two categories: Music and Other.

Music

Q: You call *that* music?

A: To paraphrase Spike Lee at Sundance—a little early in the morning for that question.

Q: You and your father play seven-string guitars. What is the seventh string, and what are the advantages of playing this unorthodox instrument?

A: That's more like it.

I love the sound of the seventh string itself. It is a low A below middle C. When George Van Eps invented the seven-string, it was to add a low end to the guitar, similar to that of a piano. A real advantage (and, at the same time, an oddity) is that listeners believe they are hearing a bass player in the mix. A radio interviewer a few years ago wanted to know about a specific guitar solo on "Paper Moon" that I had played à la Van Eps from the *Live at Birdland* CD. After an extended setup, here was his eventual question—"How does Martin know how to follow your every chord? It's amazing." I had to correct him—there was no bass during that solo—just the low A and some low chords on the seven-string. My father said that someone once said of his duo performances with George Barnes: "It sounds like two great guitarists and one mediocre bass player."

As I think of it, the seventh string provides the depth of the bass notes lower than the E on the standard guitar, which makes it highly versatile in the studio. You can hear it in the verse I play with McCartney on "Home (When Shadows Fall)."

Written in the early 1930s by Peter Van Steeden, Harry Clarkson, and Jeff Clarkson, "Home (When Shadows Fall)" was not a new song in Paul's hands. It was a regular part of the live sets for both the Quarrymen (the band started by John Lennon and some pals) and the Beatles in their various incarnations between 1957 and 1960. You might recall the version by Henry Hall and the Gleneagles Hotel Band during the dream sequence in *The Shining*, as well as two recordings by Louis Armstrong (1932 and 1957) that are essential in contrasting Pops's approach to the same song at opposite ends of his career. And both McCartney and Armstrong made the same brilliant musical decision forty-four years apart— they chose to sing the verse.

Q: If you could bring back a piano player from all time to accompany you for one track, who would it be?

A: John Bunch.

I know, I know—I could have Fats Waller, Oscar Peterson, Teddy Wilson, and George Shearing. But I had a similar choice in 1990 at the Rainbow Room when they hired me for the twelve-to-four Easter Sunday brunch. When they said they'd spring for a piano player, I told them I wanted John Bunch. To this day, it was one of the most musical and enjoyable gigs I've ever been part of. Bunch, Martin, and me. The brunchers were talking, brunching, paying little or no attention—and there was John following everything I played and sang, as though he were playing for

Tony Bennett at Royal Albert Hall (which he had done on many occasions). We were on Top of the Rock *and* on top of the world. I caught myself welling up in tears at one point at how lucky I was to have such a brilliant player and elegant man behind me. George Simon captured it when he called John "the Fred Astaire of the piano." He always raised my game when we played together, and on the breaks he made me laugh. An underrated genius.

If I were just going to listen to a piano player, it would be Dave McKenna, hands down. And that's knowing that Art Tatum is available as a choice. For my listening ear, there was nothing like McKenna's monster left hand leading the rhythm, while he played melodies that would, in many cases, define how I heard that song in my head from that day forward. And his medleys tested your command of the Songbook—the Time Medley ("Time After Time"/"Time on My Hands"/"Some Other Time"/"A Time for Love"); the Rodgers & Hart songs; women's names (sometimes ten in a row); the Knowledge Medley ("I Didn't Know What Time It Was"/ "I Wish I Knew"/"I Don't Know Enough about You").

Q: Where was the wackiest place you've ever played?

A: Probably the two shows that incorporated marine life into entertainment back in the 1990s. For one, they set us up next to the first-floor penguins' pool and habitat at the New England Aquarium in Boston. The other was next to the sixty-four-thousand-gallon seal tank in Central Park (don't laugh—it was a sold-out show—that's what we told the penguins). We timed our breaks to coincide with feeding times—seriously. Note: These shows never look as bizarre on paper and in the contract as they get when you arrive for the gig, and you are faced with the animals who are providing vocals. No mention of this beforehand. And let's just say the aroma of performing seals—it wasn't "faint."

Q: What makes for a good arrangement with (a) your quartet and (b) a big band?

A: We usually arrange for the quartet in general because that's the setting for the vast majority of my shows. When we arrange for something bigger, we build it out from a trio or quartet arrangement. The *Our Love Is Here to Stay* CD is an example of Don Sebesky writing a number of those big-band arrangements around our original trio arrangement. This way, the intimacy and excitement of what we do with the group doesn't get lost when we play the songs with a larger band. Sebesky and Dick Lieb have been very keen not to lose sight of what we do with a small group when writing our charts for orchestras and big bands.

Usually we try to find a voice for the arrangement depending on its setting. If it's a quartet arrangement, we may think Oscar Peterson or Nat Cole Trio as the basis for what we are trying to do. If it's a big-band chart, maybe Basie or Woody Herman, depending on the song and where we want it to go.

Q: What was the feeling in, say, "Ring-a-Ding-Ding?"

A: In that case, I knew nothing about how things would turn out. I told John Clayton that I wanted to use the tune and that he should write it for his band and me. When John writes, he takes his cue from what I might say but certainly gives his band their voice inside of the orchestration as a complement to me. Sebesky, on the other hand, sets out to give the listener some surprises, as he does on "Witchcraft," with the loud burst of brass and crescendos throughout.

Q: What are the main components of a great jazz solo?

A: I always feel that the solo is a story. But unlike a story one reads, there is often no set number of notes or pages in a jazz solo—sometimes you just know when it's over, and you should get out while the getting is good. My quartet's mantras are "Tell your story and get out" and "We don't need any home runs here, just singles and doubles." A great solo can be eight bars or eight choruses. I guess it depends on how well you think your "story" is going. Perfect jazz solos are hard to come by, but the striving for perfection makes for the great ones.

I think the story *does* change depending on the song. Based on what you're playing, you might want to play only eight bars and get back to the tune. As a vocalist and a guitarist (and the person calling the tunes), I am aware that delivering the tune is often more important to the structure of the show than any solo we can play. Look at Tony Bennett's live performances. How many one and out solos do the guys play in his shows? And Ella's *Twelve Nights in Hollywood*—Herb Ellis doesn't play one chorus. In seventy-something tracks! If there is going to be a solo in a Tony Bennett or Ella show, it had better be something pretty special.

Q: What are your favorite jazz guitar solos?

A: Bucky played two great single-note solos on *Swinging Sevens*—one on "No Greater Love" and the other on "In a Mellow Tone." Brilliant, from top to bottom. Wes Montgomery's solo on "Love Walked In" (with George Shearing) is as great as it gets. Pat Metheny excels on any number of things—"Phase Dance," "Are You Going with Me?" and "If I Could." Also, George Van Eps on "They Can't Take That Away from Me," and George Barnes on "Rose Room" on the *Town Hall, 1971* record with Bucky. Then there's Oscar Moore's "Body and Soul" chorus with the Nat Cole Trio.

Q: Best old-school guitarists? Best of the modern-day or modern-style guys?

A: Old-school—Tal Farlow, Joe Pass, Oscar Moore, João Gilberto, George Benson, George Barnes, George Van Eps, Bucky.
Modern-day—Pat Martino, Wes Montgomery, Pat Metheny, Romero Lubambo, Toninho Horta, Russell Malone, Howard Alden, Frank Vignola.

Q: What do you like about the more modern guitarists? Why do you believe Pat Metheny has been so successful?

A: I like how the modern guys have taken their love of the instrument and put their own stamp on it. Metheny always mentions Wes Montgomery as an influence. Not that I hear it in his playing, but he took that love of Wes and moved from it to create a unique voice on the guitar. I think Metheny has really carved out an amazing niche for himself, both as a guitar player and as a composer. He has written songs that are melodic and accessible, but they're still challenges harmonically for his group. And his solos are as good as the melodies he writes. That's a pretty winning formula.

Toninho Horta is one of the unsung kings of the instrument, at least to my ears. His approach to chords and voicing of those chords and his compositions is staggering. Ask Metheny. The way Toninho sings and plays on his own speaks to why the guitar is so beautiful an instrument. He makes the guitar sound like, well, everything—and when he adds his voice over that, it is a religious experience. Powerful stuff.

Q: How do you come out regarding improvisation? There is the Lee Konitz school of complete improv, that solos must be "organic," as opposed to those containing "figured-out stuff." Is complete improvisation worth the risk? What is a musician's obligation on a solo?

A: You know, Bucky plays almost the same chorus on "Nuages" now all the time, and it always kills. But there was a first time he played that solo, too. Those "figured-out things" started organically some-where—at a rehearsal, strumming on the porch, being shown a chord by another guitarist. I think it's all great. I don't come out on one side or the other on this, but the total improv thing of, "I'll play something weird, you follow same, and then we all make up stuff for seven minutes" is questionable. Audiences are all for 100 percent improv in theory—until they have to sit through it. I have never heard that work well. It's managing within a structure that makes improvisation so difficult.

Q: How do you see yourself in terms of your responsibility as a preser-vationist of the American Songbook? Would you like to take more of an active role, as Feinstein does?

A: I never thought of myself as a revivalist or preserver. I should take more care than I have at times with melodies and lyrics. As I have gotten older, I have become more conscious of this. Feinstein is an ace. There is no one like him. I *do* believe the music will survive because of its excellence and how it lends itself to interpretation. Everyone sounds different singing "All of Me" or "It Had to Be You." Everyone has ideas about it. Rock songs come and go because (a) the songs aren't as well written and don't hold up and (b) the listeners are so familiar with the original versions and aren't nearly as open to new ideas. Not so for the Songbook.

Q: Where would you rank your identity in the public's mind (and in your own mind) as a singer and as a guitarist?

A: I think a majority of the public would see me as a singer first. The jazz public and press would likely consider me more of a guitarist. The goal is to have your own voice, and I think I have developed that. I'll never be Paulo Szot, and I'm okay with that at this point. The great Joe Mooney joked about himself— "I haven't got a voice, just have delivery." And that's someone Sinatra used to run to see between his sets at the Waldorf. Maybe Jonathan Schwartz is right—perhaps I have simply worn down the public.

Q: How do you see your evolution as a guitarist from when you were a kid?

A: Since the banjo beginnings, I was always comfortable with the guitar. I think I know my limitations on it now, while realizing that I've mastered pieces I never thought I'd be able to play. My work on Don Sebesky's *I Remember Bill* CD (Bill Evans tribute) is like that. And I still work on chord melody things at home just as though I were in my parents' basement as a thirteen-year-old, slugging it out with my uncle's tablatures. My confidence has grown through the years to the point where I almost enjoy throwing myself into the fire to see if I can play myself out.

Q: How did your musical development go while you were in the house with Bucky?

A: I listened to records to lead the way, be it jazz or pop or bossa nova. He would stick his head in whatever room I happened to be playing in and give me a thumbs up or down or, "move the index finger over one . . . that's it" and be gone. His uncles had taught both of us, so we were always approximately on the same page— and if not the same page, at least the same book.

Q: Did you let your playing evolve, or was part of you determined not to sound like Bucky?

A: There was no way I wasn't going to sound like Bucky. He once sat in on my guitar at an audio show, and without changing a setting, sounded like he was playing *his* guitar through *his* amp! And we played together all the time during my formative years. That said, I play with him all the time, I know his sound and I know mine—and in many ways they are worlds apart. Once in a while, someone will pick up on this, either in a concert hall or a recording studio, and be able to articulate some of the same differences I hear.

Q: There is a little more twang (in a good way) in your playing than in Bucky's. I hear some George Barnes. Your thoughts?

A: I wish there was even more George Barnes in my playing than there is. Along with Frampton, he was the other guitarist from whom I was trying to "appropriate licks" back in the mid-seventies, especially when it came to playing duets with my dad. George played melodies better than anyone I'd heard. Thirty-five years later that is what you hear in Bucky's playing. He's playing brilliant melodies these days. Big fat notes singing out—gorgeous stuff.

Other

Q: What's the wildest thing you have read about yourself in the paper?

A: In what I still suspect was an elaborate practical joke, an article in the *San Francisco Examiner* quoted Tony Bennett as saying he'd want me to play him should there ever be a film of his life story. "I would play the second half myself," he told the paper. "That's just a dream right now."

Q: You're a New York/New Jersey guy, yet you are a fan of the Boston Red Sox? Care to explain?

A: Sure. The Yankees of my youth had just entered the post–Mickey Mantle era, which you will recall was characterized by some awful teams in the late sixties. Horace Clarke, Jerry Kenney, Jake Gibbs, Johnny Ellis, Frank Tepedino, Ron Woods, Thad Tillotson. Probably nice enough guys. The writing was on the wall for them when Finley bought the A's and shut down their unofficial farm system, also when baseball instituted drafting of players in the early sixties.

Anyway, the Yankees were always on the TV in our house during those days, but it wasn't exactly what you would call a winning tradition. I loved baseball, but my loyalty was a free agent through much of the seventies. I didn't like what the new owners had done with Yankee Stadium when it reopened in 1976. And I never found myself on the bandwagon of those late-seventies Billy Martin teams either, even when they were winning.

Then around 1981 or so, I happened to meet two friends at the same time who were avid, die-hard fans of the Boston Red Sox. To my astonishment, both men carried wounds still fresh from the Bucky Dent one-game playoff in 1978. (One of the friends even wrote a book about the game.) After a couple of visits to Fenway Park, I was hooked. Idyllic ballpark, organ music, someone's ne'er-do-well uncle as the PA announcer, a hand-operated scoreboard, and a left field wall that broke hearts. And with no championships in sixty-three years, no one could say that I was jumping on any kind of bandwagon.

Q: I see you are a foodie, striking up friendships with many of the boldfaced celebrity chefs. You must have some favorite wines. Please recommend.

A: Keep an eye on my website and Facebook page for ongoing recommendations. But let's start in Napa Valley—some of the best wines I drink from there are also owned, operated, and made by some of the nicest, most generous people I've ever met. Paradigm has great cab, the best merlot around, Heidi Barrett makes the wine, and Ren and Marilyn Harris are wonderful people. Maddie learned to ride a two-wheeler in the vineyard behind their home. Crocker & Starr, made by Pam Starr, has three killer wines (cab, cab franc, sauvignon blanc), Gemstone is just as good as when our pals Paul and Suzie Frank were there. And the Dotzlers at Outpost are doing great stuff from their vineyards on the top of the world . . . and Tom Seaver made his ninety-seven-point wine there. Finally, the Miners have always been great friends of Bucky's (and the wine is fabulous). Full props to Lou Ginsburg all those years ago for opening his wine cellar, serving us Chateau Montelena and Silver Oak, and weaning us off of the Boone's Farm.

Q: What did you get on your SATs?

A: Drool.

Q: How come it took two authors to finish this thing while it only took one to write *Anna Karenina*?

A: Tolstoy didn't have our deadlines.

Discography

LEADER

I'm Hip (Please Don't Tell My Father) (Stash, 1983; rereleased on Pony Canyon, 2002)

Hit That Jive, Jack! (Stash, 1985; rereleased on Pony Canyon, 2002)

Sing! Sing! Sing! (Stash, 1987; rereleased on P-Vine Records, 2003)

My Blue Heaven (Chesky, 1990)

All of Me (RCA Novus, 1991)

Naturally (RCA Novus, 1992)

Best of John Pizzarelli: I Like Jersey Best (Stash, 1992)

New Standards (RCA Novus, 1993)

Dear Mr. Cole (RCA Novus, 1994)

After Hours (RCA Novus, 1995)

One Night with You (Chesky, 1996)—Compilation

Our Love Is Here to Stay (BMG/RCA Victor, 1997)

Let's Share Christmas (BMG/RCA Victor, 1997)

John Pizzarelli Meets the Beatles (BMG/RCA Canada, 1998)

John Pizzarelli Meets the Beatles (BMG/RCA, 1999)

P.S. Mr. Cole (BMG/RCA Victor, 1999)

Kisses in the Rain (Telarc, 2000)

Let There Be Love (Telarc, 2000)

Live at Foxwoods Resort Casino (Telarc, 2002)

Best of John Pizzarelli (BMG, 2002)—Compilation

Live at Birdland (Telarc, 2003)

Bossa Nova (Telarc, 2004)

Knowing You (Telarc, 2005)

Dear Mr. Sinatra (Telarc, 2006)

Rhythm Is Our Business (BMG Special Projects, 2006)—Compilation

With a Song in My Heart (Telarc, 2008)

Rockin' in Rhythm (Telarc, 2010)
Double Exposure (Telarc, 2012)

COLLABORATIONS

With George Shearing:
    The Rare Delight of You (Telarc, 2002)
With Rosemary Clooney:
    Brazil (Concord, 2000)
With Bucky Pizzarelli:
    2 × 7 = Pizzarelli (Stash, 1979)
    Swinging Sevens (Stash, 1984)
    Complete Guitar Duos (Stash, 1992)—Compilation
    Nirvana (Laserlight, 1995)
    At the Vineyard Theater (Challenge, 1996)
    Solos and Duets (Jazz Classics—City Hall, 1996)
    Contrasts (Arbors Records, 1998)
    Passion Guitars (Groove Jams, 1999)
    Passionate Guitars (LRC Records, 2001)
    Twogether (Victoria, 2001)
    Under the Stars (Great Connecticut Jazz Festival, 2004)
    Generations (Arbors Records, 2007)
    Sundays at Pete's (Challenge Records, 2007)
    PIZZArelli Party (Arbors Records, 2009)
    Family Fugue (Arbors Records, 2011)
With Bucky Pizzarelli and Martin Pizzarelli (The Pizzarelli Boys):
    Desert Island Dreamers (Arbors Records, 2010)
With Bucky Pizzarelli and the West Texas Tumbleweeds:
    Diggin' Up Bones (Arbors Records, 2009)
    Back in the Saddle Again (Arbors Records, 2011)
With Harry Allen:
    Harry Allen Meets the John Pizzarelli Trio (BMG/RCA, 1999)
    Plays the Hits of Stage and Screen (BMG Japan, 2004)
    Tenors Anyone? (Slider Music, 2004)
With Ruby Braff:
    Relaxing at the Penthouse (Victoria Records, 2002)
    Ruby Braff and the Flying Pizzarellis: C'est Magnifique! (Arbors
        Records, 2007)
With Buddy DeFranco:
    Cookin' the Books (Arbors Records, 2004)
With Rick Haydon:
    Just Friends (Mel Bay Records, 2006)

With Aaron Weinstein:
    Blue Too (Arbors Records, 2008)
With Dave Mooney:
    Last Train Home (Challenge, 2009)

AS GUEST ACCOMPANIST/VOCALIST

Phil Bernardi Band: "I Like Jersey Best" (Homemade 45 rpm, 1981)
Pee Wee Erwin: *Playing at Home* (Qualtro Music, 1981)
Slam Stewart: *The Cats Are Swingin'* (Sertoma, 1987)
Daryl Sherman: *I've Got My Fingers Crossed* (Audiophile, 1992)
Lady Be Good Soundtrack: "Little Jazz Bird" track (Nonesuch, 1992)
Rosemary Clooney: *Do You Miss New York?* (Concord, 1993)
Various Artists: *A Soap Opera Christmas* (RCA, 1994)
Various Artists: *Forget Paris* (Elektra Entertainment, 1995)
Stéphane Grappelli: *Live at the Blue Note* (Telarc, 1996)
Natalie Cole: *Stardust* (Elektra/WEA, 1996)
Boston Pops: *Runnin' Wild* (RCA Victor, 1996)
Barbara Carroll: *All in Fun* (After 9, 1996)
Various Artists: *Swing Alive! At the Hollywood Palladium* (Drive, 1996)
Various Artists: *The Songs of Johnny Mercer* (Valley Ent., 1997)
Karen Angela Moore: *All the Wrong Things to Do* (M-Pire, 1998)
Rosemary Clooney: *70: A Seventieth Birthday* (Concord, 1998)
Don Sebesky: *I Remember Bill* (RCA Victor, 1998)
Judy Barnett: *Swingin'* (Slider Music, 1998)
Various Artists: *Gershwin: Standards & Gems* (Nonesuch, 1998)
Matt Catingub: *George Gershwin 100* (Concord, 1998)
Dawn Upshaw: *Dawn Upshaw Sings Vernon Duke* (Nonesuch, 1999)
Don Sebesky: *Joyful Noise* (RCA Victor, 1999)
Various Artists: Soundtrack for the Film *Guinevere* (RCA Victor, 1999)
Various Artists: *Montreal Jazz Festival: 20 Ans de Musique* (FIJM, 1999)
Tom Wopat: *In the Still of the Night* (EMD/Angel, 2000)
Various Artists: Soundtrack for the film *Two Family House* (BMG/RCA, 2000)
Rickie Lee Jones: *It's Like This* (Artemis, 2000)
Roy Gerson: *Gerson Swings Disney* (2001)
Ray Kennedy: *I'm Beginning to See the Light* (Victoria, 2001)
Harry Allen: *Christmas in Swingtime* (Koch International, 2001)
Jessica Molaskey: *Pentimento* (Image Entertainment, 2002)
Ray Kennedy and Bucky Pizzarelli: *Swing Kings* (Victoria Records, 2002)
Ray Brown: *Some of My Best Friends Are Guitarists* (Telarc, 2002)
James Taylor: *October Road* (Sony, 2002)

Monty Alexander: *My America* (Telarc, 2002)
Cincinnati Pops: *Got Swing!* (Telarc, 2003)
Jessica Molaskey: *A Good Day* (P.S. Classics, 2003)
Monty Alexander: *Impressions in Blue* (Telarc, 2003)
Skitch Henderson and Bucky Pizzarelli: *Legends* (Arbors, 2003)
Original Cast: *Fine and Dandy* (P.S. Classics, 2004)
Jessica Molaskey: *Make Believe* (P.S. Classics, 2004)
Martin Pizzarelli: *Triple Play* (Victoria Company, 2004)
Manhattan Transfer: *Vibrate* (Telarc, 2004)
Debby Boone: *Reflections of Rosemary* (Concord, 2005)
Rickie Lee Jones: *Duchess of Coolville—Anthology* (Rhino, 2005)
Various Artists: *Salute! The World War II Tribute Album* (Curb Records, 2005)
Various Artists: *Songs from the Neighborhood* (MemoryLane Syndication, 2005)
Aaron Weinstein: *A Handful of Stars* (Arbors, 2005)
Grover Kemble: *Live at Shanghai Jazz* (Shanghai Jazz, 2006)
Bucky Pizzarelli: *Around the World in 80 Years* (Victoria, 2006)
Erich Kunzel and the Cincinnati Pops: *Christmastime Is Here* (Telarc, 2006)
Cheryle Bentyne: *The Book of Love* (Telarc, 2006)
James Taylor: *James Taylor at Christmas* (Columbia, 2006)
Jessica Molaskey: *Sitting in Limbo* (P.S. Classics, 2007)
Curtis Stigers: *Real Emotional* (Concord, 2007)
Kurt Elling: *Nightmoves* (Concord Records, 2007)
Jessica Molaskey: *A Kiss to Build a Dream On* (Arbors Records, 2008)
Kristin Chenoweth: *A Lovely Way to Spend Christmas* (Sony, 2008)
Paul McCartney: *Kisses on the Bottom* (MPL, Concord, 2012)

Note: Cuts featuring John Pizzarelli as both singer and instrumentalist appear on numerous compilation, best-of-label, and limited-edition CDs or digital equivalents that may not be listed here.

Index

NOTE: Page numbers in *italics* indicate photos.